THE GIFTS OF FRANK COBBOLD

Arthur W. Upfield

ETT IMPRINT
Exile Bay

THE GIFTS OF FRANK COBBOLD

This edition published by ETT IMPRINT 2015

Copyright © William Upfield 2008, 2015

ISBN   978-1-25416-21-3 (ebook)

ISBN 978-1-25416-22-0 (paper)

Cover design and artwork, The Design Shop
First published 2008 by
Number 11 Publishing

for the Cobbold Family History Trust

CONTENTS

INTRODUCTION

Although the Cobbold Family History Trust was not settled until the Spring of 2004 I had been collecting books and papers about the family for some years, but the reality was that I *knew* very little. Amongst those papers was a manuscript pedigree in the distinctive hand of Clement Cobbold (1882-1961) whose excellent work expanded that already carried out by his uncle Felix Thornley Cobbold (1841-1909).

Tucked away at the bottom of a page I noticed a footnote,

NB   *Francis Edward Cobbold of Melbourne died 1935 leaving no children. He left the residue of his fortune to the Royal United Kingdom Beneficent Association for Suffolk domiciled gentlefolk of reduced means.*

By chance, whilst sorting some papers I came across a Christmas card sent previously by my very dear godmother. She had purchased the card in support of Rukba so now I knew their address. Thinking that it sounded interesting and that I might thereby be able to confirm what I had noticed, but with very little anticipation of what might be revealed, I wrote to Rukba in October 2005 to ask for information. The reply amazed and encouraged me in about equal proportions. I continued my researches and within six months the Trust had acquired an original portrait of F E Cobbold and a typescript copy of his biography by Arthur W Upfield.

I thought it was a fascinating story that was worthy of at least limited publication so application was made to the author's estate for permission. This was granted to the Trust for 300-350 copies.

The thread of the story is the selfless way in which Frank Cobbold made his money but the garment is the thousands of people whose lives have been improved as a result of his generosity and Rukba's skills. 'Go on or go under,' he used to say. He would be pleased to have been heard and heeded.

Anthony Cobbold
Keeper, The Cobbold Family History Trust
September 2008

CHAPTER ONE

1853 to 1867
Early Years

1.

Francis Edward was born in Ipswich, Suffolk to Arthur and Sarah Cobbold. At the same time, the settlers of north-eastern Australia were agitating for separation from the huge southern state of New South Wales. Not only was he the seventh son of his parents, but he was the seventh son of a seventh son. This traditionally accepted sign of good fortune was to be substantiated through a long life of adventure and endeavour on the sea, among the islands of the New Hebrides, and in that part of Australia which Queen Victoria named 'Queensland' in 1859, when Francis Edward Cobbold was six years old.

Australia was to claim the boy from an early age and during this period it was rapidly emerging from being the depository for England's overcrowded jails. The great influx of free settlers was beginning to have its effect on the quasi-military form of government, and the public concern for democratic and responsible government resulted in colonies destined to be among the brightest jewels in the Queen's empire.

This new Eldorado beneath the Southern Cross called for men of grit and stamina, and did not fail to get them. British factories were demanding ever-increasing supplies of wool for their younger colony of Victoria when McArthur established the fact that sheep were ideally suited to be reared in Australia. The eyes of all adventurers in the world had begun to turn towards the south and the people of the British Isles were starting to realise that Australia was not, after all, a mere conglomeration of convict settlements but a land of great promise for those possessing initiative and determination.

It was only natural that one of the Cobbolds of Suffolk should be caught up by the enterprising stream flooding from England across the world to Australia.

2.

The earliest surviving records of the Cobbolds go back to Robert Cobbold of Tostock, a Yeoman farmer who died in 1603. He was followed by a succession of Cobbolds in direct line to Thomas

Cobbold, who started a brewing business at Harwich in 1723. At this period, the water supply at Harwich was very unsatisfactory; Thomas Cobbold soon recognised the fact that successful brewing depended upon a pure water supply and arranged for water to be conveyed to Harwich down the river Orwell from Holy Wells Springs, Ipswich in especially constructed barges.

That condition of affairs did not satisfy him for long, however. It was not good business economics to bring the mountain to Mohammed, so he decided to go to the mountain, and the brewery was moved to the same water supply at Ipswich where the first Cliff Brewery was established in 1746. There, Thomas Cobbold extended his enterprises, becoming a farmer, a merchant, and a ship owner, determined to command the transport of merchandise and raw materials necessary to his business.

His son, young Francis Edward's great-Grandfather John Cobbold, extended his father's activities by a wharf and then building his own ships to be sent out to engage in foreign trade. At least eighteen units of this fleet carried the Cobbold house flag to the distant harbours of India and China. In size, they ranged from the 50 tons spritsail, *Cliff*, to the 366 tons barque, *Dorsetshire*, and an old picture shows the *John Cobbold*, 200 tons, helping a vessel in distress in a great storm in the Atlantic.

1. John Cobbold (1771-1860)

Determined to secure water rights for his brewery at Ipswich (named the Cliff Brewery) John Cobbold purchased the Holy Wells Estate in 1780, built a mansion on it and afterwards extended the boundaries of the property. The house was to witness the succession of five John Cobbolds in direct line, the last to live there being John Dupius Cobbold who died in June 1929. The sixth John Cobbold and his son, the seventh John

4

Cobbold, now reside at Glemham Hall, ten miles distant from the old home of the family.

2. *Holy Wells, Ipswich*

John Murray Cobbold (1897-1944) was killed when a flying bomb hit the Guards Chapel during Sunday morning service on 18th June 1944 and his son (the seventh) John Cavendish Cobbold (born 1927) died in 1983. Glemham Hall passed to younger brother Patrick Mark Cobbold (1934-1994) and thence to the present owner Philip Hope-Cobbold.

From the Tostock yeoman farmer sprang a dynasty as proud of its history and of its family as any that ruled an empire. The traditional line of descent was rigidly maintained, the eldest son automatically inheriting the major portion of his father's estate. The records of the family prove that its strength has never diminished, and that the attributes of business flair, foresight, and rigid rectitude have been passed down from one generation to the next.

In course of time, the original brewery was replaced with one fitted out with all the most approved appliances and constructed by the Cobbold staff from the Cliff building yard. The resources of the river were developed and the Cobbold docks, warehouses and maltings spread out over ground which had originally contained riverside gardens and merchants' houses. The Cobbolds grew with the growth of Ipswich, which they assisted to grow. As Punch pertinently put it:

Why is Ipswich like an old shoe?
Because it is Cobbold all over.

5

3.

On 17th October 1831, Mrs Bowditch Lee wrote to a young lady about to take her place as a governess in John Cobbold's family. She gave vivid little character sketches of every member of the family, and of the master of the house she wrote:

'Mr Cobbold is a fine, handsome man, between 50 and 60, full of native talent and shrewdness, abounding in kindness, liberality and generosity, indulgent to his children, full of honourable and manly feelings, and replete with that excellent quality, common sense'.

Of Mrs Cobbold, Mrs Lee wrote:

'Mrs Cobbold, who must have been beautiful, is a stout little woman, with a countenance beaming benignity ... her whole life is spent in doing kind actions to others, or trying to do so ... there is not a creature that she ever heard of that she does not wish to make happy. Having reared fourteen children, all of whom are living, you will readily suppose that her energy of character and her bodily activity have been constantly called into action'.

At this time the eldest son, John, was *'High Bailiff and a lawyer in great practice'*; the second son, Henry, *'is a complete contrast to Mr John. He tries to hide a great deal of good and fine feeling under a blunt and rough manner ...'*; a married daughter is *'a charming person, full of talent, taste and kindness'*; and Frank is a *'perfect hero in person, and is highly gifted with ability and taste, and he is a good conscientious clergyman ....'*

Mrs Bowditch Lee goes on to list and describe in detail other members of the family, thus: *'Mrs David Hanbury, another married daughter, is an elegant-looking, handsome woman ....'*; *'Kate is one of the sweetest, the mildest and best human beings ....'*; *'Agnes is beautiful and extraordinarily gifted in every respect ....'*; *'Emily is not so handsome, but quite enough to turn a person's head ....'*; *'Harriet is a dear pale, black-eyed, silk-ringletted girl, bounding about like an antelope ....'*; and *'Kate is engaged, but obstacles exist at present on the side of the gentleman's family'.*

The youngest of the family was Arthur, then aged 15 and at school at Boulogne. He was the seventh son and was to become the father of Francis Edward Cobbold, whose career is to follow.

3. Arthur Thomas Cobbold (1815-1898)

6

4.

A picture of Francis Cobbold's father Arthur, made during the closing years of his life, shows a strong family likeness to his ancestors – the same strength of mind and the same physical strength, the same determined jaw, and the same facial sternness when in repose - a sternness somewhat belied by the straight nose and the widely placed eyes. Born in 1815, he lived to reach his eighty-third year – longevity being another feature of his forebears.

In due time he married Sarah Elliston who, like her husband, lived to a ripe age and reached her eight-sixth year. They had ten children, the subject of this biography being the eighth child and, as mentioned earlier, the seventh son.

The Ellistons were a yeoman family of Suffolk – the earliest recalled being Robert Elliston of Monks Eleigh – and more than

one member of this family distinguished himself. One of Sarah Elliston's uncles was a naval lieutenant under Admiral Boscawen when he defeated the French fleet off Gibraltar in 1759; he had reached the rank of Commander when he retired. Another uncle – William Elliston - was a member of St. John's College, Cambridge, receiving his degree in 1754 with the distinction of fourth wrangler and in 1760 he was elected Master of Sidney Sussex College, a post he held until 1807.

4. *Sarah Cobbold, nee Elliston (1814-1899)*

Yet another uncle, Robert William Elliston, was a comedian-actor, manager who was at one time the proprietor of Drury Lane Theatre. Of him it was said: 'He had never been excelled and seldom equalled'.

> *Issue 18 of Phaeon, the Sidney Sussex Newsletter, described William Elliston as 'the Master from 1760 to 1807 who transformed the College into a place of high standing in the University after a hundred years in the shade'*

7

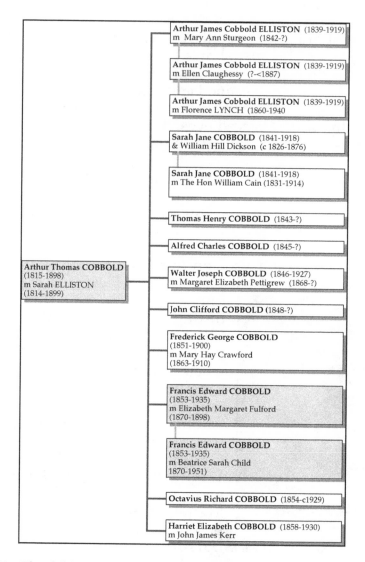

Arthur James Cobbold ELLISTON (1839-1919)
m Mary Ann Sturgeon (1842-?)

Arthur James Cobbold ELLISTON (1839-1919)
m Ellen Claughessy (?-<1887)

Arthur James Cobbold ELLISTON (1839-1919)
m Florence LYNCH (1860-1940

Sarah Jane COBBOLD (1841-1918)
& William Hill Dickson (c 1826-1876)

Sarah Jane COBBOLD (1841-1918)
m The Hon William Cain (1831-1914)

Thomas Henry COBBOLD (1843-?)

Alfred Charles COBBOLD (1845-?)

Walter Joseph COBBOLD (1846-1927)
m Margaret Elizabeth Pettigrew (1868-?)

John Clifford COBBOLD (1848-?)

Frederick George COBBOLD
(1851-1900)
m Mary Hay Crawford
(1863-1910)

Francis Edward COBBOLD
(1853-1935)
m Elizabeth Margaret Fulford
(1870-1898)

Francis Edward COBBOLD
(1853-1935)
m Beatrice Sarah Child
1870-1951)

Octavius Richard COBBOLD (1854-c1929)

Harriet Elizabeth COBBOLD (1858-1930)
m John James Kerr

Arthur Thomas COBBOLD
(1815-1898)
m Sarah ELLISTON
(1814-1899)

5. *The children of Arthur Thomas Cobbold and Sarah Elliston*

5.

It can never be fully established that the seventh son of a seventh son is definitely lucky. After all, luck is much less a matter of chance than the result of long planning, and the sense to take a firm hold on an opportunity before it passes by. It is also preferable to be born lucky than to be born rich - this truth may be illustrated by the incident of Francis Edward Cobbold's visit to the engine house of the Old Colchester Brewery at the early age of seven.

The main reason for the visit was the coldness of the east wind and the warmth of the air coming out through the open door. Once they arrived, however, the great attraction was the gleaming engine flywheel turning at high speed. For several moments Francis stood still and silent and partly hypnotised by the revolving metal. Then a strong draught of air blew through a second door, and whisked the ends of the scarf wound about his neck against the lynch pin of the wheel. To the child, time ceased to be. He watched the woollen strands revolving with the wheel shaft, saw how they were twisted round and round like the strands of a rope, and he saw how the rope of his scarf tautened, grew rapidly shorter and then began to drag him towards the wheel. There would have been no subsequent career to record if the engineer in charge had not come in at that moment, sprang to the boy's side and, with superhuman strength, torn the scarf away from the ponderous revolving mass of metal.

In 1860, when Mr Arthur Cobbold and his family were living near the little village of Waldringfield, ten miles from Ipswich, Francis attended a dame's school. From there he went on to an Academy kept by Mr Frost and his sister at Colchester and, at the age of eleven, he joined his brother Fred at Colchester Grammar School, which at that time was run by Doctor Wright, DCD assisted by Doctor Bates (the Classics Master), Mr Harrison (the English Master), Herr Gunst (the German Master), Sergeant Atkins, who instructed the pupils in drill, and Mr Callaghan, the gymnastic instructor.

If the two learned Doctors despaired of Francis Cobbold, their state of mind was not shared by either Callaghan or Atkins. These men were concerned only with young Cobbold's physique, not his mental development. They saw, with the vision of experts, the physical man the child was destined to become, and they delighted – when the Doctors frowned – in moulding the boy's muscles, hardening his body with constant exercises, training it to accept hardship without complaint - precisely as though they knew in advance the demands that life was to make of him.

Though mentally alert, the boy was not quick to learn from books. Like many other boys, learning did not appeal to him because he could not understand - and no-one took the trouble to explain - how application to study can exercise the mind and make it easier to grapple with life's inevitable problems. Loving most branches of field sports – he won the quarter mile race and the gymnastic trophy for boys under fifteen – nonetheless he still managed to assimilate a sound education which was to be of use to him in understanding, appreciating and adapting himself to the tremendous changes he was to witness, and in which he was to play a large part.

Though familiarity with Latin, Ovid and Virgil may not teach a man to bake a loaf of baking powder bread successfully in the hot ashes of a camp fire, it will still assist in building up a comfortable philosophy cheerfully to accept a blackened loaf, in the centre of which the flour and the water still remain a glutinous mass!

The smell of tar, of canvas and of salt water had an inevitable effect on the growing boy. The sea called softly and insistently, and it was to the sea that Francis Cobbold turned in holiday freedom. The holidays were spent among the fishermen on Mersea Island, when golden days were lived on the smacks at sea; or on the river Deben, near Waldringfield, where the family possessed a sailing boat in which cruises were undertaken to Felixstowe and up river to Woodbridge; or on yachting cruises in Mr Cobbold's cutter-rigged boats, the *Stag* and the *Dewdrop* which were kept at Harwich.

The house at Waldringfield was situated on the riverbank, and in winter it was often used as a shooting box for wildfowl. Mr Cobbold was a keen sportsman, who inculcated in his sons the intelligent use of firearms, and created in them an intense interest in the wildlife found on and in the vicinity of the river.

6. *Waldringfield on the River Deben from 'The Maybush',
October 1995 (a favourite haunt of Giles, the famous British cartoonist)*

A powerful telescope set up in a top room was used to mark the arrival and landing on the marshes of flighting wild-fowl, and expeditions were taken in the flat-bottom duck punts in which the boys were trained in the craft of stalking ducks –

pushing the punts gently and soundlessly through the narrow water-passages among the tall reeds, or hugging the low bank of a mud flat to gain position within gun range.

Sometimes their father took the boys over the surrounding fields and sea-flats, Mr Cobbold carrying the twin barrelled 'Joe Manton' he used so expertly, seldom failing to bring down the zigzagging, darting snipe rising from the sedges. In those days the custom of driving birds was not practised; intelligent pointer dogs being used to 'put up' a covey of partridges, and the liver-and-white Clumber spaniels to retrieve the wild-fowl.

In this way, the boys were taught not only to exercise their mental powers in combating the cunning of birds – especially the alert ducks – but also to cultivate the virtues of patience and pertinacity. Their powers of observation were trained, their minds were widened, and tolerance and goodwill were established in their characters.

If the snow lay thickly on the ground, the hunters donned old white suits and hats, the colour harmonising with the background and making them difficult to be seen by the watchful and suspicious birds. When the Joe Manton was replaced by a more modern pin-fire action type of weapon, the boys accepted it with admiration, and increased their proficiency with its use.

The atmosphere of the sea and foreign countries breathed by Francis, together with occasional visits to his grandfather's ships at Ipswich, definitely planted in his soul the restless urge epitomized by the travels of Ulysses. As his mind and body grew, so did his ambition to go striding across the world.

At first perplexed by this urge, not understanding it and yet spiritually delighting in it, he read Marryat's novels with engrossed interest. He came to know ever more clearly what he wanted to do, what he wanted to be – he wanted to own and sail his own ship through the Southern Seas which had called and had claimed his eldest brother.

On making known this ambition to his parents, he received a severe check. Poignant memories of the fate of her firstborn naturally caused Mrs Cobbold to rebel against the idea. The sea had claimed one of her children: it should not claim another. Mr Cobbold tried to dissuade his son from following such a course, and with much earnestness he painted in vivid colours several careers having greater promise.

Yet the sea was too strong for even this powerful combination, and in the end his parents came to understand the strength of their son's determination to go to sea. They recognised that his ambition was not just obstinate opposition to their wishes but something entirely beyond human control, so they surrendered. At the tender age of fourteen, Francis joined the *Ann Duthie* as an apprentice. She was a full-rigged clipper built at Aberdeen, was owned by Messrs Duthie, and was engaged in the ever-increasing Australian trade.

It was this ship that cut the knot binding Francis Cobbold to comfort, security and an assured future. It carried him away to a life of strenuous endeavour and no little danger for which, quite unconsciously, his school drill and sports teachers and even his own father had prepared him so well.

Arthur James Cobbold Elliston was the eldest child of Arthur Thomas Cobbold and Sarah Elliston but chose to retain his mother's surname. According to his son Edgar: "…when finished his education [he] *entered clerical and office work, it did not appeal to him so he went to sea in the grandfather's sailing ships, later he qualified as 1st Mate. He then went on voyages with cargoes to Baltic Ports, then to the St. Lawrence river Canada, China, Australian ports.'*
'He was buffeted for three weeks around Cape Horn before they got a favourable wind. One voyage was to Melbourne, then to Dunedin. Hearing of the gold rush, he left the sailing ship and went to the Otago gold rush where he stayed a while, later moving up to Christchurch where there were a large party of Diggers going around to Hokitika in the ship 'City of Dunedin'. He was asked to go with the party but declined, saying he was tired of the sea and would go overland. The 'City of Dunedin' has not been heard of from that day to this."
Though his parents may have thought they had lost him, Arthur remained in touch with some of his family through his sister Sarah, who had moved to Melbourne. During the influenza epidemic in 1918, Arthur James Elliston worked tirelessly helping to stop the spread of what he termed 'the plague'. Ultimately, however, he caught the virus himself and died on 24th July 1919 in Reefton, New Zealand, aged 79. At his funeral all business houses and public buildings flew their flags at half-mast as a tribute to '… an Esteemed Pioneer's passing on.'.

CHAPTER TWO

1867 to 1868
Apprenticed to the Sea

1.

Young Francis Cobbold joined the *Ann Duthie* during the slow transition of sail to steam in ocean transport. The Act of Parliament had recently been passed which created the Plimsoll Mark, defining the limit of loading any ship could take.

One day late in 1867, Mr Arthur Cobbold took his youngest son to the London Docks, probably in a growler carrying a heavy sea chest in addition to the two passengers. The sight of a forest of tall masts would not be strange to the boy, who was familiar with his grandfather's ships, but the sight of the *Ann Duthie* must have stirred his heart with admiration.

She was a lovely ship and brand-new. Her cargo was stowed and final preparations for the long maiden voyage were

being rapidly completed. In the forecastle, the crew of fourteen able-bodied seamen were in several stages of intoxication, while on the deck the First Mate was roaring and ranting at everyone - his appearance and his expletives shocking and terrifying the new apprentice.

7. *Model of the Ann Duthie*

This latest addition to the famous Australian wool clippers weighed about 750 tons and, beside the captain and his three officers, it carried a bosun, a sailmaker and a carpenter, six apprentices, the fourteen seamen, two second-class passengers and about a dozen saloon passengers. She had been built by and was owned by Messrs Duthie of Aberdeen, Scotland – a well-reputed shipping firm who owned, among other ships, the well-known *William Duthie*, the *John Duthie*, the *Abergeldie* and the *Cairnbulg*.

Mr Cobbold and his son entered the maelstrom of activity and the cacophony of shouted orders on the deck of the *Ann Duthie*, and eventually reached Captain Birnie, who was engaged in the feverish business of getting his ship to sea and anxious to catch the tide.

"He is small and thin, but you will find him active," Mr Cobbold said to the captain when presenting his son.

Birnie was a man of light stature, with a straggling light-brown beard and cold penetrating grey eyes. He was quiet and efficient, cynical and sarcastic, and he eyed the boy up and down as a man might look over the points of a horse. Since he appeared to show no great interest in Francis Cobbold, father and son went forward on the deck among the crowd of riggers, the maze of ropes and tackle, and the seeming general confusion. During the short period of time at his disposal, the elder Cobbold earnestly talked with this son whom he had wished to keep at home and who had maintained a steady determination to go to sea.

Perhaps the boy did not hear all that his father had to say, for the first mate was addressing the riggers in lurid language, and someone troubled himself to apologise by saying: "That's only 'Dafty' Donaldson's gentle method of urging the workers to greater efforts."

As the old saying had it, Francis Cobbold had long insisted on making the bed on which he was to lie.

2.

A tug took the ship in tow till well beyond Dover and by this time a sufficient number of the hands had been sobered up to enable the mates to get some canvas on her.

The passage down the Channel was made in squally and cold weather, the crew grumbling and fumbling in their bemused mental condition and, after a short and sharp attack of seasickness, the youngest apprentice engaged in the general labour of working the ship. In the morning, after a deck watch spent during a wild and wet night, the muster of men called to the poop for a tot of rum included him. Looking down and observing the thin, shivering boy, the cynical captain shouted: "Rum! I think a coffin would fit you better!"

Not a very kindly man, he probably practised the use of sarcasm without finesse to hide an inferiority complex – he may well have been an embittered man, and certainly his judgement of the material placed in his hands was poor.

14

What youth, having gained his sea legs, would not delight in every hour of the beginning of such a voyage, experiencing the glow of ambition realised! The whine of the cold wind through the rigging, and the wash of water crashing against the clipper's dainty bows would be music in his ears, while the manner in which order and discipline evolved from chaos in just a few hours would be a revelation and a never-to-be-forgotten lesson.

Within the space of a few days three significant facts were impressed on the mind of this boy thrust into a rough, albeit new and romantic, world. The first was the quick acceptance of and obedience to every order; the second, that the officers and the crew were kindly men beneath their rough exterior; and the third was the terrible quality of the food served to both the apprentices and the men and the manner in which the food was eaten. And in those days, no ship could be sailed without orders expressed in fluent and excessively adjectival language.

'Dafty' Donaldson was then in the prime of life, with an erect posture and fine physique. A full black beard and bold brilliant eyes gave him the appearance of ferocity which went no deeper than his skin – or further down than his tongue. Appalled at first, young Cobbold quickly came to see that he was a dog who delighted to bark and seldom bit, and that the manner in which Donaldson carried out his job was entirely divorced from his natural disposition. Bred and reared in a hard school, the First Mate merely applied his experience to his trade of driving men and assisting to sail a ship. Though master of his trade, he was not mastered by it.

The second officer had learned his trade in a harder school. By sheer strength of mind and tenacity of purpose he had, as it were, crawled through the hawser pipe of a collier to reach the poop of a clipper. His junior was quite a young man, having but recently gained his second mate's ticket. He, too, was a sailor of the Second Mate's stamp.

Here then were young Cobbold's sea-going school masters: the Captain maintaining aloof isolation - an unknown ogre in a secluded cave, ruling the destinies of all on board the *Ann Duthie* through his officers. The three mates were like the school form masters, in much closer contact with the 'young varmints' who had to be kept subdued and made to learn their sea lessons.

15

The sailmaker and the carpenter had a much more familiar relationship with the six apprentices. Hard-bitten, yet kindly seamen, these two sub-officers were always ready with advice and encouragement; it is possible to imagine their benevolence, their patience, and their secret admiration of the 'young gentlemen', who in the future might well command their ships. Both were excellent specimens of the seafaring types existing in those days. 'Chips' was an Aberdonian, dour, deliberate and efficient, while 'Sails' hailed from Sweden, gloried in his trade, and was seldom seen on deck without his palm and needle and hardwood fid. He appears to have been a man possessed of common sense, for the first piece of advice offered to the youngest apprentice was: "The finest equipment a sailor can have is a sharp knife and a clear conscience."

The working conditions of the seamen of today do not bare comparison with those operating in the late 1860s other than for the purpose of contrast. Modern steamer sailors on the Australian coast in the 1920s have much to thank progress for: fourteen pounds a month and overtime; duty shifts of four hours on and eight off; no possibility of being summoned from their warm bunks to go aloft in the middle of icy and wind-tormented nights to spend hours reefing or stowing sails; and a menu which contains fresh meat and vegetables and even bacon and eggs for breakfast.

Among the crew of the *Ann Duthie* were men of a fine type. Some were studious and ambitious to become officers, and they had with them sextants and books on navigation. Not a few were hoary old salts whose life experience was bounded by long voyages, alternating with short and lurid periods spent in a mental haze of women and alcohol. Their meagre pay having been spent at the millionaire rate, it was then the cry of the boardinghouse keeper: "Get out Jack and let John come in, for I see you're outward bound!"

There was a small minority of the crew, half-starved wretches who spent most of the voyage malingering in their bunks. They could hardly be blamed for this, since on the outward run they were between the regular sailors and the passengers in that they were merely working their passages and received only one shilling a month. Their purpose was to reach Sydney, where they would be taken in charge by the boardinghouse keepers until a berth was obtained for them on a homeward bound wool ship on which their wages would be four pounds a month. When the chits had been paid to the boardinghouse keepers from this low wage, there was nothing much for them to draw on arrival at an English port.

Soon after clearing the Channel, one of these unfortunates seems to have made up his mind that he had reached the end of life's tether - or it may be that he had been shanghaied and could not contemplate the months of absence from England. Whatever the reason, he rushed suddenly out of the forecastle, looked round wildly, and then dashed to the bulwark over which he sprang into the sea.

The ship was hove to, but the man was indeed homeward bound.

3.

With the crew reduced to thirteen able seamen, some of whom in practice were distinctly unable, the *Ann Duthie* proceeded south to the Azores and into finer weather, her cargo of rails for the New South Wales railways keeping her well trimmed.

Young Cobbold quickly became accustomed to going aloft with his fellow apprentices to handle any one of three skysails or to assist the sailors working in the standing rigging or the three tall masts when manhandling the royals, the skysails, and in reefing and stowing the topsails or courses. They were never allowed to work on the jibs out on the jib boom, that being considered too dangerous for boys in training.

The run to the Cape of Good Hope was accomplished in favourable weather, and before this latitude was reached the youngest apprentice had fallen into his place on board the ship and was fast becoming seasoned in and by this environment. The only distasteful dish on life's otherwise delightful menu was the atrocious food served alike to the apprentices and the crew. They lived on hard salt junk one day, odoriferous pork and watery pea soup another day, and rice on Saturdays. They never saw fresh meat and vegetables, and instead of bread they received brick-hard biscuits made of bran and meal – often weevilly. There was water to drink, of course, but limited to three quarts, and an occasional tot of rum and more frequent issues of limejuice to defeat scurvy; hence the nickname of the sailing ships – hungry limejuicers.

The midship dock house was devoted to the cook's galley, aft of which on the port side were the cabins occupied by the sub-officers. The apprentices occupied two cabins on the starboard side – three to each cabin – and here the boys slept, ate and lived when off watch. At the head of each bunk hung the occupant's hook pot which was taken to the galley at meal times with a plate and brought back containing the same food served to the sailors, who took theirs away in a kid - a wooden tub.

For a while, the boys did fare better than the crew with the addition of the contents of hampers provided for them by knowing parents, but when the hampers gave out nimble minds sought other avenues of supply – and there was one in the lazarette.

The leading or senior apprentice was a young fellow named Bob and, although he'd never hesitate to fire the bullets he himself made, he was considered by authority to be too sophisticated to carry out a certain duty better suited for the youngest apprentices.

Every day, one of them had to visit the lazarette and there fill the bread barge for the crew – in other words, to fill a wooden box with the weevilly biscuits kept in several iron tanks. To reach the lazarette, the boy first had to enter the saloon at the break of the poop deck, pass through it to reach an alleyway on to which opened the cabins occupied by the officers and the Chief Steward. He then continued to the hatch which gave entry down into the lazarette at the stern of the ship. The lazarette did not contain only weevilly biscuits.

The layout and the nature of the stores were well known to the observant Bob. To the guileless apprentice appointed to visit the lazarette, he quickly described the opportunities waiting there for any sensible person.

"You will find yourself among cases and boxes of all description and of great variety," he was always careful to explain. "The cases are all marked 'For the Crew' and 'For the Passengers'. Those marked 'For the Crew' are, of course meant for us and, as the Chief Steward has a bad memory and often forgets to serve out the food contained in those cases, we are entitled to repair the omissions. You delve into some of them, and then the Chief Steward, who is really a decent old sort, will never experience poignant regret."

Young Cobbold set off on his first visit to the lazarette, a slight youth carrying the empty bread barge through the gauntlet of the passengers in the saloon, then slipping by the officers' cabins keyed up with excitement. Arriving in the lazarette, with haste and trembling he carried out Bob's careful instructions, delving into this case and that until a layer of 'luxuries' – tinned milk and jam, raisins and currants and bottled fruit - covered the bottom of the bread barge, and were then hidden beneath the quantity of biscuits.

The return journey was even more thrilling, and no gun or whiskey runner ever enjoyed the game of running contraband as the youngest apprentice on the *Ann Duthie* enjoyed bringing the bread barge from the lazarette, having to pass the open door of the Chief Steward's cabin, perhaps an officer, and then the passengers in the saloon.

Every crewman knew what was underneath the ration biscuits, and on the way to the forecastle the bread barge had to be halted at the dock house for removal of part of the contraband for the apprentices, the remainder going to the seamen. To their credit there was not one among them to give away the show. All honour to them, although it was honour among thieves.

Perhaps the Chief Steward was not so blind after all - he must have known the leakage at the end of every voyage when he checked the stores. Doubtless he chuckled every time a white-faced boy slipped by his open door with the laden bread barge, and possibly he was torn between the economy laid down by the owners and his naturally generous heart. Anyway, he never placed any restrictions or obstacle in the way of this 'luxury' running which, after all, could not be regarded as theft because the 'luxuries' rightly belonged to the crew.

Despite the unwholesome food, life at sea had a beneficial effect on the youngest apprentice. The winds and the sun, allied to the constant physical occupations, began to harden and toughen his body and, when the ship had passed the Cape of Good Hope and began its run down the Easting, his nerve and his courage were tested.

Though heavy following seas, raised by a succession of gales, assisted the ship on her way across the Southern Ocean, they made her steering more difficult than normal against the wind blowing from a few points ahead of either beam. The helmsman's task was therefore made more laborious, so young

Cobbold was sent to assist him. Because of the experience gained on his father's yachts, he quickly became proficient at steering, or assisting to steer, an ocean-going ship, taking two-hour shifts at the lee wheel.

Day after day and all through the long nights, the high seas raced after the heavily-laden ship, hovering threateningly above the stern, then bending down to shoulder her forward on the surge as though impatient of her slow speed. Her decks were constantly boarded by tons of white water necessitating the rigging of a safety gangway from the break of the poop to the after end of the deck houses to which life lines were secured, and from the foreward end of the deck houses to the forecastle head. As much as possible of the running gear was removed from the often-submerged deck to the gangways fore and aft of the deck houses, as well as to the higher elevated poop and forecastle head, and thus the crew were saved many a sousing as well as the hazard of being washed overboard. The doors of the cook's galley were battened fast and a square hatch cut in the roof, the cook having to climb a ladder to reach this unusual ingress.

This was not an easy school for any boy to attend.

It was the practice among the apprentices for those who spent the watch below to lend any article of apparel to a member of the watch on deck. Early one dirty night it began to blow harder than ever. Those boys and members of the crew taking the deck watch huddled into whatever shelter they might find, then were ordered aloft to reduce even further the canvas carried above the top gallant sails. Young Cobbold was directed to the foremast.

As has been stated, the *Ann Duthie* was a full rigged ship. Beside the usual square sails on each mast – the courses, the double topsails, topgallant sails and royals – she carried skysails above each of the royals, and hence she was known as a 'flash ship'. Whether or not the skysails were of any material assistance in driving her is problematical, but they certainly gave her a smart appearance and revealed in her captain what in modern parlance would be termed 'swank'.

Given a new ship, where the gear was not only new but stiff, and given a skipper anxious to show what he could do with her, every stitch of canvas she could carry was piled on, even up to the royals. About midnight on one pitch-dark night, when the violence of the gale was continually increasing, the Chief Officer warned the skipper, who reluctantly consented to allow the royals and the topgallant sails all to come in together. The order then was to let go the topgallant sails and royal halyards, get on to the clew lines, and go aloft; apprentices to the royals, able seamen to the topgallants, one man or boy to each sail. Away went young Cobbold up to the fore royal, Brown to the main royal, and Fraser to the mizzen. The boys were followed by the able seamen of the watch, who would stow the topgallant sails.

In the teeth of the hurricane wind, Cobbold was lying alone across the fore royal yard, maintaining the folds there by the weight of his body and the strength of his bleeding hands, and at times having to let go the canvas in order not to be pulled bodily across the yard. Suddenly, above the shrieking gale came the dreaded cry "Man overboard!"

The seaman working on the main topgallant yard underneath the apprentice Brown had heard his yell, and in the pitch darkness he had sensed that the boy on the royal yard above him had gone down to the sea.

All hands were ordered to the deck and the Captain sent was for. Birnie quickly appeared, to stand at the break of the poop looking up at the shivering sails. He was seen to shake his head. The carpenter was cutting loose and throwing overboard anything that would float.

The inexperienced boy and the unimaginative crew waited for the order to lower away a boat, unable to appreciate the distance that the ship had covered from the moment of the accident, and the impossibility of locating the sea's victim in the absolute darkness of the night, even had a boat been successfully launched.

The victim in this instance was the apprentice Brown, sent aloft to stow the main royal; and, picturing the unfortunate lad struggling in the wild waste of water far astern and frantically screaming for help, it was like a blow between the eyes to be ordered aloft again to complete the job of furling the sails, and to know that the ship was speeding on her way leaving the human flotsam to die, if death had not already claimed him.

Afterwards, the crew heatedly discussed what they considered was the Captain's callousness in making no effort in locating and rescuing the lad. However, in view of the darkness of the night, the running sea, the speed of the ship when the accident happened, the amount of canvas she was carrying at the time, and certainly the great risk in bring his ship about in such weather with the weak crew at his disposal, Birnie had no alternative but to act as he did. Even had he accepted the risk and endangered all the lives in his keeping, the odds of locating the lad, even if still alive, were ten thousand to one against.

For the first time in his short career, Francis Cobbold was brought face to face with life in the raw; perhaps also for the first time, he was made aware of both the cheapness and frailty of human life when one of the apprentices, on being aroused and told the news, sleepily said: "Why, Brown had on my sea boots!"

4.

The wild westerlies blew the *Ann Duthie* across the Southern Ocean to Australia in a quick passage averaging 300 miles a day – according to the cook who got it from the Captain's steward. Certainly the wind was favourable from the longitude of the Cape of Good Hope to the longitude of the Leauwin, south-western Western Australia.

Fremantle was then a small settlement maintained by the hated convict settlement system and for several years the eastern States had refused to have anything to do with these residents. The *Ann Duthie* did not call there, or at either Adelaide or Melbourne, and when she arrived off the Victorian coast fine weather was experienced all the way to Sydney, which was reached on the eighty-fourth day out from London.

Sailing up the harbour, when the wind was soft and off the land, the cries of cocks from the fowl runs were delightful to all hands. Entranced by the beauty of miniature promontories, islands and bays guarded from the Pacific by the frowning Heads, Francis Cobbold beheld the youthful city and its surrounding hills covered with their natural bottle brush and fuchsias that, in the years to come, were to give place to the streets and houses.

Having to wait for an available berth at Circular Quay, the anchor was dropped in the harbour and almost immediately the ship was blessed by the arrival of the meat boat, which also brought fresh vegetables and potatoes. Passengers were eagerly looking forward to the promise of this beautiful land after the long and arduous voyage; the apprentices were high-spirited and boisterous; and the 'round-trippers' of the crew were estimating the amount of money due to them and looking forward to a short burst of a full life in the company of harpies and perfumed with strong drink. Only the poor shilling-a-month sailors who had come all the way from England for the privilege of working a wool ship home were not exactly overjoyed by this landing. Immediately the ship was berthed, they were paid off with less than three shillings each, submissively to approach the boardinghouse keepers for food and shelter until a ship could be found when they would have to seek an advance with which to recoup their hosts.

After the more fortunate sailors had been discharged, the work of unloading the ship began, and continued in the leisurely fashion of the day when harbour charges were more sanely reasonable. The Colony's wool was then loaded into the empty ship, the loading done even more leisurely, as at that time there were just a few waterfront warehouses and much time was spent in waiting for the arrival of the many consignments.

Altogether, the *Ann Duthie* was in Sydney for three months, and if the time passed slowly for the Captain and the Chief Steward – with their visions of irate owners to whom economy was almost religion – the weeks passed pleasantly enough for young Cobbold and his fellow apprentices.

They all had a little money entrusted to the Captain by their parents, and this was doled out to them as pocket money. The meagre income was augmented by the sale of excess clothing to a Johnny Allsorts, who would purchase anything from the ship's cat to the lead off her keel and who was no doubt eager with advice regarding the expenditure of the money he paid over.

Naturally, now that they were in port none of the youngsters thought to do his own washing, and a source of expense lay in connection with this hated task, which was given to an old lady who visited the ship. She was a shrewd businesswoman, and evidently a student of psychology in her humble way, for on every visit she took with her articles and delicacies she knew would be appreciated – and willingly paid for.

The berthed *Ann Duthie* was at this time situated directly opposite the Paragon Hotel that still remains with no visible alterations to this day. About her were other famous ships: *The Paramatta*, frigate built, all her ports painted white; *La Hogue*, a similarly built ship; the smart *Damascus* and, in the harbour, the

23

John Duthie of the same line as the *Ann Duthie*. The apprentices of both ships often visited each other.

Although Francis Cobbold and his fellows had nothing to do with the actual loading of the ship, they were not allowed to be idle. They were kept employed by unbending and sending

down the sails, overhauling the running gear, and washing down the deck at the end of each day. A favoured duty was that of night watchman when, after all the officers had come on board and retired, it was customary to curl up in the companion way and do the watching in their dreams.

8. The Paragon Hotel, Sydney

Eventually the *Ann Duthie* sailed from Sydney and the days mounted into weeks, governed by the renewed routine of sea life aboard a clipper. The inevitable high seas and strong winds were encountered as the ship approached the Horn.

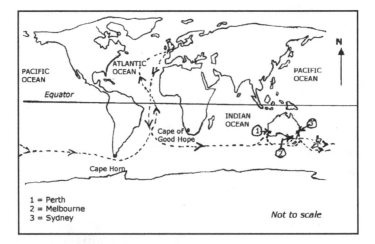

9. The Clipper Route followed by ships sailing between England and Australia/New Zealand

Each successive gale was more violent than the one before, and Francis Cobbold's earlier experience of the sea became as nothing to the roaring tempest which almost overwhelmed the ship when rounding the Horn. The darkness of the night hid the white, serrated summits of the mountainous waves, while above the deck the sails which could not be taken in were torn to ribbons and blown away one after another.

Night shut down on the ship like the lid of a box. The cacophonous elements took charge of the vessel wallowing in the troughs and shuddering on the heights. Out of the surrounding blackness, the white-capped walls of water sprang into ghostly visibility like the hands of demon spirits trying to pull the ship down to the bottom. In the saloon, the passengers held continuous service to God, beseeching his mercy and succour, some of them weeping, others terror-stricken and silent, a few courageous souls singing and praying and calmly prepared for death.

At the break of the poop stood the Captain, his white face surrounded by his wind-whipped whiskers and hair. The carpenter stood by, his hands clamped about the haft of his broad axe, waiting for the order to cut the lanyards that held the standing rigging of the foremast and thus let everything go.

All night long Birnie stood at his post, tensed and reluctant to give the order to Chips, delaying the decision until it should be inevitable. Many others in his position would have accepted defeat. When dawn came, however, the wind moderated and the grim captain had won. By then, the carpenter had waited through almost two watches for the order that was never given.

Afterwards, he told Cobbold that it was the worst storm he had ever experienced.

Expecting to encounter ice at any time, the reliable Swedish sailmaker was entrusted with the keeping of the forecastle head watch during the long and dark nights. His broad figure would be pressed into the lee bulwark, his keen eyes constantly trying to pierce the gloom out of which might spring the ghostly shape of an iceberg. Conscious of his responsibility, he was worthy of it.

One Sunday, when Francis Cobbold was about to go off watch, the weather was not particularly boisterous but a squall threatened and the Chief Officer sent the lad below to call the

Captain. Birnie came on deck to look aloft, first at the sky and then at the full load of canvas that was driving the ship forward. In that instant, as though the sails were a passing cloud, the fore topmast and the fore top gallant mast and the main topmast all went overboard.

The watch below were called, and the men then had to slave all that day to cut away the gear, to let the spars drift clear of the ship and then recover them. Being the youngest person aboard, Cobbold was listed with the night watch over the deck, during which he had to strike the ship's bell every two hours and call the cook at five o'clock.

After this delay, affairs went well with the *Ann Duthie* until, shortly after having crossed the Line, a series of further squalls again brought down the repaired masts. Once again the crew had to slave for hours in cutting away the fouled gear and repairing the damage. From then on, the sea was kind to her and the weather remained fine. Off Dover, she was taken in tow in the company of the *Donald McKay*, a ship that had left Sydney the same day as the *Ann Duthie*.

Thus ended Francis Cobbold's first voyage. And for the crew it was the boardinghouse keeper's cry: "Come in John – let Jack get out, for I see you're homeward bound!"

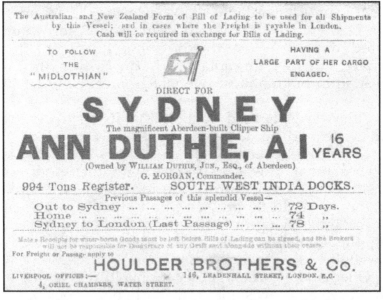

10. *Flyer advertising a voyage of the Ann Duthie from London to Sydney*

CHAPTER THREE

1868 to 1869
'Swallowing the Anchor'

1.

During the period the *Ann Duthie* was in the London docks discharging her cargo, being re-fitted, and taking in cargo for her second voyage to Sydney, Francis Cobbold spent an enjoyable holiday at his family home. His travels had partly drawn aside the curtain shutting off the far Southern World from the Old World, and what had been revealed to him provided food for reflection.

Though still only 15 years old, the decision resulting from this reflection demonstrates that Francis Cobbold had inherited sound foresight as well as an ability to assimilate and profit by hard facts. The ambition with which he had first sailed in the *Ann Duthie* was based on what he had seen and learned when visiting his grandfather's ships. That fleet of ships belonged to one owner, when other owners possessed single ships. It had been young Cobbold's ambition to sail his own ship in trading ventures among the alluring islands of the South Sea at a time when it was only just becoming clear that opportunities for trade in that part of the world might be as great as they were in both India and China.

At a much later date, private shopkeepers were to feel the keen competition of trading corporations and chain stores. In the same way, in 1868 private ship owners were feeling the competition of shipping lines owned by recently-formed joint stock companies. The lad saw this trend in ocean traffic and recognised its potential growth. Ships were becoming even larger, and already his grandfather's biggest ships were small in comparison with the newest ships launched from British slipways.

The prospects of becoming an independent trader were rapidly dwindling, and there was nothing ahead of a ship's apprentice but the prospect of slowly rising to the position of a ship's captain - subservient to the will of an owner or a combination of owners. Beyond that a sea career went no further.

Slow promotion and wretched pay lay ahead of the *Ann Duthie's* apprentice, who at that time would most certainly not have been able to envisage his advancement to the bridge of an Atlantic liner driven by steam turbines and owned by a joint stock company capitalised with millions of pounds. Steam at this time was regarded as an auxiliary to sail, and the most up-to-date mail and passenger liner running to Australia was the steamship *Great Britain*, an auxiliary vessel still relying mainly on sails for driving power.

So when Francis Cobbold sailed again for Sydney, he was determined to leave his ship in Australia, though he refrained from telling his parents of this decision.

2.

On reaching Sydney, Francis Cobbold packed his kit and walked off the ship. There was nothing to hinder him. The owners of the *Ann Duthie* had, of course received the £60 for his apprenticeship and they could not hope to get anything further. If the lad chose not to complete the sea education they had contracted to give him, it was no concern of the ship owners, to whom further sums of sixty pounds were being offered by parents wishing to apprentice their sons. Also, at that time Australia was comparatively a free country, access to which was open to everyone. There was then no White Australia Policy, no immigration restrictions whatsoever, and ships' captains were not held responsible for their crews and faced with a heavy fine should a member of a crew elect to stay in the country. So many sailors left their ships to take part in the gold rushes, or take up more remunerative work ashore, that often homeward bound ships found difficulty in obtaining crew.

From Sydney, the lad took passage to Melbourne in the *Dandenong*, a steam ship of about 500 tons. The cost of the passage was about thirty shillings, and the trip occupied six days or so.

3.

When he arrived in Melbourne, Francis Cobbold visited his sister, who had just recently come to Australia. She was the wife of Mr William Dickson, the founder of Dickson Brothers and Company, Importers of Flinders Lane. Cobbold accepted a position offered by his brother-in-law in the wholesale importing

28

house - to enter commerce proved to be another decision which was to benefit him throughout his life thereafter.

His sister was Sarah Jane Cobbold, born 24th March 1841, who came to Australia from South America and has married William Hill Dickson (c 1825-1876) in Colchester on 8th July 1869. The business was located at 23 Little Flinders Street, which was also known as Flinders Lane. Sarah married a second time in April 1877. Her husband was the Hon William Cain (1831-1914).

His job at the warehouse was to enter into a journal the lines called out by the entry men. His fellow clerk at the same desk was the invoice clerk concerned with despatching invoices with outgoing goods. Their work was inter-dependent, and young Cobbold learned how to write quickly and legibly and accurately run up the pounds, shillings and pence columns simultaneously. Should there occur a discrepancy at the end of the day, they had to work back until it was discovered - naturally in the beginning there were many, for the entry man was constantly calling for more speed which meant higher proficiency or employment elsewhere. Cobbold came to owe a debt to a fellow clerk named Wingate, for Wingate gave him a good deal of assistance and encouragement.

But it was not the type of work that appealed to him. Life on the *Ann Duthie* had roused the wanderlust in his soul, and very soon he was seeking an avenue of escape from the desk in the warehouse.

Australia was in closer proximity to the islands of the South Sea than England was; it was then the jumping-off place for all those glamorous tropical countries just being opened up to unrestricted trade. The tales of fortunes won and to be won were rife and seemed more realistic than they had seemed at the other side of the world.

The American Civil War had recently dragged to its conclusion. The price of cotton had risen to two shillings per pound, and through the commercial houses in Melbourne and Sydney went the tale that the Islands of Fiji were the coming place for anyone possessing spirit and enterprise to grow cotton.

The Islands! The South Sea Islands were painted with the bright colours of romance, adventure and wealth far more then than today. Had not Tasman sailed those seas in search of islands of solid gold? Certainly neither Tasman nor any one of those ocean explorers who followed him had ever found those islands of gold but - there is never smoke without fire. The heart of Francis Cobbold was stirred, and his distaste of the indoor, sedentary life of a commercial man became intensified.

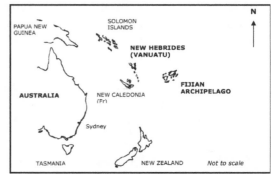

11. *Australia and the Melanesian Islands*

His fellow invoice clerk was a young fellow built on his own lines and he, too, was spiritually restless – dissatisfied with a clerk's life and yearning for something more rewarding. Often these two discussed the price of cotton and the prospect of the cotton market for a long way ahead, and eventually they decided to leave Dickson's and migrate to the Fijis in search of fortune. They resigned on the same day and shortly afterwards arranged passages - it was during this period of waiting that Francis Cobbold met with an aggravating misfortune, breaking his arm while trying to jump a horse over a three-rail fence.

It was two months before he was able to use the injured arm again. Still determined to try his fortune in Fiji, he sailed for Levuka via Sydney and New Zealand on the *City of Auckland* – a smart steamer having a cutaway yacht's bow.

The voyage was pleasant, and he made two good friendships on board ship. One was with an Italian surveyor named Martinelli and the other was with a Mr Wingate, whose brother had been so helpful to Francis Cobbold at Messrs Dickson's. They, too, were going to Fiji, their object being to survey eight thousand acres of land on the Island of Viti Levu for a Melbourne syndicate.

4.

Together with other groups of islands in the immense Pacific Ocean, the Fijian Archipelago is unique in formation and colourful in its history. According to geologists, back in a tremendously far distant age a great part of what is now the Pacific Ocean was an extended land mass, while the Continent of Australia was still submerged except for the Great Dividing

Range running down its east coast, the Mt Lofty and Flinders Ranges in South Australia, and the south-western portion of Western Australia. A cataclysmic upheaval caused the Pacific 'continent' to sink beneath the sea and the sea to drain off the land about the Australian 'islands', thus raising one continent while lowering another.

Certainly the study of any modern chart of the Islands of the Pacific gives the impression that a continental mass has subsided, leaving only its most elevated portions above sea level in the shape of islands. In the Fijian Archipelago, there are over two hundred and fifty islands, and they vary enormously in size from Viti Levu, with its mountains and rivers lying in an area of 4,053 square miles, to a mere rock. In many cases, not even a rock or sand cave is left above water to indicate the position of former islands. However, around the sites of these original islands the coral insects have built reef walls that enclose still lagoons from between two or three feet to fifty fathoms in depth, generally with a precipitous edge to the deep water.

In calm weather, when no breaking surf marks the submerged reefs, they are extremely difficult to locate. During his epic voyage of some 3,600 miles in an open boat into which he and eighteen companions had been forced by the *Bounty* mutineers, Captain Bligh sailed across an unsuspected reef above which was just four feet of water - a reef capable of wrecking any ship.

Nowhere in the world are there more reefs and shoals in proportion to the size of the Archipelago than Fiji. Even today, when in command of a steam-driven ship and when supplied with accurate charts, a sea captain seldom deviates outside known channels of deep water - the hazards presented to ships dependent on the wind can be clearly appreciated.

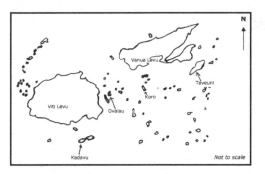

12. *The Fijian Archipelago*

31

5.

During the 1840s common sea adventurers arrived in the Fiji Archipelago. They were a roaring, fighting, buccaneering crowd, and when Francis Cobbold reached Levuka, then the chief port and the largest native town on the islands, they had not quite passed on. Blackbirding was rampant and murder a common crime.

> *Blackbirding refers to the recruitment of people through trickery and kidnappings to work on plantations, particularly the sugar cane plantations of Queensland (Australia) and Fiji. The practice occurred primarily between the 1860s and 1901. Those 'blackbirded' were recruited from the indigenous populations of nearby Pacific islands or northern Queensland.*

Cobbold's age at this time demands comment. When modern boys are studying for their school leaving certificate, he was working in the rigging of a clipper; when the modern boy is venturing from the parental home to study at a high school or university, Cobbold was sailing to an archipelago not fully charted or even fully explored, little known to the outside world, and populated with proven savages. At the age of fifteen he had embarked on a venture undertaken only by grown men of the roughest and the wildest natures. It was not as though he were an orphan kicked out into the world to fend for himself or go under, or that his people were needy, or that circumstances drove him. Nor was he sufficiently affluent to travel for pleasure, or for the excitement to be gained from visiting out-of-the-way places. If further proof of a dauntless spirit is needed, it will be found in full measure in his subsequent history.

At Levuka he met a charming family – a Mr Whalley and his wife with their two sons of about his own age and their daughter, aged twelve years. Whalley had been a government servant at Geelong, Victoria, and apparently the lust for adventure had seized upon him. Tall and thin and sure of himself, he and his courageous wife accepted Francis Cobbold with firm friendship.

Walking one day on the beach at Levuka, he was presented to a quite famous personage - none other than King Cakobau, pronounced Thakombau, the true King of the Cannibal Islands. Of striking physique, His Majesty expressed his delight at the introduction, smiling broadly and revealing his nicely filed teeth. The eating of human flesh was not then fashionable at Levuka, but it was suspected that the First Citizen often indulged his craving.

At the Whalley's invitation, Cobbold accompanied them to their plantation - or what was alleged to be a plantation. He and the entire family left Levuka one evening in an open boat fitted with a lugsail and the usual complement of oars for the home on the Ra Coast of the Island of Viti Levu. For a one time civil servant, Whalley revealed marked ability as a navigator for, steering by the stars all night through, he beached the small boat quite close to his house, a native hut built with bamboo and thatched with grass.

Only a small portion of the plantation was cleared, while no planting had been done. They lived chiefly on yams, coconuts and fish. He had no money - or very little – but very little money was needed other than for development of the plantation.

The only labour performed during young Cobbold's visit seems to have been the construction of a bamboo pipeline for carrying water from the nearby hills for domestic purposes.

Several other settlers were neighbours of the Whalleys, among them being an old Scotch gentleman named Carstairs who possessed a wonderful baritone voice and a plantation in the maturing stage. Accompanied by Mrs Whalley on her piano – imagine the determination and the struggle to get it there from Geelong! – Carstairs often sang 'Jessie's Dream' in which she hears a Highland Regiment rushing to the relief of Lucknow, and out across the tropic beach and the slow-heaving sea would roll in rich Highland accent:

"I hear the pibrochs sounding!"

Francis Cobbold's visit to the Ra Coast was both pleasurable and memorable and not a little instructive. It formed a prologue, as it were, to the play of many acts that was to follow.

> *Ra is one of the fourteen provinces of Fiji, occupying the northern area of Viti Levu. Ba is a province covering the north-west sector of Viti Levu; the name Ba is also used for a province, a tikina (a native Fijian administrative region comprising several villages), a town and a river.*

CHAPTER FOUR

Years 1870 to 1871
The Coral Island

1.

When he returned to Levuka from the Ra Coast of Viti Levu, Francis Cobbold took up an appointment as bookkeeper to Messrs Unwin & Nieman, the proprietors of the Albion Hotel.

This was before any kind of government had been established in the Fiji Archipelago. While Levuka was the chief port of the islands, and at this time was a conglomeration of native and European houses, it was not imagined that Suva would eventually become the chief port and the Seat of Administration.

The houses in occupation by the whites at Levuka were constructed in the rather crude Fijian fashion, with bamboo walls and thatched roofs. The whites had contributed two general stores, four hotels, and a dozen or so private residences to the township. There was little money in circulation, drafts on Australian business houses forming the major portion of currency. There were no civil servants, no costly transport facilities, no national debt, and consequently no taxation. Always off shore would be several schooners at anchor, while their crews would be found in the hotels, along with settlers from the Ra Coast and from neighbouring islands.

13. Levuka Town, 1890s

Life was red-raw and red-toothed. Fights were frequent among the whites, and many suffered from *delirium tremens*. A complex society was quite unknown other than by dividing the population of Levuka into three classes: the natives, the seafarers, and the more sober-minded and respectable of the settlers. A narrow, curved, white beach lapped by the gentle waves of a reef-protected shore, while back from the beach the few houses, the stores and the hotels were hemmed to the west by hills covered with dark-green profuse vegetation – this was Levuka as seen through the eyes of Francis Cobbold.

He worked at his books in the leisurely fashion of the time and place. He came to know well the people living there - the people who came there to trade and to drink, and the seamen who came chiefly to drink and to pick up any trade going, whether in goods or in black ivory. If a man became obstreperous in the Albion Hotel, there was the immensely stout Mr Unwin - semi-clothed in duck and perpetually perspiring - ever ready to invite the quarrelsome one outside to take a fall or two in a wrestling match. There was Mr Unwin's charming daughter to supervise the native domestic staff, and there was Mr Nieman who had married Miss Unwin and who was content to be always overshadowed by his enormous father-in-law.

The wildest, hardest-drinking, blasphemous, good-for-nothing and yet good-natured ruffians ever beheld in the South Sea staggered and lurched from pub to pub; men afraid of nothing, capable of anything, reliant and resourceful; Irishmen, Englishmen, Scotchmen and Australians, Bluenoses and Yankees and Dutchmen and Germans; ex-naval men, or whalers, ex-clerks and ex- everything else. The impact of an iron fist against a stubby chin was more often heard than a 'beg pardon!'

Francis Cobbold had stepped on to this colourful stage in his sixteenth year, and after him came a young man just a few years his senior in the person of J G Pilbrow. Pilbrow had recently left New Zealand where he had been a sheep shepherd for a while - an employment appearing at odds with one who certainly was a cut above minding sheep. A stickler for the dress proprieties of the decade, he demanded equal fastidiousness from others, taking pride in confessing that never once had he started a day's shepherding without wearing a clean starched collar.

About this time, Cobbold met another lad, the son of the captain of a topsail schooner, the *Margaret Chessel*. Young Wetherall was a year or so older than Francis Cobbold, and these three youths, living in a community of matured, hard bitten men, naturally drifted together. Pilbrow, by virtue of seniority, became their leader.

While Francis Cobbold had come to the Fiji Islands with the main objective of growing cotton, he was less impetuous than Pilbrow to make an immediate start. Pilbrow appears to have been one of those men ever impatient of delay, over-impulsive, none too cautious and in possession of a great faith in himself. It was his opinion that land in the Fiji Archipelago was much too dear, and he offered the proposal that the three young men should sail to the New Hebrides without loss of time, and there select land and proceed to get rich with remarkable facility.

Having become used to working in the presence of men much older than himself, Cobbold at once agreed with Pilbrow's suggestion, while young Wetherall also showed no hesitation about going. In port was a Captain Pollard who hailed from Wivenhoe, Essex, where Cobbold had spent many a golden day with the fishermen. Knowing that the Captain was about to sail for the New Hebrides in his 60-ton schooner, they arranged for their passages with him.

Elated by the prospect of action, the three youths pooled their resources and talked to Mr Doig who owned one of the two stores. They found Doig to be a typical Australian backcountry storekeeper, shrewd in business and an able judge of character. Middle-aged, and with a fair beard, Doig provided them with the necessary goods to the amount of their capital, and then was good enough to grant them credit for a further amount. It does seem that in those days businessmen were good gamblers, always willing to accept a chance even when a chance was a grave risk.

So three very young men set sail on the *Colleen Bawn*, their purpose being to land among savages on some islands of the New Hebrides group, and create a plantation there. Looking back from the assured safety and the humdrum conditions of life today, this venture appears to be one of the most sublime as well as the most harebrained ever undertaken by courageous youth.

2.

Levuka is situated on the east side of the small island of Ovalau, which lies some miles east of Viti Levu - the largest of the Fiji islands. From this port, protected by the usual reefs of coral from the wild sea sometimes raised by the trade winds, the *Colleen Bawn* sailed south round the main island before steering a course south of west. Holding to this course for some ten days she finally dropped anchor in Port Resolution in the island of Tanna, one of the southernmost of the islands in the New Hebrides.

Port Resolution is dominated by an active volcano, and after less than twenty-four hours the deck of the *Colleen Bawn* was covered with an inch of grey dust. Here in 1870, Francis Cobbold saw part of a ringbolt embedded in a rock, which had been used by Captain Cook's ship *Resolution* when he put into the place to re-caulk her sides in 1774.

The appearance and behaviour of the natives did not encourage settlement of Tanna. They had an evil reputation, which still clung to them for many years after Cobbold's visit. They murdered, one after another, the white men who settled among them. The most determined was a Scot named McLean, who maintained a bodyguard of local boys. His turn came, however, and like his fellows, he suffered indirectly through the sins which the early voyagers and sea ruffians had committed against a wild and primitive people.

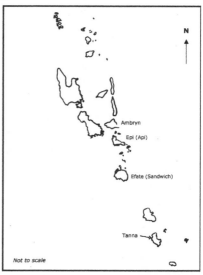

14. *Vanuatu (formerly the New Hebrides)*

From Port Resolution, the *Colleen Bawn* sailed to Efate, or Sandwich, and there she anchored in Sou'-West Bay early in October. The bay forms a deep indentation in the south-east coast, and from its base juts a low, bush-covered, headland forming a lesser bay on its other side. Off the beach, in each of these lesser bays, lies a small island – that to the north-west being called Mali and the other Vila. The headland masks each from the other.

Cobbold and his two companions were landed on the main beach opposite the island of Vila, together with their stores and baggage. The day was brilliant. The sunlight was reflected by the dancing water of the bay, the gleaming white beach edging the land, and the dark-green vegetation of the jungle which in places was impassable. It was a little world of peace and beauty – on the surface of things.

Immediately after the *Colleen Bawn* had sailed through the heads of the Bay outward bound, Vila canoes put out which brought a crowd of excited natives to the new settlers led by a particularly truculent ruffian who announced himself to be 'Jimmy' and who boasted of having sailed in a whaling ship. Of his whaling ship experience there was no possible doubt, for his knowledge of English was confined principally to the lurid adjectives to be heard on such a ship.

Here then were three white lads, their boxes and goods near, and round them a horde of naked savages armed with bows and arrows and clubs, gesticulating and excited, and led by a coloured gentleman having a whaling ship's education. It may have been due to this education that the settlers were not slaughtered immediately.

Jimmy, however, was a crafty blackguard who retained a modicum of respect for the white man and the white man's firearms – in this instance a sporting gun and eight ancient and obsolete 'Tower' muskets that were more dangerous to their users than to any object fired at. He sat himself down and proceeded to establish himself as a good lawyer in attempts to extract from the new settlers a portion of their goods.

Lucidly, and in a manner still further emphasising his one-time association with the crew of the whaler, Jimmy pointed out that the land on which the party had landed was really private property belonging to the members of his illustrious tribe. It was unfortunate, but property rights existed on the island of Sandwich, rights which had to be respected.

When it was argued that he was referring to land on the main island of Sandwich and that obviously he and his fellows lived on the small island of Vila, he replied that their settlement there was dictated by fear of the bushmen who lived inland and who sometimes raided them and their neighbours on the island of Mali. Here, his adjectives were employed even more extravagantly.

By mutual consent, the subject of land purchases was dropped for the time being, and some of the natives were paid to erect a bamboo shelter, plaited with the leaves of coconut palms. The cased goods were turned into walls, providing a shelter should the weather break, and slight protection should the savages decide to make a night attack. Jimmy was given a present, and he retired to think out further points for continuing his argument on property rights.

Accordingly, he presented himself again on the following day. He said he had called on a little matter concerning a transfer of land, and he desired to know what was going to be done about it. It would be a sad culmination of local hospitality if the people were forced to maintain their property rights with arrows and clubs. As far as he was concerned, the white men were welcome to all the land they wanted, but the common people on the island of Vila were most ungenerous. He urged the wisdom of a settlement of some kind.

After conferring among themselves, the lads parted with a considerable portion of their goods in payment for an area of land sufficient for a plantation and, the land question then being settled, Jimmy was asked to supply labour. In this matter he was as emphatic as in the matter of land purchase, pointing out that no Vila man could possibly work in his own country for others - no Hebridean gentleman could do that.

Here, as on the islands of Fiji and elsewhere in the South Pacific, the natives held it to be beneath their dignity to labour for strangers in their own territory; Jimmy, however, was obliging enough to offer to bring a party of bushmen to work for the white men.

This suited the lads, and that evening ten or a dozen men from the hills presented themselves and expressed willingness to assist in developing the plantation. They were allotted a space on which to build a shelter for themselves, and were given the first instalment of their rations. Then, at the usual hour, Cobbold and his two companions turned in, thankful that they had been farsighted enough to bring mosquito nets. That night they slept well, confident of the integrity of Jimmy and his followers.

On rising the next morning no bushmen were to be seen. The lads crossed the thirty odd yards separating the two camps and, instead of finding the sluggard natives peacefully sleeping, all they did find was broken spears and clubs and a few arrows, and many significant splashes of blood.

It is difficult to understand how the white settlers could have slept through the certain uproar when a number of natives were butchered within thirty yards of them, but it was so, and the evidence was strong that the bushmen had fought hard for their lives.

Jimmy then arrived and expressed both astonishment and indignation. That his people could have committed such an act was, of course, impossible. Those Mali men were quite capable of doing it - in fact, they would murder their mothers when life became boring, or when they felt too tired to hunt their fellow men for meat. Having castigated his neighbours with the adjectival fluency of the whaling ship he retired, overwhelmed with horror.

Then came men from the island of Mali to disclaim with equal fervour their guilt of the atrocious crime. Pilbrow conducted a kind of Court of Inquiry, and the verdict favoured the Mali men. He then suggested – and his suggestion was accepted – that they move camp out of the Vila men's territory some two miles into the territory of the Mali men. With the assistance of the Mali men, they transported their goods and persuaded the natives to assist them further in erecting a substantial house of wooden uprights, walled with bamboo and roofed with coconut grass. That done, they erected a paling fence and enclosed the house in an acre of land.

A further portion of their remaining goods were paid out for the land owned by the Mali men, the payment in goods for the land purchased from the men of Vila being written off as a dead loss. They now, however possessed their own 'castle' and they were far more firmly established.

The house was built none too soon, however, for the monsoon rains set in with terrific thunderstorms. Fever vapours rose from the drenched earth and the humid heat made life almost unbearable. Repeated earth shocks rattled their crockery so badly that many pieces were broken.

One after another the boys went down with malaria or ague fever, despite the large and repeated doses of quinine. The fever, plus the lack of fresh meat, quickly began to have inevitable effects on their constitution, while their strength was further sapped by enforced inactivity caused through the incessant rain. To attempt to labour in those weather conditions would have been fruitless. The lack of fresh meat was more keenly felt than anything else. Even if they had brought with them a small boat from which to fish in the Bay, they would have been unable to distinguish between poisonous and non-poisonous fish.

They bought a pig from a native on the condition that he slaughtered it for them. He gladly undertook to do this, taking the wretched animal into the sea and drowning it. The killing, while being both simple and effective, prevented efficient curing, however. For the purpose of a communal feast it would have been an excellent method and one giving a minimum of trouble, but since the pig was not bled properly, the curing was a dismal failure, and for one meal of fresh pork the deal with the native pig breeder was costly.

3.

The health of the youthful settlers was not good when the rains ceased and the weather improved. Naturally, men suffering ill health put off until later those things normally healthy men would have done on the day. Pilbrow appears not to have been a strong leader, and already the fire of enthusiasm for cotton growing was dying within him. As neither he nor Wetherall had ever handled a gun, it devolved to Francis Cobbold to take the single barrelled shot-gun into the dripping jungle, and there try to bag a pigeon or other edible bird. Even here discouragement was experienced, for it was difficult even to see a bird in the dense foliage, and seldom did he bring back any tangible result for his efforts.

Days would pass without the lads seeing any savages. No schooner sailed into the bay, and week by week their health and strength waned. It speaks well of Francis Cobbold's courage in that he often ventured into the jungle in search of pigeons, when memory of the fate of the bushmen must have still been keen. It was probably sharpened by such incidents as that of a native wanting to barter fresh meat offered on a plantain leaf. It was not like the flesh of any animal, bird or fish he ever had seen ... Pilbrow suffered most from malaria, and Wetherall's condition did not make him a dependable branch on which to lean.

One day, a white man visited the settlers, a runaway sailor who had gone native. He arrived with his retinue of savages from the other side of the island, having heard of the 'white invasion' at Sou'-West Bay. Naked, save for a breech clout, wearing a necklet from which was suspended a boar's curved tusk, and marked and tattooed with tribal insignia, he had taken a native wife, had become a local power and had gained a satisfying life. A year earlier he had been a member of a boat's crew sent ashore for water, and while the barrels were being filled he had run off into the jungle. There he had met and been well received by the natives of the tribe from which had come the ill-fated bushmen who had volunteered to join the young settlers' labour field.

Further to wearing a native dress, he carried the New Hebridean bow and arrows and club. Although on many counts blameworthy for his racial fall, the man cannot be judged without examination of all the facts controlling it. He was an ordinary sailor and likely enough one who would not pass high in a modern intelligence test. On any ship he would be a cipher to be ordered about by the captain and the mates, and be fed with food worse than merely coarse. A quick dash into the jungle, a throw of the dice with fate in a gamble in which to lose meant death, resulted in his bruised vanity being satiated by the respect of black men and women and the wielding of a little power, both of which had been denied him all his life and would be denied him while he lived among his kind.

Towards the end of the year affairs had not progressed with the youthful settlers on Sandwich Island. There is no evidence that they did very much developmental work, and what they had done and had been done for them had been costly. A large proportion of their trade goods had been expended on land purchase, on services, and on native fruits and other things. Pilbrow still suffered more from malaria than did either of the other two, and when by chance a small steamship put in for water he decided to return on her to New Zealand. Intending to return with further supplies of trade goods when he had recruited his health, Pilbrow left Sandwich Island on the *Wainui*, taking with him the title deeds of the land bought from the natives. He did not return, however, and many years passed before Cobbold saw him again in Australia.

4.

So Pilbrow left in the *Wainui*; Cobbold and Wetherall remained at Sou'-West Bay on Sandwich Island. On the threshold of his eighteenth year, Francis Cobbold elected to carry on in the face of great difficulty, ill health, and the unfriendly savages who coveted their goods and probably their bodies.

Relations with the natives became steadily worse. Constant bickering between the Mali men and the men of Vila frequently ended in armed demonstration in support of some trumped-up grievance. Arguments would be carried on between pacifiers on the one side and excited savages on the other, when a thoughtless act or an undiplomatic word would provoke violence with only one result.

Further weeks passed. With the passage of time, the hopelessness of making good became even clearer. It was impossible to hire the natives, who would not work for others in their own territory. It was impossible to obtain labour from another island because Cobbold had no way of recruiting and transporting them to his plantation.

The time arrived when he was compelled to face the fact that to grow cotton successfully was impossible. Every day he looked for a ship to call and take them back to Levuka. Bouts of malarial fever continued to take a toll of his strength.

One day, when wandering along a native path through the jungle hoping to acquire a pigeon, he suddenly came to a clearing in which were set up many carved figures and images - objects which proved that this was a native ceremonial ground. Impelled by curiosity, he examined the place with thoroughness, and in a cavity beneath one of the carved figures he found a nest of fresh eggs. Into his mind leapt a picture of poor Wetherall's wasted face, and he marked the place in order to find the eggs on his return.

Continuing out of the clearing, he followed another native path until he happened to disturb a wild sow and a litter of well-grown pigs. He had a mental image of his earlier years in Suffolk - and the gun practice on the river Deben now proved of worth.

This was a red-letter day for Cobbold, and he set off back to the house with the carcase of the pig over one shoulder. Securing the nest of eggs inside his hat, he went on homeward slowly and with repeated halts on account of his weakened state of body, at last reaching the house where Wetherall's smile of delight at the good things he had brought was reward enough for the effort.

Fortunately for them, Cobbold had to make a trip to the nearby creek for fresh water, so the eggs were not cooked

43

immediately. He had returned with the water and was in the process of lighting a cooking fire when a mob of excited, clamorous savages, gesticulating and waving their weapons, appeared from beyond the house enclosure. It was clear that they wanted, metaphorically, only the lifting of an eyelid for the excuse to rush the house and commit murder.

Not understanding the reason behind the demonstration, the two lads crossed the enclosure to meet the natives and to find out calmly the cause of this unneighbourly show of force. It took some time before they could pacify the visitors sufficiently to learn that, by taking the eggs from the ceremonial ground, Cobbold had committed an act of sacrilege; only by returning the eggs and making many presents from their dwindling supplies was reparation made.

Even so, relations remained very strained. Incident followed incident, making life both unpleasant and filled with anxiety. Cobbold began to realise that a determined attack on their goods and on their lives would not be delayed much longer. It would only take the rash discharge of a gun for the savages to surround the house enclosure and cause bloodshed. The prospect of open warfare became ever more certain, and even if Wetherall and he did not run the risk of being murdered separately, if it should come to a siege of the house he was the only one out of a garrison of two who could properly handle a firearm.

The 1871 New Year came in. Francis Cobbold did not dare to leave the enclosure to hunt along the jungle paths, where he would be an easy target for any bowman. Months passed after the departure of Pilbrow before another ship called at Sou'-West Bay for water and, observing her to be a topsail schooner, Cobbold hurried to Wetherall to say that he thought by the cut of her she was Captain Wetherall's ship, the *Margaret Chessel*.

The visit to Sandwich Island by the *Margaret Chessel* was indeed opportune, for the two lads were in poor physical condition through the ravages of fever and an unbalanced diet. Despite frequent doses of quinine, their legs were swollen to twice their normal size and if a pit were made in the flesh with a finger tip it would remain for several minutes.

Together, they watched the ship sail up the Bay, the crowding terrors of the jungle at last beaten back by the prospect of relief from what really had become a siege. They saw the splash of water at the ship's bow when her anchor was let go, and they watched a small boat being lowered and in it three men make for the shore.

When the boat grounded on the beach, the steerman sprang out to meet them and to announce himself as Mr O'Neill, one time a Lieutenant in the Navy, and now super cargo of the *Margaret Chessel*.

5.

Within a few minutes the two lads were transported to the ship on which father and son were happily reunited. Beside the cook and two Fijian natives, there was Lance O'Neill, and his brother, who kept his eyes focussed on the house ashore. Old Captain Wetherall's mahogany-tinted face revealed concern for his son's physical condition. About sixty years of age, he was stocky and fat and satisfied with a life which offered him command of a ship at a low salary. For the command of such a ship he was ideally suited, not being very intelligent and content to obey his owners' orders without question. O'Neill, the super cargo, was entirely different from the Captain, however. Tall and slim, he was a well-born Irishman without nerves and with plenty of grey matter. These men comprised the entire crew of the ship.

The two lads had had a hard time since they were landed at Sandwich Island, but the crew of the *Margaret Chessel* had experienced a harder time. In the matter-of-fact manner of a man long accustomed to lurid experience, Captain Wetherall recited his adventures since leaving Levuka, O'Neill standing by, sometimes stern of expression, sometimes revealing a twinkle in his merry eyes.

The *Margaret Chessel* had made the island of Ambrym, in the New Hebrides, her first port of call on a voyage to recruit black labour for the Fijian plantations. On going ashore at Ambrym, the mate and two oarsmen had been immediately set upon and killed by natives. The remainder of the crew under O'Neill had at once set off in another small boat, taking what miserable firearms the ship possessed. The natives, however, instead of offering battle, fled into the jungle, and O'Neill and his companions buried the three dead men before returning to the ship with the first boat.

The *Margaret Chessel* next called at the island of Api where, just before her arrival, the *Colleen Bawn* had met with disaster and all her crew killed. At this island, O'Neill and two of the crew went ashore in a boat to recruit labour. They induced a number of natives to volunteer, and when the wages and conditions of employment had been settled, they brought off one full boatload and returned for the second load.

On deck were the cook, the two Fijians and the Captain, Lance O'Neill being down below with a bout of malaria. He had been an officer in the Army, and he was amusing himself by sharpening his old regimental sword when, from above, came sound of a scuffle. Not thinking it was anything very serious, he was very surprised to see the ponderous Captain Wetherall come crashing through the cabin skylight and thud upon the floor. Believing the Captain to be dead, Lance O'Neill rushed up on the deck and expertly pitted several of the natives with his sword, thereby relieving the pressure from the two Fijians. The cook had been knocked overboard and was not in view.

Lance O'Neill may not have come out of the fight safely if Captain Wetherall had not appeared carrying a loaded rifle. The apparition of a man, supposed to have been effectively killed with a club before making such an undignified entry to the cabin, so unnerved the savages that they broke away and dived overboard.

Yells and cries from the shore drew the attention of the visitors, and through their glasses Wetherall and Lance O'Neill observed the other O'Neill and his two companions fighting desperately with a crowd of savages. Even while they looked, before they could rush to a boat to go ashore and render assistance, the three shore men were knocked down to the beach where they lay quite still, and the victorious natives hauled their boat high up the beach.

Concluding that the super cargo and his companions were dead, Wetherall decided to clear out. The cook clambered aboard, and the five men set to raise the anchor. The anchor, however, had probably become stuck in a coral crevice; they could not break its hold and were in the end obliged to slip it by unshackling it. Having hoisted the headsails, the ship slowly came round, enabling a course to be set and more canvas put on.

Lance O'Neill then thought he heard a faint cry and, mounting the rigging, he saw through his glasses a man swimming desperately after the ship. Every possible measure then was taken to slow down the *Margaret Chessel*, and a boat was lowered to return and pick up the swimmer, who proved to be O'Neill's brother and not much worse for a severe crack on the head. He had come to in time to see the savages standing watching the ship getting away, and he had taken the opportunity presented by the distraction to run past them and into the sea.

6.

Efforts to recruit labour in the circumstances described above tend to draw aside the curtain on what, even in its most favourable aspects, was a brutal labour system and in its worst aspects was nothing more than slavery. The methods employed by Wetherall in this uncontrolled labour trade were gentle in comparison with those adopted by many others of his sort; indeed America had recently staged a civil war on this question.

The Captain urged his son and Francis Cobbold to abandon their ambition of growing cotton and to return with him to Levuka. Fully realising the futility of further effort, Cobbold agreed with young Wetherall to accept the offer of transportation and consequently the remainder of their goods were brought on board. From them one case of brandy and two of port wine were given to Wetherall in payment.

The two lads now found themselves on a ship short of food and short of men to handle her, and Wetherall decided to put in to Black Beach, on the island of Tanna. It was a place notorious for the murderous instinct of the natives but O'Neill, despite his recent experience at Api, volunteered to take a boat ashore to trade with the natives for enough food to take them part of the way to the home port. The Fijians rowed the boat, and Cobbold went along with a rifle in order to protect the super cargo while engaged in barter.

"If they rush me," O'Neill explained grimly, though still with an eager twinkle in his eyes, "you drop the first man coming at me and leave me to get to the boat the best way I can. In no circumstances come right ashore for me. Make no mistake about dropping the first one who rushes."

Once he was landed with the trade chest, the Fijians pulled the boat a little way off the beach. Cobbold set in the stern, the rifle pointed at the gathering of savages halted a short distance from the super cargo. They were well armed and by no means friendly and, in view of what he had gone through, it speaks well of O'Neill's courage and coolness in that he calmly opened negotiations for trade with the backing only of a boy of seventeen armed with a single-shot rifle. In the event of a rush to kill him and capture his trade chest, Cobbold could only hope to stop one, since the affair would be all over before he could re-load, and O'Neill would be either dead or swimming out to the boat and doing his best to dodge a flight of arrows.

Without haste, and certainly with no sign of perturbation, he traded for several pigs, coconuts and yams, and eventually the boat was backed to the shore and the provisions transferred to it, Cobbold continuing to cover O'Neill's retreat.

Thus was a most ticklish piece of business successfully concluded, and thus did Francis Cobbold take his departure from Sandwich Island in the New Hebrides.

CHAPTER FIVE

1871
Stormy Days and Wild Men

1.

The fine weather continued all the way from Sandwich Island to Levuka Harbour, but it was then at the beginning of the hurricane season and the Fiji Archipelago lies well within the hurricane belt.

The toll of lives and ships taken by the Fiji hurricanes is very heavy. Several days before reaching Levuka, Wetherall sensed a potential weather change. The day the *Margaret Chessel* dropped anchor in Levuka Harbour, the peculiarly leaden sky and the long, oily rollers sweeping by from the south-east told him that the hurricane was coming.

It was towards the end of February 1871 when Francis Cobbold went ashore and once again put up at the Albion Hotel; there were seventeen or eighteen vessels in Levuka Harbour. The enormous Mr Unwin showed his fatherly interest, and his daughter – seeing the ravages of malaria - served him with her best culinary efforts. The hurricane struck Levuka one morning, coming out of the south-west with a rising scream of wind and a wall of white water at its foot. Of the anchored vessels all but three were driven ashore and wrecked, the three fortunate ships being the *Margaret Chessel*, the *Meteor Barge* - a regular trader from Sydney - and a steamer that only escaped by steaming hard up to her anchors.

Houses were flattened as though built of cards: others were whirled away. The Albion Hotel rocked like a boat at sea and was one of the few buildings of any consequence that escaped destruction. Cobbold saw the ships come piling ashore, watched house after house being destroyed, and witnessed palm trees growing on the brow of a hill being whirled away like wisps of straw. It was one of the worst hurricanes experienced during the settlement of the white man in the Archipelago, its entire centre having passed over the western part of the group.

When life at Levuka again became normal, the lads brought their remaining goods ashore and settled their account with Doig with part of them. They deposited the balance with the British Consul - a Mr Marsh who had recently arrived. For some time they waited for Pilbrow to turn up and, when he failed to do so, they dissolved the partnership.

2.

During this time the schooner *Swallow* came into Levuka Harbour, commanded by Captain Bartlett, who for most of his life had been a mate on a whaling ship. 'Bluenose' Bartlett was old, tough and bitter, powerfully built and of medium height, a heavy drinker and, to use an Australian aphorism, a hard case. However, despite the man's apparently wild nature, Francis Cobbold found a certain amount to admire in him, and after several weeks of slight acquaintance he agreed to sail with Bartlett on his next cruise.

Meanwhile O'Neill – the ex-naval officer – had left the *Margaret Chessel* and been appointed to the command of King Cakobau's Royal Yacht. She was formerly a well-known crack Sydney craft, and had been brought to Fiji by a businessman who had decided that a place without bailiffs would be ideally suitable for him. O'Neill had to go to the island of Taveuni on the King's business and, since that island was just over a day's sail from Levuka, Cobbold accepted the invitation to accompany him to fill in time until the *Swallow* was again ready to go to sea.

The cruise continued beyond Taveuni, and eventually Cobbold became anxious that he would miss the *Swallow*. Accordingly he took passage in a trading cutter bound for Levuka where, to his consternation, he was informed that Bartlett had left.

That was a fortunate miss for him, since if he had sailed on the *Swallow* he might well have left his bones on a New Hebridean island where savages attacked the ship in the night. They had swum out from the shore and had gained a footing on the deck before they were discovered. Bartlett managed to escape from the ship and hide in the jungle, where logically he should have been found and butchered by the savages. However, coincidence is far more prevalent in life than in fiction, and after a further two days spent in the jungle he was rescued by the crew of a schooner that had put in to the same harbour for water.

Unscrupulous recruiters of labour for the plantations had inflicted so much trickery and violence on the natives, and so much success had been gained by the savages in their acts of retaliation in treachery and murder, that in 1874 no less than twelve labour-recruiting vessels returned to Levuka from the New Hebrides with their crews reduced by attacks made by the natives.

3.

Malaria having got a firm hold on Francis Cobbold, he visited the only chemist in Levuka, a Mr Thomas Parker, who advised him to take a long sea voyage during which he should not land at any malaria island.

Messrs Unwin and Nieman were both enterprising men who owned, beside the Albion Hotel, a plantation on the island of Taveuni. It so happened that they were fitting out a 20-ton ketch, the *Trent*, which they were despatching to the Gilbert Islands – a thousand miles or more north of the Fijis – to engage in trade and to recruit labour for their plantations. An interview with them secured an agreement on terms whereby Cobbold was to sail with Captain Bruce in no particular capacity.

Captain Bruce was a little old Scotchman and one of the finest navigators who ever sailed the Pacific. He plotted his course with unfailing accuracy with the assistance of only a sextant and a chronometer, and throughout the voyage on which Cobbold sailed with him he never proved to be out of his reckoning when drunk or sober. Like so many of his class and time, he was a hard and persistent drinker.

It should be remembered that it was a drinking age, before tea became popular; an age which had begun with the Georges and at this time had not yet ended with Victoria. Proper allowance should be made for the early white Fijians such as Bruce, Bartlett and Wetherall - and many others who Cobbold met during these years. All kinds of spirits were both cheap and plentiful. Life was extremely uncertain and death always lurked round the corner. Malaria and ague were fevers easily contracted and difficult to banish, and the hard spirit drinkers appear to have been better able to withstand these fevers than did those who were more moderate.

The mate of the *Trent* was of German nationality and as good a sailor as Bruce. He was superior, however, in that he was sober and upright in his dealings. In addition to the Cockney cook, the crew comprised Kanakas – young Melanesian boys. There was one other passenger in addition to Francis - a gentleman named Clark, who was determined to reduce his addition to alcohol by going native on one of the islands at which the *Trent* would call. Drunk, he was a squalid beast; sober, he was a refined, likeable fellow.

Their first port of call was Wairiki on the Island of Taveuni, where Captain Bruce managed to exchange two casks of beef for two cases of rum. He then proceeded to enjoy himself, with Clark to keep him company, and until the rum was consumed the Mate took the Captain's place while Cobbold acted as Mate. One might have thought that the consumption of two cases of rum at one sitting would be sufficient to ensure the Captain's retirement from this world, but long before the ship reached the southernmost of the Gilbert group he was as chirpy as usual.

Arurai, or Hurd Island, is formed of coral and sand, with no harbours and no anchorage like those to be found at the island further north, and for nine or ten days the *Trent* lay on and off beating up against the mild trade wind and set of the current. To land was a difficult and dangerous undertaking because of the tremendous surf always beating against the reef.

The natives were particularly skilful at bringing their canoes through the reef surf which, though probably not too dangerous for themselves since they were such expert swimmers, nonetheless could easily have caused the destruction of their craft. Being an old man, they especially favoured Captain Bruce by taking him ashore in a canoe several times, but if any other member of the crew wished to go ashore he had to be content to go as far as the reef in the ship's boat and swim through the surf to the land.

Francis Cobbold tried it – once. He would have fared badly but for the Kanakas with him in the water. The mate, being unable to swim, remained on board the ship but Clark, liking the look of the place, decided that it was his spiritual home. He was landed with his few belongings to work out his destiny - which ultimately proved not to be to his liking.

Sailing north from Hurd Island they passed Rotcher Island away to starboard, and eventually sighted Byron Island - named after a sailor who had either deserted his ship there or who had been marooned for bad conduct. The place had an evil reputation, created no doubt by its overlord, Byron Bill, who came off to meet the *Trent* in a native-built whale boat manned by eight native paddlers. A man of conspicuous, if wild, appearance, he came to meet the visiting ship as should a gentleman of the South Sea – accompanied by a dozen native canoes each with two to six paddlers. Whale boat and canoes skimmed over the crests of the green water mountains and cut down through the valleys, the paddlers working madly and urged to even greater efforts by Byron Bill standing at the great steering oar, a huge semi-naked man whose unkempt hair and beard were whipped by the breeze. He was a man not easily forgotten.

The island fleet surrounded the *Trent* with vociferous welcome in what appeared a friendly manner. Captain Bruce, however, would have none of them. He had not been sailing those seas for several years to remain unsophisticated; he had heard reports of Byron Bill and his 'subjects' which, true or not, did not encourage trust. The canoe crews began throwing their grapnels on board, while Byron Bill in his whaleboat metaphorically expressed concern for the Captain's health. Acting on orders, the crew of the *Trent* severed the grapnel lines with hatchets as soon as they were heaved on board. Despite the apparent welcome, it was more than likely that the intention was to drag the ship on to the reef, where the crew would be murdered and the ship quickly broken up by the sea leaving no trace – after her stores had been transferred to Byron Bill's camp. Byron Bill must have been a picturesque ruffian, and one who was not likely to die peacefully in his bed.

The next call the *Trent* made was at the island of Beru, re-named Francis Island, where Bruce bartered for a score of flying fish and a quantity of coconuts. Trade was done in the open sea

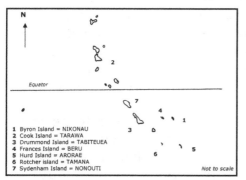

as there is no harbour, and when the island was left astern the *Trent* bore away on a north-west course for Drummond Island, which differs in formation from those at the southern extremity of the group. Narrow and curved like a horseshoe, its enclosed lagoon is well protected by a reef in

15. *The Kiribati Islands (formerly the Gilbert Islands)*

53

which there are only one or two passages large enough to pass a ship into a splendid anchorage.

The week spent at Drummond Island was occupied chiefly in paying and receiving visits to and from the crews of the Yankee whaler and the Sydney trader. Francis Cobbold saw that the Gilbert Islanders were different from those of the Fiji Archipelago. Their black hair was long and straight, whereas that of the Fijian is crinkly and fuzzed into a mop. They were also of lighter build and colour, handsome, well-shaped and well-built fellows.

Many of them were suffering from the unsightly disease known as 'scaley', due to lack of oil in the epidermis, which caused the skin to peel and fall off in minute flakes. The disease was doubtless caused by their diet, for they appeared to subsist only on fish and coconuts, the fish being caught at night when the canoes would go out into the open sea with flares to attract the flying fish.

These Drummond Islanders were a likeable people. Cobbold got on well with the young men, and vied with them in their diving exploits. Naturally they were more expert than he was in the water, but it is worth noting that he could reach greater depths than they could. To establish superiority in one branch at least of aquatic sport, Cobbold would amuse them and himself by going down the anchor chain hand over hand until he could touch it. His white body flashing in the translucent water was keenly watched by his dusky admirers on deck until one day, when half way down, a swift passing shadow sent him quickly to the surface thinking he had seen a shark. The watchers stated that it had not been a shark but an immense swordfish estimated to be at least twenty feet in length.

At Drummond Island, twelve men were recruited for indentured labour in Fiji, and four more were secured at the next port of call, Ipawara Island. Having called at Tarawa Island, or Cook Island, the *Trent* sailed south-west back to Hurd Island - their first port of call in the Gilberts, where they had left Clark to go native at his leisure.

Poor Clark had found life on Hurd Island to be much worse than merely boring. His self-imposed separation from alcohol had proved too much to bear, and he had invented a still from an old musket barrel with which he succeeded in manufacturing a most potent spirit from the native toddy. His efforts delighted the natives who encouraged him to such a degree that they kept him at work with threats of diverse pains and penalties should he attempt to go on strike. He became perpetually drunk: they held parties at which they waxed both excited and violent, so much so that many of them received broken hands, while Clark was slashed with shark's tooth swords and prodded painfully with spears.

The still was maintained at full capacity production and, when the *Trent* arrived, the natives were almost speechless and Clark was in *delirium tremens*. Unable, of course, to leave him there to certain death - either by the still or by a shark's tooth sword - Captain Bruce had him brought on board to return to Levuka.

By this time the ship's stores were becoming low, and Bruce shaped a course for an island where it was hoped to barter for yams and perhaps a pig or two. When they were a mile off the shore of this island the Mate, with the cook and Cobbold, took the ship's boat ashore and landed about a quarter of a mile from a native village.

The cook was ordered to remain by the boat, while Cobbold and the Mate walked to the village where they were received with unmistakable signs of hostility. The only defensive weapon between them was an old pepperbox revolver carried by the young man, who was the more expert shot. The inhabitants seemingly did not understand a word of Fijian, yet this was the only dialect known to Cobbold. The Mate knew not even that. All the natives were armed with spears and shark's tooth swords, and they appeared much more inclined to fight than to negotiate. There was nothing else for it but to make a strategic retreat, backing all the way to the boat while Cobbold menaced the crowding natives. This way, they reached the boat and were able to row safely back to the ship.

From Wairiki, the *Trent* sailed to the island's southern extremity, where they landed at Vuna Point. In the course of his stay, Francis Cobbold met a Mr Davene, who was the manager of Holmehurst, the principal plantation.

However, he did not rejoin the *Trent*. The voyage made in her had distinctly improved his health and the urge to be up and doing something, to be getting on with the serious business of life, was again burning in his heart.

CHAPTER SIX

1871
Fijian Adventure

1.

If it not been for the impulsive and unstable Pilbrow, it is unlikely that Francis Cobbold would have placed the cart before the horse as he did by consenting to go to the New Hebrides with two very young and inexperienced men. The decision was out of character, but perhaps the plain fact that circumstances largely control any man's life must be taken into account. In 1870 there was not the same opportunity as occurred the following year, when circumstances directed him to the Island of Taveuni where he met the manager of Holmehurst.

Two hundred acres of cotton were planted on Holmehurst, with further acreage being added every year. This was an efficiently run cotton plantation, with a staff of six white men under the manager, who controlled a Kanaka labour gang of some two hundred. His knowledge of the Fijian language, and experience of the natives, ensured that Cobbold secured the position of Second Overseer.

The men on the staff with Francis Cobbold are worth noting. The Chief Overseer, William Hazlett, was a native of Moonee Ponds, near Melbourne. An athletic, well-built young fellow, he had drifted to the Archipelago and to Holmehurst. He was something of a boxer and, when visiting Levuka for a spell, he met and thrashed the then bully of the beach, a Captain Weiss. On another occasion, his brother fought with one of the estate carpenters and, getting the worst of it, Will Hazlett stepped in to take his place, at which the powerfully built carpenter walked off. A likeable man, and one of sterling character, Hazlett left Holmehurst to go on a recruiting voyage to the Solomon Islands in the schooner *Dancing Wave*. The very first day he landed with the boat's crew he was killed in a desperate affray with the natives.

The third Overseer, George Fairweather, was a huge man physically, though slow in thought and action. Tom Drew, one of the estate carpenters, had been in the *Galatea* with the Duke of Edinburgh on that voyage when he was shot in Sydney Harbour. The second estate carpenter was an Aberdonian who had received his early training in shipyards, and then went to sea in the ships he helped to build, eventually retiring to a shore job with a chief officer's certificate. The engineer who ran the power plant and attended the cotton gins was yet another white man.

> HMS Galatea, a wooden steam frigate, left Plymouth on 24th January 1867 for a world tour with the Duke of Edinburgh in command. She arrived in Australia on 31st October and whilst there the Duke was shot by an Irishman. The Duke survived but James O'Farrell was found guilty of attempted murder and was hanged.

Of the Kanakas, one tenth were sent daily into the jungle to forage for food for the remaining nine tenths. What they secured was supplemented with a meagre ration of pork and rice, while on Sundays all hands engaged in sea fishing.

One of the several owners of the plantation, Lieutenant Hamilton, late of the Royal Navy, appears to have been a forthright John Bullish, no-nonsense gentleman of the period. Having married, and come to stay temporarily at Holmehurst, he brought with him two ancient muzzle-loading cannons and had set them in position in front of his house. The de facto Government having been established, it inevitably followed that taxes had to be levied and collected. Captain O'Neill was in command of the *Vivid*, King Cakobau's Royal Yacht, and called at the plantation for this purpose. However, when informed of the reason for the visit, Hamilton had the muzzle-loaders trained on the ship and threatened to blow it and O'Neill out of the water, damning O'Neill and Cakobau and the Government in full measure. The taxes were not collected.

Three brothers named Drury owned a plantation to the rear of Holmehurst, and Francis Cobbold visited them almost every Sunday. The oldest Drury had been a high official at the Mint in Melbourne, while the other two were formerly officers in the British Army.

Not far from them were two brothers named Young, the elder of whom became a successful businessman in Tahiti. The younger brother eventually became the Chief Inspector for one of the largest Pastoral Companies in Queensland. The Youngs owned a green-painted cutter with a gold band named the *Annie Young*, and at one time every available man in the native village of Vuna, together with the plantation hands, was conscripted to haul the cutter high and dry in order to scrape the barnacles off her bottom. The time for the pull was taken from the chorus of the Fijian Meke Meke. Years later, when Young and Cobbold met in Queensland, it was by recalling this picturesque instant that Francis Cobbold made himself known.

16.   Meke is the Fijian expression for a traditional dance, usually performed by a group arranged in one or more rows, with music provided by singers and instrumentalists seated behind them.

On the east side of the island was a former infantry captain named Jones, and a settler named Maitland who had left New Zealand to find out if he could grow cotton better than he had grown wool. Another neighbour, J V Tarte, was one of the few to survive the ultimate cotton debacle by developing his plantation into a good paying coconut and cattle concern.

Two other young men, Whittaker and Williams, owned a property close to Tarte's plantation. Whittaker met a tragic end when sailing his cutter, *The Peri*, from Levuka with sixty indentured Solomon Islanders on board. By concerted action, the labourers overwhelmed the crew of the cutter and murdered them all, intending to steal the boat and sail it back to their own home. When overhauled by HMS *Basilisk*, however, there were only fourteen Kanaka survivors in the last stages of starvation and exhaustion.

For the white man, death always lay in wait just round the corner. Even so, life was attractive and had many compensations. Set down among these gorgeous tropic islands, or sailing over the often placid sea, men lived a wider life than was and is possible in the city. Untrammelled by conventions and to a certain extent bonded together by the growing treachery and the savagery of the natives, there was none of the aloof reserve and the consciousness of class among the settlers that is found among men living an ordered civilised life.

One very windy night the alarm was given at Holmehurst that the cutter had broken loose. Francis Cobbold, Tom Drew and the Third Overseer manned the dinghy and set off after the cutter. It was lucky for them that they reached her, for they might well have found it impossible to row back against the tempest blowing off the land and increasing in violence every minute.

Having boarded the cutter and fastened the dinghy's painter astern, they hoisted sail - only to discover that the cutter was too lightly trimmed to beat against the wind. Having escaped from the danger of being swamped in a small and open dinghy, there was no alternative but to sail the cutter so that the distance from the island would not increase, and hope for the wind to drop. It was most important that they make the island before darkness fell the next evening, as they were due to attend a ball given in honour of the opening of a new cotton house on a plantation – a plantation owned by a man blessed with a bevy of pretty daughters.

In the morning, Taveuni was below the horizon and hope of attending the ball rapidly faded. The day wore on, and still they were unable to sight the island or gain much against the wind and sea. However, the Aberdonian carpenter, guessing the plight of the dinghy's crew if they were still alive and had managed to reach the cutter, put the case to a neighbour named Moore who owned a powerful boat. Moore loaned the vessel to the Aberdonian and, quickly gathering a crew, the Scotch carpenter set off in pursuit.

Finding the Holmehurst cutter, the carpenter bore down on it, ran alongside, transferred some of his crew and took off the whites. With every inch of canvas that could be carried, Moore's boat was sent thrashing against the gale and, with the loss of only the bowsprit, they landed by eight o'clock that evening – in time to rush home and dress and hurry to the ball.

2.
When he had been at Holmehurst for some six months, Francis Cobbold decided that he knew all he wanted to know about cotton, or at least sufficient to start growing cotton himself.

Knowing that Lieutenant Hamilton and his wife had recently arrived from Sydney bringing a weighty bag of sovereigns, the Second Overseer resigned and drew his pay in good red gold instead of the usual money order, or calabash, drawn on some bank or other in Sydney.

He purchased a centre-board cutter called the *New York* and, with a friend and two Fijians for crew, sailed north-east between Taveuni and the Island of Vanua Levu (the second largest in the Archipelago), set a course north-west between Vanua Levu and Rambi Island (a sea strait containing a name of shoals and reefs) and so into the great Natewa Bay which bites into the north-west coast of Vanua Levu.

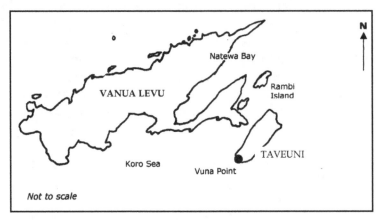

17.   Vanua Levu and Taveuni

Putting into a natural harbour on the west coast of the bay, he met two brothers called Vane Tempests who had recently arrived from England and were establishing a plantation there. They made him most welcome, but after a stay of only a few days, he sailed away out of the bay and back on the course he had followed since leaving Taveuni until, coming to the Koro Sea, he steered westward round the cost of Vanua Levu for some miles to land at an inlet beside which a certain Captain Henry was developing a plantation.

Captain Henry was married to a charming half-caste Tonga woman, by name Maram, meaning in Fijian 'Lady'. Cobbold so liked the look of the country that he purchased 125 acres of land from the Captain, for one American dollar per acre. The deal completed, he sailed for Levuka with the intention of procuring indentured labour. However, there was none available, and he was detained so long that his capital dwindled and finally vanished, and in the end he was obliged to sell the *New York* for an amount only half of what he had paid for her.

3.

Francis Cobbold's eldest uncle, John Chevallier Cobbold, had married Lucy Patteson, aunt to Bishop Patteson who was working in the South Sea Islands. Towards the end of 1871 Mr Arthur Cobbold wrote to his son, care of the British Consul at Levuka, enclosing a letter addressed to Bishop Patteson.

Francis Cobbold received his father's letter and the enclosure when he had occasion to call on the British Consul, but it was then too late to deliver the letter to the Bishop, for his lordship had been murdered by the natives of the Island of Nukapu in the Santa Cruz Group. He died by the hands of those who he had championed for years, and who he had gone to save from the usual conspiracy directed by the labour recruiters.

18. Bishop John Patteson in a photograph signed by his brother

Purely and simply, the blackbirders had resorted to the diabolical tactics of impersonating missionaries to facilitate kidnapping. Bishop Patteson protested vigorously and unavailingly to the authorities at home against this and other iniquities committed by the recruiters. On hearing that a particularly evil recruiter had sailed for the Santa Cruz Islands, he decided to make a rush visit there and, if possible, forestall the recruiter. He arrived at Nukapu on September 20th 1871 where, at the request of two savages and in order to show confidence in them, he transferred from his ship into one of the native canoes which took him ashore.

As soon as he was hidden from those on his own ship by the reef, a volley of arrows was fired at the Bishop's ship, wounding some of the sailors and mortally wounding the Bishop's Chaplain. A short while after that, those on the vessel saw the natives on shore turn adrift a canoe; when they overhauled it they found the dead body of the Bishop, rolled up in a mat to which was stuck a branch of a coconut palm with five knots. According to the native custom, this signified that the Bishop's life had been taken in revenge for the five native lives taken by the kidnappers whose visit had been made just prior to that made by Bishop Patteson. There were also five wounds on the unfortunate cleric's body.

Subsequently, it was elicited that the Bishop had been taken into a hut and clubbed to death. The majority of the islanders, however, strongly disapproved of the murder, and they banished the assassins. The man who struck the first blow fled to a neighbouring island, thence to Santa Cruz Island where the Chief, on learning of the crime and having always been friendly with the Bishop, had him executed.

The admiration and the respect of all civilised men is due to Bishop Patteson, and to many others who laboured to regenerate the savages of these island groups who hade been made even

more savage by the blackbirders. They were armed merely with a simple faith in god; they never equalled the glory of a soldier on the battlefield, but with pagan savages as their building materials, they worked to build an honest society, though constantly attacked by blackbirders and thwarted by the indifference of civilised governments.

19. *The Patteson Memorial Chapel*

They built better than they knew. On the Island of Nukapu, in 1884 Bishop John Selaya erected a cross to the memory of John Coleridge Patteson, Bishop of Melanesia; while a bas relief erected in Merton College, Oxford, where he was a fellow, represents the martyr recumbent with a palm branch in his hand.

St Barnabas' Chapel, sometimes known as the Melanesian Mission Chapel or the Patteson Memorial Chapel was primarily established as a memorial to John Coleridge Patteson, Bishop of Melanesia, who met his death as a martyr in September 1871. Such was the affection and regard in which Patteson was held that when the Patteson Memorial Fund was set up, the donations were sufficiently generous to establish several memorials. The chapel, for the Mission College on Norfolk Island, was a dream long cherished by the Bishop himself when he was alive.

4.

As has been stated, in 1871 a *de facto* government was set up, and the natural corollary of government is the making and breaking of laws. A Mr Freeman came to Levuka, who was admitted by the local authorities as the first Barrister and Solicitor in Fiji. It was not long before he met Francis Cobbold, whose little capital, general ability, and 'tone' given him by a good school duly impressed him.

The young man was induced to join Mr Freeman as his managing clerk, Mr Freeman painting in glowing colours the easy emoluments held out by the law in Fiji. However, money was scarce, and Mr Freeman was an ill paymaster. Cobbold never succeeded in getting a penny out of Mr Freeman, or out of the business into which he had put the last of his capital.

The alleged luck of the seventh son of a seventh son most certainly did not touch Francis Cobbold during his stay among the South Sea Islands. One after another, projects to which he turned eager hands failed, due less to any lack of a business sense than to the rude conditions of affairs in general and to the universal lack of money in particular. By nature he was not sufficiently ruthless and conscienceless to compete with conscienceless and ruthless men.

Before the period of what was a kind of war between the whites and the savages, the natives of the South Sea were always eager traders. It had been a generally accepted belief that the Fijians killed and ate all 'saltwater' men – any men of any colour who either through circumstances or choice landed among them. This was a fallacy. Inter-island trade was widely carried on before the blackbirding pirates arrived to disorganise it, and in many instances the very early voyagers traced the natives of one island to another to which they had been swept by the prevailing

63

trade wind and hurricanes. In their reports, both Captain Bligh and Bellinghausen stressed the willingness of the native trade - although their reports do not ignore the readiness of the natives of some of the islands to commit acts of piracy and homicide.

The period of Francis Cobbold's visit to the islands saw the transition from the old native 'empire', under such head chiefs as Cakobau, to the ordered state of British suzerainty.

Undaunted by his failures, Cobbold approached Mr Doig, the storekeeper, with a plan to which Doig readily agreed. Cobbold was fitted out with a large box filled with articles for native trade and, accompanied by two native carriers who also acted as guides, he set off on foot for the Raicola country of Viti Levu.

At the end of the first day of the journey, he halted at a native village and his guides returned home. On the following morning, fresh guides from this village took him on to the next village, then returned to their own. Thus, from village to village, did he progress with his trade goods to the head of the Rewa River almost in the centre of Viti Levu.

The climate differs much on this island - the north and west being comparatively dry compared to the south and the east, where there is much rain and high humidity. In no respect was Francis Cobbold's journey easy or pleasant – inland from the Ra Coast he was off the settled belt and in the country footing the Koroboya Range. Without doubt, when in his seventeenth and eighteenth years, Cobbold revealed admirable initiative, courage and resources.

At the head of the Rewa River, down which he proposed to raft the goods he secured by trading with the natives, he was fortunate to find a village at which the Ratu or head man proved to be a friendly fellow and honest. The young trader made known to the Ratu the purpose of his visit, which was to barter for yams, coconut mats, curios, and anything they had for sale. He was taken to the communal house and the news broadcast by the beating of a lali or native drum.

The natives quickly gathered from all directions: young men and old, matrons and maids, rich and poor. They were harangued by the Ratu, and Cobbold's goods were spread out on the mat, each article plainly priced. There, for all to see, were shining hatchets, knives, calicoes, beads, mirrors, and many other things - and then there occurred a wild scramble in which everything was snatched up and carried off.

Poor Cobbold was aghast. Here was the end of his trading venture. He could see no hope of ever recovering his goods or goods in payment for them. The old Ratu, however, remained quite unconcerned, and with a chuckle assured the youthful trader that eventually everything would be paid for, the rafts would be made and pilots provided for the return journey down the river.

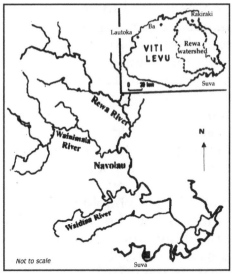

20. The Rewa River, Viti Levu

Notwithstanding the Ratu's genial assurance, it was insufficient to ease Cobbold's mind. His goods had been grabbed and carried off, and that seemed the end of them so far as Doig and he were concerned. As though to recompense him for the loss of his goods, he was taken to watch the slaughter of a pig, the heating of the cooking stones, and the entire process of cooking the carcase whole. Women brought tare, yams, plantains, coconuts, fruit and slabs of vakalolo – a native arrowroot pudding - and then, a meke meke was arranged, with native dances and liberal potations of yaqona. At the close of a most convivial evening in the company of 'thieves', Cobbold retired to the hut occupied by the young men, where he was supplied with native sleeping mats and a pillow.

In parts of Polynesia the drinking of Yaqona (pronounced Yangona), is a common ceremonial and social custom. Yaqona is made from the root of a pepper tree. In times long gone, the Yaqona was prepared by the young girls of a village who chewed the pieces of the root into a soft pulpy mass before the water was added. Today the root is pounded in a pestle and mortar or by machine. After the water has been added, the gritty pieces are strained through a bundle of vegetable fibre, usually the shredded bark of the Vau tree.

The following morning, after the usual swim in the creek, he was invited to an excellent breakfast and then led along the native path to the riverbank where, to his astonishment, he found waiting for him piles of goods rendered in payment of his own. Moored to the bank were bamboo rafts, hastily yet efficiently constructed to transport the goods down river.

Bidding a warm farewell to his native friends, and with the assistance of two pilots to steer the newly loaded rafts, Francis Cobbold began the long journey downstream, over the many rapids and skirting dangerous eddies until the smooth and tranquil reaches of the river were gained when the pilots left him to return to their village. Keeping the rafts in the centre of the water-way, Cobbold was taken down by the current to the next village where he hired two pilots to take him on to the next. Travelling from one village to the next, he brought his goods down to the delta of the Rewa River where he found a trading steamer, the *Pride of Viti*.

When remembering the acts of violence being committed by both blacks and whites all over the archipelago, it is worth noting that throughout the entire expedition Francis Cobbold had not one moment of trouble with the natives from one end of the river to the other. Apart from the one night of needless anxiety, he had traded with honest men, and had passed through the hands of many honest men whom he had hired as guides and river pilots.

In the Captain of the *Pride of Viti* he met yet another courageous fighter of these times. Captain Page hailed from Nova Scotia; he had converted a sailing ship into a steamer, having built the paddle wheels and installed an ancient portable engine in the hull. Page made regular trips between Levuka and the Rewa River, in the proximity of which were several settlers, and he would always accept a towing job, or anything that offered in the way of transport. Beside his shipping activities, he owned land and cattle, and was a man of sound financial standing, being considered to be worth at least five thousand pounds, which was a big sum in Fiji in those days.

Through the *Pride of Viti*, Francis Cobbold delivered his goods to Doig in Levuka, but when they realised a profit of only seven pounds he determined that the trading venture was not worth continuing. And so another failure must be debited in the ledger of his life.

CHAPTER SEVEN

1872-1873
The Fiji War

1.

Late in 1872 Francis Cobbold found himself in the little settlement established at the mouth of the Rewa River. Again with a little capital, he hired a boat from an old beachcomber and bought goods for a trade box with which to do business with the natives of the several islands off the south coast of Viti Levu. The boat was old but seaworthy – an open cutter with a codfish bow, carrying just a mainsail and a foresail.

An Australian bushman, who had drifted to the Rewa settlement, approached the young man and asked to be taken on the trip so, with this white man and one Fijian boy, Cobbold set a course for Mbengha Island where it was hoped to secure beche de mer, tortoise shell, yams and coconuts. The weather was squally, however, and the choppy sea quickly made the bushman violently ill.

> *Bêche-de-mer, also called Trepang: boiled, dried, and smoked flesh of sea cucumbers, used to make soups. Most bêche-de-mer comes from the south-western Pacific, where the animals are obtained on coral reefs.*

Keeping the coast of Viti Levu on his starboard beam, Cobbold steered for the dark hills of Mbengha, which rose to meet the tossing cutter. To the north, far back from the reef-guarded shore, towered Bligh's Coxcomb Hill – 3,960 ft high and so named because of the likeness of its summit to the jagged tips of a cock's comb. The boat proved herself and created confidence in her captain, but the Australian bushman was too ill to appreciate her.

Surrounded by the usual coral reefs, which extend far out to sea on its westward side, Mbengha was eventually reached - to the very great relief of Cobbold's companion who decided that the firewalkers were preferable to the angry billows. Consequently, having done what trade he could among the local population, Cobbold and his crew of one native boy set sail for the island of Vatu Leile, some eighty miles further west.

Tourists and seamen who have visited Suva will know the Kandavu Passage. From the bridge or the deck of a steady-going, steam-driven ship, the Passage is seen at an entirely different angle from that seen in an open cutter boat, where the horizon is constantly masked from the gunwale by walls of water, even in calm weather. On leaving Vatu Leile, Francis Cobbold set his course south-east against the strong trade winds to make the hundred miles crossing with only a pocket compass to guide him through the dark night.

When it is recalled that on more than one occasion young Cobbold had acted as cover for another white man trying to trade with hostile or treacherous natives, one wonders at his temerity in attempting to trade when he had no cover and only one native boy manning his small boat off the beach. It was not as though he were ignorant of the possibility of being overwhelmed by savages, covetous not only of his goods but also his body, for although the reputation of the Kandavuans was not fully established they were neither better nor worse than the natives of other islands.

Trade was moderately successful and in due time he returned to the Rewa River Settlement via Mbengha. There he picked up Smith, the Australian bushman, who was less sick on the short homeward run as the weather was calm.

2.

A Mr Burns had established a plantation beyond the mountain country where Francis Cobbold had traded at the head of the Rewa River. Early on the morning of Tuesday February 4th 1873, several of his indentured native labourers arrived at Rarawai with the news that natives from the mountains had descended and slaughtered Burns and his wife and two children.

Mr McIntosh at Rarawai despatched two white overseers and forty of his black labourers to investigate and to render what assistance they could, and in under an hour they reached the Burns' house to see the Mountaineers moving freely about the homestead. On seeing the two well-armed white men with their retinue of servants, the murderers impudently and without haste walked off in the direction of the river. The white men followed as far as the river permitted them and managed to drop one of the savages at long range.

Returning to the plantation, they found the body of Burns some distance from the house. He had been clubbed and tomahawked. His brains were beaten out, his bottom jaw was smashed, and two deep cuts had been inflicted on his left breast. Investigation among the plantation natives revealed how one, a Tanna Islander, had gone to his assistance when a Mountaineer had forced his tomahawk from Burn's left hand. The Tanna native in turn had taken the tomahawk from the Mountaineer, and Burns had then shot the latter dead. Other mountain natives had rushed in to surround Burns, who managed to shoot several before he was butchered.

When discovered, the body was stripped of its clothing. It was during the diversion this act produced that the Tanna man slipped away and ran to safety in the river.

The body of Mrs Burns was found some distance from the house; it too was entirely naked. She must have suffered great agony before death came to her, for she had received two awful cuts with an axe or a tomahawk on the top of her left shoulder, and in death her left hand was raised in a fixed position to the wounds. Another cut had been inflicted under the jaw and several of her teeth were forced down her throat. A nine-foot spear found beside the body had made two gaping holes, one on each side just above her hips. It was deeply stained with her blood for three feet up its shaft. Death had been directly caused by a club, the blow from which had smashed in her skull.

She had been attacked and killed in a corner of one of the rooms, and the pieces of her broken hair comb lay in a large pool of blood. The savages had stripped the body of clothing but had overlooked her wedding ring, and then they had dragged the body on its face to where it was found, evidently with the intention of taking it away and eating it.

The plantation natives said that the unfortunate woman had seen her husband attacked and killed, and that she had then sat down to write a note to be despatched by one of her house servants for assistance. Her cook, a Tanna Island woman, had implored her to escape with her, and Mrs Burns had pointed out that all the boats save one had been taken by the indentured labourers in their flight, and that the boat left was too big and cumbersome to be managed. The cook had fled, and Mrs Burns was left alone with her babies. She realised that with them she could never hope to reach the river; she would not, however, go without them.

The savages surrounded the house, stormed it and carried on their fiendish work. The little boy was found outside the dwelling, his head clubbed to a pulp; the girl, younger than the boy, had been seized by the ankles and whirled round to have her brains dashed out by a doorpost.

Besides the Burns family, ten Erromanga men, five Tanna men and one Solomon Island woman were killed. Two Tanna natives were found with their legs cut off and these, with the bodies of several others, were discovered at some distance from the plantation. The mountain savages had been forced to drop them by the pursuing whites while trying to take them away to eat. The condition of both the exterior and interior of the house was terrible to see. Clubs, spears and waddies and pools of blood were lying everywhere, mute evidence of the work of murder and destruction which had fallen as quickly as a thunderbolt on the unfortunate family.

When the news of the atrocious affair reached the settlers on the Rewa River -and soon afterwards reached Levuka and Pau - a formidable force of native warriors was formed with Major Harding in command and Mr Carew, the Private Secretary to Adi Quila (King Cakobau's sister), as interpreter. The force was transported to Rewa River in cutters, schooners and native canoes, while the *Pride of Viti* brought the white officers and the staff and much of the equipment necessary for such a punitive expedition.

At Carew's invitation Francis Cobbold accompanied the expedition, but he and it were not destined to see much fighting. As it was only possible to make progress through the jungle near the river, the staff went up the river in boats and the natives tramped along the natural paths bordering the river. The warriors were proud to fight under white men, and thrilled at the prospect of indulging in true savage violence from which they had been restrained for many years by their proximity to the white settlements. They were armed with clubs, spears, muskets and bayonets and wore their full war regalia.

After the first day's march, the boats had to be dragged up rapid after rapid - the same rapids down which Cobbold had sailed his loaded rafts the year before. In some of the river bends a little ambushing and sniping were carried out between isolated parties of local natives and the advancing host. Day after day the expedition drew nearer to the ranges in which lurked the murderers of the Burns family, and beyond which the River Ra flows in a north-westerly direction to the Ra coast of Viti Levu.

70

When they arrived at the head of the Rewa River, the staff was compelled to abandon the boats, and the whole force moved on up into the ranges which culminate in the Koromboya mountains. However, here in the Kai Colo country the warrior inhabitants of the stockaded villages gave way; they retreated with little resistance and suffered few casualties. Considering the nature of the country, the staff decided to disband the force and re-form it again in another district from which the Kai Colos could be more easily reached.

3.

It was fully realised that failure to exact justice for the murders of Mr and Mrs Burns and their two children would place the life of every settler in the Fiji Archipelago in jeopardy. To permit such an atrocity to pass unpunished would result in the loss of respect for the white man's superiority in the hearts of natives to whom homicide was a virtue, and further murders would assuredly follow the obliteration of that respect.

However, while the objective was most desirable, the means of achieving it were primitive and the obstacles almost insurmountable. The jungle covering the lowlands of Fiji's largest island, and the dense forests split by deep ravines that covered the mountain ranges, offered the inhabitants of the Kai Colo country every facility for escaping an enemy. Months passed before the punitive force was again created, but the idea and determination to avenge the murders of the Burns family were never sidetracked. The new force was taken round the island and landed on the Ra coast, and there followed a war in which many of the guilty natives were killed. The ringleaders of the attack on the Burns family were not taken, however.

On August 6th 1875, under the heading 'The Native War', the Fiji Times reported: "A very sharp fight took place on the 19th inst. – July 19th – near Na Cula, a mountain town, when Mr Phillip Jack, planter of the Ra River, and Mr Gresham, planter of Raki Raki, were killed … several others were severely wounded … There were several natives killed and wounded on the Government side, and a great number also of the Kai Colos.

"The forces had to make their attack up a steep hill. Awaiting them, the Kai Colos lay safely ensconced until the troops approached, when a front and flank fire was opened on them by the mountaineers, and then the opposing forces met in a hand to hand encounter in which bayonets, axes and clubs, did deadly work. The struggle was too hot to last long, however, and the Kai Colos threw away their weapons and everything they had, and ran for their lives. Two or three whites, with a number of natives, followed them up towards Na Cula, shot several in their chase and three in the town which the Kai Colos set fire to before the Government party reached it. Three natives of the Government force had been shot a day or two before, and taken to this town to be cooked and eaten. Their hands were found stuck upon sticks and their bones placed on the side of the path in sight of every passer-by. Joe Trenchard was one of the first to arrive in the town, and he had the bones collected and buried ...

"The notorious Rokoquera and his uncle, who it is said murdered Macintosh and Spiers, have at last been killed and eaten ... A number of mountaineers from a place called No Gaga, at the head of the Sigatoka River, joined the Government side and fought the Kai Colos well, rendering great assistance as guides. They lost several of their numbers, but felt perfectly satisfied with the revenge they had on these people that have been persecuting them for years. It is very evident that the Kai Colos have got such a lesson that they never dreamt of.

"The (Kai Colos) have already commenced to quarrel amongst themselves; those who had nothing to do with the murders of the Burns family are accusing those who did the deed of bringing all this trouble upon them by murdering the white man. A great number are hanging about, waiting to give themselves up, but don't seem able to have the nerve to do so. Patu Dradra, Chief of Karawa, has sent in a breech-loading double barrel gun belonging to the late Mr Burns, also some cartridges belonging to it. The gun was taken from the Burns's house on the morning of the murder. Dradra says he would like to give himself up, but is both afraid and ashamed to do so.

"The natives report that Teloko, the man who murdered Mr Burns, and Tawasi, the chief or principal leader of the people that murdered the Burns family, are still at large, and are camped at a place called Natuwai. They have Burns's revolver with them."

The 'war' over, Francis Cobbold returned to Levuka and shortly after his arrival he sold the land on Vanua Levu which he had purchased from Captain Henry.

The money offered him means of escape from the Fiji Archipelago. The word 'escape' is the right word, for he was beginning to understand that someone possessing just a small capital had little, if any, chance of either increasing it, or of getting out of the ruck of the dipsomaniacs who haunted the Levuka beach, the ranks of the knockabout schooner seamen, and the poor struggling settlers. The cotton bubble had burst when a genuinely United States of America turned back from civil war to the business of growing cotton once more, and now the best of the Islands' cotton was down in price below the cost of production. A large percentage of the growers were faced with ruin.

There was also, as has been stated, no real money in Fiji: the currency of IOUs and paper calabashes was normally only worth about twelve shillings in the £. Gold or bank-backed notes was seldom seen and much less handled.

Francis Cobbold was not nineteen years old, and the last six years had crowded the experience of a normal man's lifetime into his observant brain. When many young men of his age find that just to drift, to live for the day only, is sufficiently alluring, Cobbold was becoming alarmed by the fact that if he had not been actually drifting he had made no headway in life. The fictitious prosperity ruling in 1869 no longer existed now because the opportunities for development had not been backed by the same sort of outside capital which was pouring into Australia.

Someone at some time had said to him: 'My boy, go where the money is. There is none here.'

Abruptly, with the swiftness of making decisions which was to stand him in good stead in later life, he decided to return to Australia before his small capital dwindled and vanished. Money! There was money in Melbourne. There was money in Sydney. There was money in wool and cattle, but there was no money in cotton. 'Go where the money is' was what the wise old man had said.

The *Pride of Viti* happened to be in port, and Cobbold learned from Captain Page that at Suva there was a brig about to sail for Melbourne. She was shorthanded and there were excellent prospects of working a passage and thereby saving money. It was from a native canoe that Francis Edward Cobbold figuratively shook the cloying dust of the Fiji Archipelago from his feet, against the dark background of Viti Levu with Bligh's Coxcomb Hill rising darkly into the northern sky. He was to return years later as a successful businessman on holiday.

On board the *Nil Desperandum* he was signed on as an able seaman. The voyage was uneventful until the south Victorian coast was reached, when the ship was buffeted by a succession of gales - not unusual in these waters. Like most of the old tubs of those days, however, she was strongly built. She had plenty of beam and was not over-mastered, and she was able to ride out heavy weather as well as the best of modern steamships provided she had plenty of sea room.

On reaching Port Phillip, she sailed up the bay to what then was called Sandridge and which is now Port Melbourne, where she was taken in tow by a tug and moved to a berth in the upper Yarra River. Cobbold went ashore with the rest of the crew, and duly received his discharge of 3 VGs, meaning very good for Ability, Character and Sobriety.

CHAPTER EIGHT

Years 1873-1874
Cobbold takes up Surveying

1.

When Francis Cobbold returned from Fiji on November 1st 1873, there were ten million sheep in Victoria, Sir G F Bowen GCMG was Governor, and the Colony had enjoyed eighteen years of responsible government.

Forty years before, the gum trees grew on the slope gently falling to the creek which today is Elizabeth Street. Thirty-five years before, Melbourne was a tiny village patterned on an English model; in 1873 four-storied buildings lined the young city's business block, round which were driven hansom cabs and broughams in charge of liveried servants. It was before the telephone, gas was a new invention and the cable trams were yet to come.

21. Bourke Street East, Melbourne, c 1870

This was Melbourne as seen by Francis Cobbold after four years spent in the Fiji Archipelago. Here lounged policemen in uniforms looking as though they slept in them; here walked men wearing tail-coats and high-crowned bowler hats; here sauntered ladies arrayed in wasp-waisted, long-sleeved, high-necked costumes and little poke bonnets. Here reigned ordered security, here life was unhurried. Little more than two thousand miles away, the Burns family was being murdered by savages, and kidnapped native labourers were slaying the Whittakers in order to capture schooners and attempt to sail back to their homes, only to perish of starvation and thirst.

From the day when he set sail as an apprentice on the *Ann Duthie*, Francis Cobbold was destined not to live all his life in the locality of his birth, nor indeed in the country of his birth. There could have been a slight possibility of settling down to a life of ordered existence after that first voyage, but in undertaking the second voyage Cobbold proved himself to be made of sterner stuff.

On board the *Ann Duthie* it seemed to him that he had escaped from a house which was by no means uncomfortable into a garden which was by no means unbeautiful. From the house he had seen the garden, but from the garden he was able to see the rolling fields and the green forest and the broad highway which was the world. The house and the garden lacked the power to hold him.

22. *Queen's Wharf, Melbourne, c 1870*

His experience of clerical employment in Melbourne was too much like the house, from which he had seen the light and the air of the garden, to have been one of permanent duration. Confined within the walls of an office, Cobbold had been pulled by two opposing and powerful influences: the wish to please his parents through his sister by achieving success in business, and the desire to follow the world's highway. Desire being the stronger, it led him to Fiji, to the New Hebrides and to the

Gilbert Islands. For a little while, desire held sway, but after a rule of four years it relaxed its hold when the wish to mould his life in accordance with the ideas of his forebears gained in strength.

It produced the second period spent in Melbourne but, like the first, it was not to be a long one. Like that rolling stone gathering no moss, the average man suffering from wanderlust fever does not acquire many of the world's goods. However, if 'mental cobwebs' are substituted for 'moss' we have a different meaning from the rolling stone never doing any good for himself. A rolling stone gathers no mental cobwebs. The wanderer's mind is never entangled, enmeshed, or enchained by the web which slowly and surely cramps the mind of the stay-at-home. The wanderer gains mental wealth even if he does not in all cases gain material wealth.

In Francis Cobbold we have the example of one bringing together not only the wish to enter and succeed in business, like all his Cobbold ancestors, but also the desire to be ever on the move. The inherited instinct for business failed to be submerged by the wanderlust. Although the majority who succumb to it remain drifters through life, a select few become workers and planners.

In the fourth quarter of the last century, Australia was in the process of being moulded into a nation. It offered the workers and the planners great rewards if they would just roam over its vast area to see and to hold the countless opportunities. After that first voyage on the *Ann Duthie*, Francis Cobbold never would have made life successful in England. It was not possible to make it successful in Fiji because the opportunities for work and planning did not exist owing to the lack of outside capital.

In Australia the soil was excellent, the season was right, and the climate was suitable for the Cobbold sapling to take firm root and to grow to robust maturity.

2.

After a few days in Melbourne, its busy streets and bright shops had their reaction on the young man. Again he felt the urge of the restless quest. Out from the tropic islands of Fiji came the whispered words 'Go where the money is', and although there was money to be found in Melbourne shops, offices and factories, this was distasteful to someone who had sailed an

77

open cutter twice across the Kandavu Passage, where the winds are strong and clean.

1851-1861 was the decade of gold, during which precious metal to the value of 93 million pounds had been gained from the earth. This was followed by a decade of surging immigration, but the gold phase was passing and the agricultural phase was beginning by 1873, when the roads to fortune via trade and commerce were full of men establishing their positions. There were too many in Melbourne who had failed to win a fortune from gold. There were too many immigrants who had been robbed of their small capital, or who had become desperately disillusioned, to encourage any but the hardened prospector to continue seeking easily gained wealth on the fields.

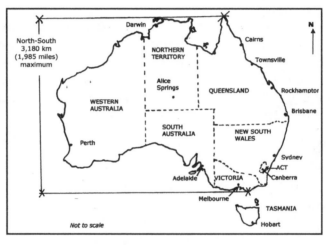

23. *Australia*

Hearing of an opening at the Lands Department, he applied for and gained the vacant position. Leaving nothing to chance to make a success of surveying, from the day he entered on his duties he took coaching lessons twice a week, finding an excellent tutor in a Mr Mackay who was an able mathematician. And as his father, Mr Arthur Cobbold, and the sports instructors at his school had unconsciously prepared the young man for those four years in the Fiji Archipelago, so Mr Mackay unconsciously fitted him for the several decades he was to spend in the west and north of Queensland.

Francis Cobbold proved to be a good pupil and one well worthy of his master. The tuition in drawing given him in his early boyhood was now of incalculable value, and in a remarkably short space of time he was promoted to the office of Mr A C Allen, the Inspector General of Surveys. Here, his job concerned the work of the District Surveyor's Offices, where up to that time the surveys of the land selections had been done in anything but an accurate manner.

At this time the field surveyors were haphazardly carrying out their work with the old fashioned Y theodolite, and the Inspector General decided that all licensed surveyors must replace their Y theodolites with modern transits and, further, that each should provide himself with a Chesterman Steel Tape for testing and adjusting the link chain. In order that the steel tapes in turn should be periodically tested, accurate measurements were marked off on the granite curbing outside the Lands Office.

The general survey of Victoria at this time had been accomplished in a manner which was both superficial and inaccurate. Large areas in the north, the north-west and the north-east of the Colony were being steadily cut up into 640-acre blocks for selection, and in these districts fresh surveys revealed instances of over-lapping in every direction, and in other cases wide spaces between boundaries. When the rush for land took place at Brandy Creek – now Warrigul – the chaotic methods of surveying then in fashion produced many disputes and much confusion.

The Inspector General and his Departmental Minister decided that far more accurate methods of surveying had to be adopted, and it was decided that, further to the continuance of geodetic surveys, the marked and cleared base line running true north through the Colony should be continued and completed from where it had been abandoned several years previously.

Applications were invited from surveyors competent to do the work; these applications were filed for reference by Francis Cobbold. One of the applicants who lived locally often visited the Lands Office and so came to make Cobbold's acquaintance; when this Mr Coates succeeded in winning the position he invited the young man to work with him.

Now here was an opportunity for outdoor work - an escape from confinement and ordered hours which could not be disregarded. However, the successful surveyor did not have the authority to appoint Cobbold or anyone else to the position of assistant and, in addition, an assistant had to be a licensed surveyor, which Cobbold was not. While experienced in every way to fill the position, it was still necessary for him to spend six months in the field before he could sit for his certificate.

However, through the good offices of the genial Inspector General, this hard and fast rule was waived in Cobbold's favour. He received the appointment conditional on his presenting himself for examination after the first six months spent in the field.

J J Coates had lived in New Zealand for several years but was a Surrey man and one devoted to his profession. Francis Cobbold had got so far ahead in the same profession that he was confidently able to carry out his duties as foreman, computator and draughtsman. With them was a cadet named Tilley Browne, who went out to complete his term in the field before sitting for his certificate. Beside these three, there were two chainmen, two axe-men to fell any of the huge timber that might obstruct the line, and a cook.

The Colony's great base line then ran to a point in the ranges a few miles east of Kilmore. Where it had been abandoned, the party made its first camp.

Coates was a jovial, burly-built, athletic man, an indefatigable walker and a fine leader. He never seemed to tire, and at the close of a long day's tramp he was always ready to set off hunting possums or bears to collect skins with which to make rugs. Then, before turning in, he and Cobbold would plot the day's work with all the accompanying calculations.

Before running the true north line, they also laid down the trigonometrical lines from one trig point to the others, the trigs being built with stones on the summits of the most conspicuous hills. In this way, distances and bearings were measured and computed, covering the whole of Victoria with a series of triangular base lines which, with the true north line, formed the basis of all future surveys and enabled inaccurate ones to be corrected.

It was not easy work. As well as a high order of intelligence, it called for physical fitness. Often their labours took them six or seven miles from their camp, which meant double the distance to be walked, while at the same time carrying a heavy theodolite. However, there were hours of relaxation on Saturdays, when they would walk many more miles to a distant township to dance, and then walk back to camp through the dark bush, thankful that God had ordained one day of rest in the seven.

It was a great life for any young man, and especially a young man of Francis Cobbold's temperament. It was a valuable experience for him, and without doubt he would have risen high in the Lands Department if destiny had not thrown a stone against the wheel of his life in the person of Mr Nicholas Sadleir, the manager of one of New South Wales' greatest sheep stations.

In 1874 Albermarle Station comprised roughly one and a quarter million acres. During the course of the years, however, closer settlement under the various Land Acts, as well as by the terms of the lease had reduced the area of this great property to three quarters of a million acres. In 1874 the station carried about one hundred thousand sheep and two thousand head of cattle, beside a large number of horses. Today it carries no cattle, just a few horses, and only some fifty thousand sheep.

Francis Cobbold met Nicholas Sadleir through the manager's brother, Inspector John Sadleir of the Victorian Police who was afterwards prominent in the capture of Ned Kelly. The meeting took place when the young man was on a trip to Melbourne after he had been with Surveyor Coates only four months. It resulted in Cobbold not completing his term of six months in the field, and in consequence he did not sit his certificate. Again the wheel of destiny had been halted and turned to roll along yet another track.

Sadleir had evolved a scheme for watering a part of the huge Albermarle run from the River Darling on which it fronted, and he was looking for a surveyor to make a feature survey of the country to be watered before he began to put the scheme into effect. The work of the survey was offered to Cobbold, who at once appreciated the possibilities of the scheme should the survey prove it to be practicable, and he agreed to leave his government post to undertake it.

Leaving Melbourne for Albermarle Station in November 1874, he took the train to the golden city of Bendigo, which was then the railway's northern terminus. At Bendigo he boarded a coach for Swan Hill, a town situated on the southern bank of the River Murray. It was a vehicle patterned after those held up by Dick Turpin, and even more closely allied to those which figured so romantically in Western America. Cobbold left Bendigo at nine o'clock in the morning, and with continuous change of horses travelled all that day and night and all the next day.

When the gold fever was sweeping through Victoria in 1852, a certain Freeman Cobb arrived from America bringing with him a fleet of handsome leather-sprung coaches and a company of daredevil drivers. He had heard of the great gold rushes: he came, he planned, he conquered. His coaches rolled into the Gippsland Mountains, across the western downs country, and over the great northern plains. They rumbled along the bush tracks of New South Wales and Queensland, South Australia and Western Australia; gold-digger, magistrates, civil servants, pastoralists and traders lolled inside them or swayed about on their roofs. The romance clinging to Cobb's coaches will live as

long as the nation, for they have become the central figure of the brilliant picture of those days of gold. The last one to be taken off the road was that running in 1924 between Yeulba and Surat in Queensland – yet another victory for the internal combustion engine.

24. *Chinese leaving for the diggings,*
Cobb & Co coach, probably c 1865 - c 1871

The day following his arrival at the Murray township, Cobbold took another coach which ran down to Euston, one hundred miles. The country through which he passed was for the most part covered with dense mallee shrub and held by a squatter named 'Money' Miller. At one point, the driver pulled back his horses and shot a dingo for the scalp; this would earn him five pounds, these wild dogs being great killers of sheep.

From Euston the journey was continued further down the Murray to Wentworth, just below which is the junction of the Darling River tributary with the Murray. At Wentworth he was obliged to spend the night in order to catch another coach scheduled to run to Menindie, 180 miles up the Darling. The young man put up at the best of the several hotels. This was kept by a man who would not shake his customers' hands with his right hand and, on seeing nothing wrong with the right hand, Cobbold was interested in knowing the reason. His host explained that: "Me right 'and was once took be the Dook of Edinburgh, and it shall never be taken by the 'and of a lesser man."

Towards the evening of the sixth day after leaving Melbourne Cobbold, with other passengers, arrived at a little hamlet named Pooncarie. At the hotel the landlady explained away the atrocious dinner by saying: "Everyone's on the booze and there ain't time for no cookin'."

The following day he reached Menindie, a small township lying over a wide sand belt which stabs the river from the west. Today the gum tree is still there beneath which the ill-fated Burke and Will exploration expedition camped in 1860 on their way to explore the continent from south to north. Bone-weary by the long journey, during which for some fifteen hours each day he had been jolted by the rough tracks, Cobbold was glad enough to arrive at his destination.

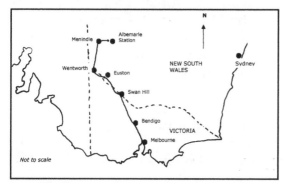

25. *The journey from Melbourne to Albemarle Station*

4.

The homestead of Albermarle Station, then and now, is situated on the east bank of the river Darling, some eighteen miles up from Menindie. Today its southern east-west boundary comes into the river approximately opposite the township, but in 1874 it joined with Talarno Station, thirty odd miles below Menindie. Within its forty miles of river frontage and eighty miles of depth lies a chain of large dry lakes filled by high floods of long duration through a narrow and shallow creek, which joins the northernmost lake of the chain to the river above the town of Wilcannia. The main lake, Victoria Lake, lies almost due east of the homestead and is fifty miles from it. Then, some few miles south of Wilcannia, a by-creek or anabranch leaves by the river to run more or less parallel with it at a distance of twelve to twenty miles until it crosses the river a few miles below Menindie. It cuts right across the major stream, to run south-west and then south to the Murray, east of the junction of the Darling with the Murray. Above the crossing, the creek is called Talywalker; below the crossing it is known as the Anabranch. The actual crossing is a remarkable feat of nature.

At this point the banks of the Darling River are straight and evenly sloped. The banks of the crossing creek are formed so symmetrically as to give the impression that they have been created by machine scoops. Only when the river is in flood does the creek run water. The level of the bed of the crossing creek is much higher than the bed of the river, and it was Sadleir's dream to throw a bank across the creek where it met the parent stream, and then to lift water into it from the river with a large-capacity pump. He thought that when the water level in the creek was raised sufficiently high, water would be forced back into a series of small and shallow dry lakes, billabongs and depressions.

After two days' rest, Francis Cobbold set about the work of making a features survey, and it did not take long for him to become convinced of the impracticability of the scheme. Even if it had been feasible, it is almost certain that Sadleir's proposed dam would have been swept away by the first river flood, or the creek would have found and made another junction with the river. Darling River floods are not to be regarded lightly. An incalculable amount of water dropped by heavy rains on the vast watershed of Southern Queensland will widen the river below Burke to ten, fifteen or even twenty miles.

CHAPTER NINE

Years 1874-1877
Pioneers of the West

1.

On finding that Sadleir's scheme for damming the Talywalker Creek was not practicable, one might have thought that Francis Cobbold would have returned to Melbourne to complete his training as a surveyor. However, despite the summer heat, this first experience of the Australian bush charmed and held him, as it has captivated so many before and after him.

Under Sadleir's management, Albemarle became a fine property. He offered the young surveyor a position as a bookkeeper and a storekeeper who would be expected to undertake light work in slack times. When the usual run of bookkeepers would have been satisfied to keep their books and issue a few stores and spend their slack time reading novels, 'FE' - as he later became known to his business associates - made the bookkeeping position an excuse to get among the flocks and pick up the details of growing wool in the peculiar circumstances governing the industry in Western New South Wales.

The Albemarle horses have always been well bred. 'Maori Jack', a powerful half-caste Maori who broke in horses of which Cobbold was to ride several, is still remembered today. He was followed by Billy Tutor, a breaker of less renown but equal efficiency who enjoyed the nickname of 'The Murrumbidgee Sticking Plaster'. They handled the progeny of a famous sire named Circassian.

With plenty of riding, a good deal of sheep work, and a thorough insight into the financial side of a sheep station, Cobbold mastered the rudiments of stock raising in Australia with the same facility with which he had mastered the mysteries of surveying. The shearing, of course, was an education in itself - they were the days when the shearers were comparatively poorly paid but were, notwithstanding, proud tradesmen. They received only one pound per hundred sheep, each man having to contribute half a crown a week to the cook. To succeed in making high average tallies, the shearer of the 1870s had to be something of an expert when selecting his shears for a run of sheds. He had to be a good judge of his tools, testing his shears by the ring of each blade to prove if the metal was soft or hard; if one blade was softer than the other, the harder blade would quickly cut into it and the shears would become useless.

During the eight to ten weeks of the annual shearing Albemarle was much like a busy town, with forty-four shearers, thirty rouse-abouts to pick up the fleeces, the station hands, the musterers, the jackaroos and the odd men making a total of ninety. During this short period something like two thousand bales at £14 per bale were produced.

Every Saturday afternoon, those who were not too tired by the week's work took part in sports. It appears that a jackaroo (a cadet) named Hancock was a good runner, and a series of races between him and Cobbold proved that at a hundred yards he could beat Cobbold by inches, and at two hundred yards, Cobbold could beat him by feet. When Hancock returned to his home in the Western District of Victoria, he became Amateur Champion sprinter for that part of the country.

The white-faced boy who had joined the *Ann Duthie*, the malarial-smitten youth who had sailed the South Seas, now filled out in this wonderful climate of outer Central Australia. He put on weight - solid muscular weight - and turned into a lithe, fully-built young man with blue eyes and brown hair, ever anxious to know things, always ready to join in any sport going, and an attentive listener to the yarns spun around the camp fire. In those days the exploits of the bushrangers and the fate of the expedition led by Burke were fresh in men's minds. There was land to the north and to the west into which no white man had ever gone, a free country where land was not held by squatters, land waiting to be taken up and developed as sheep and cattle stations. Cobbold looked over to the empty north and west, and soon the call of it reached his straining ears and his restless spirit answered it.

Having been at Albemarle Station for only fifteen months, with his whole experience of the bush limited to that period, he tried something that many old bushmen would hesitate to do. He bought a horse with a reputation as a galloper, and a steady pack horse with all the necessary gear, asked for his cheque, bade farewell to Sadleir and all the many friends he had made, and he rode away to the empty north-west, the great south-western district of Queensland.

2.

Riding the horse, leading the packhorse on which was the sum total of all his property, and heading for the empty North, he must have expanded his chest and breathed a deep sigh of satisfaction. He was free to wander wherever he wanted, and only those who have experienced the ecstasy of perfect freedom can have complete sympathy with him. He left behind a life governed by regulation and faced a future in which he need only obey the impulse of the moment controlled by the needs of his horses. He could go where he liked, camp when he wished and travel by night if the days were too uncomfortably hot.

Calling at a station named Bellilla, below Wilcannia, he was welcomed by the manager, Mr Bowes Kelly, who was to become one of the best-known mining magnates in Australia, owning large interests in the Broken Hill mines and those at Mount Lyell in Tasmania, and rising to the directorship of many important companies.

26. The Broken Hill and District Water Supply Company illustrated their prospectus with seductive drawings of the Darling River and Menindee Lakes brimming with fresh water.

At this time, Bowes Kelly was a young man, keen on his work and a keener sportsman. The day after Cobbold reached Bellilla they set off together for Wilcannia where Kelly intended to try out a colt in one of the races at the meeting being held. Cobbold ran his horse in the same race in which Kelly rode his colt and, although the Bellilla man won the race and Cobbold did not secure a place, that was to be the beginning of a long and active interest during which he was to race horses in Brisbane, Sydney and Melbourne.

The next time these two were to meet was after a lapse of forty-three years. They had then become directors of the same Australian-wide company, Cobbold being the Chairman of Directors of the Brisbane branch and Kelly being one of the

Directors of the Melbourne branch. It was as a visiting director that FE met Bowes Kelly in the boardroom of the Union Trustee Company of Australia.

On leaving Wilcannia, Cobbold headed up the River Darling for several days before striking north-westward to reach the unique, and dry, Paroo River. Following this empty river, he crossed the border into Queensland at the little township of Hungerford and, continuing beside the Paroo, at length reached the primitive township of Eulo where he met a woman whose personality was to linger in the minds of the bushmen for many decades.

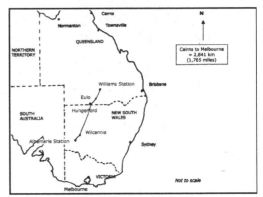

27. *Journey from Albemarle Station to Williams Station*

She was known far and wide as the 'Eulo Queen', being the

licensee of the principal hotel at Eulo. A remarkable woman, even then she was famous for her kindness and interest in every bushman. Her business instincts did not submerge a kindly disposition, and she commanded the respect of all who met her.

28. *The Eulo Queen Hotel, Queensland*

Cobbold stayed for a day or so at the 'Queen's' hotel, chiefly to rest his horses, and then continued north along the Paroo until he arrived at the junction of the Beechal Creek. He then followed the latter to Beechal Station, a run extending to the low range of hills known as the Dividing or the Paroo Range.

From Beechal, he went to Fairlie Station, owned by Mr John Howie, and still further on to Williams Station owned by two brothers of that name. These two brothers were first class stockmen and superb horsemen and bushmen, having been bred in the bush.

Having recently despatched their first draft of fat bullocks to the Adelaide market in charge of one Simon Leslie, they offered Cobbold employment as a stockman among cattle and the young man gladly embraced the opportunity presented him.

For nearly a year he remained on Williams Station, being shown all the tricks of the cattle business by two experts. It proved to be one of the most enjoyable years of his long career. The brothers – Ridley and Bob - accepted their new man as a brother.

A certain Doctor Ball was then the cook. An alcoholic almost all his life, he had steadily fallen from the position of House Surgeon in one of the Manchester hospitals to immigration to Australia, to shepherding sheep, and finally, when sheep shepherding in all weathers was forbidden by advancing age, to a knockabout cook.

The Australian bush contains many such tragedies. Not only uneducated men and misfits joined the gold rushes - among the tens of thousands who tried to win fortunes quickly were students, tradesmen, professional men and the younger sons of the English, Scottish and Irish nobility. Many of them returned to their native land having made good, while many more made good in Australia in occupations other than gold hunting. Still others became bitten by the haunting charm of the bush and elected to remain in it. Men became imbued with the desire to get rich quickly and rush home. Some of them did, while others became content to plod along the road of life in Australia, or to become submerged by the new world where men are so easily forgotten.

3.

The example of the Williams brothers pointed clearly to the goal Francis Cobbold might reach if he wanted to. They were ruled by implicit confidence in themselves and in the future of the country they were assisting to tame. Constitutionally as hard as iron, they thought nothing of hardship; they disregarded the elements where they themselves were concerned, and regarded the heat and the pests of summer as incidences of life which were redeemed by the calm, cool and bracing – albeit short - winter.

A young boy passed through the station in charge of a mob of fat bullocks, and he was known as 'The Boy Drover'. When, fifty years afterwards, Cobbold again met Bill Long it was as a fellow guest at the Hotel Cecil in Brisbane. John Howie, of Fairlie Station, only fifteen miles distant, was a visitor whom Cobbold came to admire for his superb bushmanship. He was a man of the same stamp as the two brothers, if a little less demonstrative and a little more efficient, if that were possible.

All these men had mastered the bush: they had never permitted it to master them. There was no fear in them – and there was no meanness in their souls. Among others, they were the pioneers of the cattle industry in Queensland. They were the pioneers, among others, of the real Australia - the real body of Australia on which the cities eventually came to batten, like ticks on the back of a bullock. Unlike the first pioneers, who entered upon beautiful, well-grassed, well-watered land with retinues of servants and a seemingly inexhaustible supply of convict labour, they were men who slaved and suffered. What they endured to establish themselves in a semi-arid, often drought-stricken country was a thousand times more harsh than the slight inconveniences experienced by the pioneers who landed on the shores of the continent and became immortalised as founders of cities and towns.

Batman, Henty, McArthur and others founded settlements; the Howies, the Williamses, the Boy Drovers and the Francis Cobbolds founded a continent. They discovered the water-holes and the lagoons and the gold bearing reefs; they were followed by the town builders, the small selectors, the road makers and the railway constructors. They went into an unknown, unexplored country in which running water was never seen unless after heavy rain, when an unexpectedly dry water-hole meant death. They fought off the blacks, subsisted only on damper and meat for weeks and months, planned and built, and hung on in the face of tremendous difficulties and incredible hardships, eventually to die unhonoured and unsung. While the seaside pioneers of an earlier age deserve their memorials and statues, compared with the country pioneers they are lesser men, to be credited with lesser achievements.

John Howie sold his Fairlie Station without the stock, and set off to prospect for land in the open country beyond Cooper's Creek. His invitation to Cobbold to accompany him was accepted with alacrity, and the young man reported at Fairlie Station in time to take part in the general muster of the cattle and horses. Soon afterwards the long journey began, Howie and Cobbold with two stockmen taking charge of the cattle, a cook driving his dray, another man driving a team of bullocks drawing a huge wagon laden with Howie's goods and stores, and a boy of sixteen to tail the loose horses. Not only were Howie and Cobbold destined to play important parts in the development of the cattle and sheep industry in Queensland, but the horse boy was to be none other than J B Howe, one of Australia's great landholders and an important breeder of sheep. Fifty-eight years after his journey into the Never Never with Francis Cobbold and John Howie, he was to receive Francis Cobbold at his home in Deniliquin in 1934. By this time, the boy of sixteen, now 75, had become enfeebled and tired, made so by the harshness of his life. Time, however, had barely tamed the indomitable spirit that had won him worldly success. He eagerly discussed with his visitor, and the companion of long ago, those 'days when we were young'.

> Cooper's Creek is one of the most famous and yet least visited rivers in Australia and is also known as the Barcoo River. It rises west of the Great Dividing Range on low ground as two central Queensland rivers - the Thomson between Longreach and Charters Towers, and the Barcoo in the area about 500 kilometres inland from Rockhampton.
> Cooper's Creek spreads out into a vast area of meandering channels, making its way roughly south into the far south-west corner of Queensland before turning due west towards Lake Eyre. In most years it is absorbed into the earth, goes to fill channels and the many permanent waterholes, or simply evaporates without reaching Lake Eyre. In very wet years, however, it manages to flood the entire Channel Country and reaches the lake.
> Most of the basin of the Cooper is used for sheep and cattle grazing on natural grasslands; the rainfall is much too erratic for cropping.

Spanning the bridge of years to 1876, we see the close lines of cattle moving out from Fairlie Station. The cook and his dray have gone on to the camp selected for that night. The bullocks drawing the loaded wagon strain forward beneath their yokes, the driver walking beside them, his long whip now and then bursting into a fury of reports which ring outward through the scrub trees. It is early summer, and the pioneering cavalcade winds down among the stony slopes of the Paroo Range. The cattle snatch titbits from the herbage as they pass, not yet seized by the desire to return to the country of their birth. Stony, scrub-covered hills, dry creeks and water courses which become raging torrents when it rains, blue sky and a powerful sun, and the ever-changing scene is what Cobbold is looking upon with a song in his heart. Again he is on the move.

And so, day by day, the cattle and the outfit move on westward to the Bulloo River, on and on past Mount Margaret of

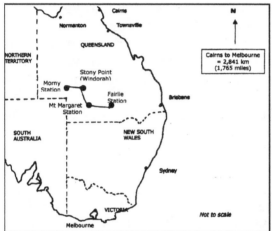

the Grey Range and from there to Kyabra Creek, down which they move towards the great Cooper's Creek which runs south-westward into South Australia to lose itself in the desert which killed Burke and Wills. It is now December. Heavy rains set in, and the Cooper's Creek is a brown flood.

29. The journey from Fairlie Station to Morny Station

It is essential to cross the creek. The rain increases in volume. The stores are safe on the bullock wagon, kept dry with tarpaulins. The men's swags are secured on the cook's dray, but the riders are unable to escape the rain, and they ignore its discomforts although the water is running down inside their clothes and dripping down their saddle-flaps.

From the north-west, rolls a succession of violent thunderstorms, but delay in crossing the creek means a possible halt of many weeks, and the creek is rising and widening and flowing faster and faster. Two of the men hold the cattle. The others assist the bullock driver, and with cracking whips, shouts and oaths, the panicky beasts are sent into the flood, straining, groaning, hauling the great wagon and its load through the white-frothed, brown water to the far side.

It is then back to the cattle, the cattle made frenzied by the uproar of the elements, beasts who have become almost uncontrollable. The men astride the intelligent horses become like madmen but have the cunning of madmen. Snapping whip thongs vie with the crackling thunder. Men shout, dogs bark, cattle bellow. Slowly the milling mob is pressed nearer and nearer the swollen creek and, stunned by the elements, dazed by the horsemen, the beasts take to the water and plough their way to the west side of the creek.

The cattle are trembling when they have been jammed into a bend of the creek where it is thought they may be easily held during the night of thunder and rain. The men are drenched and cold and hungry. The cursing cook at last manages to get a fire going and make some tea. He cannot cook anything but a stew. To bake a loaf of baking powder bread is beyond the ingenuity of any man on earth.

Storm after storm rolls down from the north-west. All night long it rains without ceasing. It is a night incessantly illuminated by lightning and made horrific by the pandemonium of celestial warfare. In shifts of two, the men ride to and fro across the creek bend in which are the invisible cattle. There is no comfort and no possibility of sleeping for those not on cattle guard. There is no dry place in this land of water and mud on which to unroll a swag.

When daybreak finally comes, however, it is clear that the cattle have gone. Somehow, the fear induced in them by the storm must have prompted them to flee, and somehow they bypassed their guards. Despite his inexperience, Cobbold volunteers to look for them and, accompanied by two cattle dogs – both as cattlewise as any man - he rides his horse into the stream. The brown flood rises to submerge the back, leaving only her head and neck and the upper part of her rider's body visible to the watchers on the bank. Swimming diagonally across the creek, they are still swept downward, the eyes of the guiding men seeking out the rushing death traps of floating debris.

The eastern shore is reached after the successive channels have been negotiated, and on gaining solid ground the plucky little mare is seen to be trembling and breathing fast. She is given short respite while her rider attends to the saddle girth, and then begins a long hunt for the missing cattle. There are no tracks: the rain has wiped them out of the sodden earth. Cobbold has to ride in a giant arc, and trust to his eyes and the dogs to find them.

The grey mare and her rider cross the mud flats, skirt the gilgie holes, flounder over the raging water gutters, climb to the summit of sand dunes to spy out the land and hope to see the dots of moving cattle. The going has been hard on both man and horse, but eventually the cattle are found, stopped and headed westward again. When the Cooper's Creek is reached they are reluctant to swim, and there is now but one horseman and two dogs to force them over the wickedly angry torrents that have expanded and joined together since the morning.

Yet the task is accomplished by a youth with just two years' experience of the Australian bush. He is watched approvingly by John Howie and his stockmen, who are unable to render any assistance – men who have lived all their lives in the bush, and who know the wiles and the whims of cattle better than they know themselves.

30. *Devon cattle crossing a stream*

This was how life was lived by the men of Western Queensland in those early days of development.

Howie and his men shifted camp to the point of the nearest mulga ridge. In years to come a township would be built there, first called Stony Point and later re-named Windorah. There they were forced to camp for some time, for a sliding sea of water twenty-five miles wide - the western overflow of the Cooper's Creek – was barring their western passage. When the weather had cleared and the water partly subsided, the crossing was attempted over the boggy ground, with the countless water gutters still flowing bank high. It took the party a full week to travel the thirty miles to the first camp on the bank of Whitula Creek, where the cattle were turned adrift. By now, the grass and herbage were springing with the astounding growth associated with the season and the rain, and it was unlikely that the beasts would wander far, following such a period of semi-starvation.

After the rains came the winged pests: the flies, the midget sand flies, and the mosquitoes. Men and animals were tortured almost to madness, and relief could only be found in the stifling smoke of fires made for the purpose. It is no unusual sight in Western New South Wales and Queensland to see men eating with their heads thrust into camp-fire smoke and their horses or camels standing close behind them, both only finding escape from the flies in smoke. On arrival at a selected camp site, the animals will stand close by and wait for the men to light a fire to which they walk immediately smoke arises from it.

When the journey was continued, the drovers and the bullock team were faced by a sea of rolling sand dunes over which progress was reduced to about five miles a day. Reaching a water-hole, another stop was made for a few days, for rain torrents vanish from the surface as swiftly as they appear. Then they at last reached a camp on the bank of a creek, some two miles from the homestead of Morny Station. Further torrential rains fell. The earth was covered by vast sheets of water and one night all hands were compelled to perch on top of the loaded bullock wagon. This flood caused another long delay, but much of this time was used to spy out the land and to decide which direction to take to reach open country.

On the advice of John Henderson, the manager of Morny Station, Howie and his outfit eventually reached a fine tract of country crossed by numerous creeks which seemed to have a good supply of possibly permanent water, and here John Howie decided to establish his run.

Cobbold's work with Howie was finished. With all his possessions lashed to the back of a packhorse, he journeyed the hundreds of miles back to Mount Margaret Station, lying some sixty miles north of the township of Thargomindah.

Described in the Sydney Morning Herald on February 8th 2004 as:
Thargomindah: *Outback town on the edge of the desert. Located 1014 km west of Brisbane and 126 m above sea level, Thargomindah is the last hint of civilisation before the traveller heads off into the desert areas of far western Queensland.*

4.

At Mount Margaret Station, Francis Cobbold met a bushman called Jack Darcy, and together they engaged with Duncan Campbell to drove a mob of fat cattle to the Melbourne market. Arriving at Durham Downs, they mustered the bullocks – 350 of them – and started south with the assistance of two other stockmen, one of whom was Leslie Ogilby, the son of a Victorian bank manager.

It was Ogilby's first trip into the bush but he manfully did his share of the work, being placed at the tail end of the cattle while the more experienced men rode on the flanks. The hours were long because the cattle had to be off the camps before daylight, and they were not camped again until it was almost dark in the evenings. It meant snatching meals when they could, and their sleep was cut to a minimum too, because the nights had to be divided into watches.

So Cobbold returned south through Bellilla, through Albemarle and Tolarno to the little township of Pooncarie, there to turn south-east over the desert road to Euston – seventy miles of poor, dry, unbroken bush country. Crossing the Murray at Swan Hill, they swam the bullocks across Australia's major river and drove them south past Bendigo and thence through Sir William Clark's paddocks at Lancefield. On arrival at Flemington, the king bullock realised £17 5s 0d at auction.

That was the first Tuesday in November 1877, and Cobbold and his friends just had time to order new suits and see Chester win the Melbourne Cup. Francis Cobbold had been absent from Melbourne for three years to the day. He left the city with the Fijian fever marks still on him; he returned hard and in perfect health. He had gone away as a youth in search of the Holy Grail; he returned as one who had at last determined his destiny and had found himself.

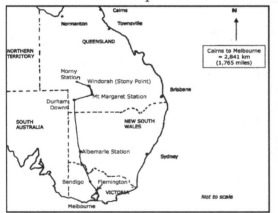

31. Morny Station (Queensland) to Flemington (Victoria)

CHAPTER TEN

Year 1878
Misfortune and Triumphs

1.

If you go into the offices and the business places of Melbourne, or of any other Australian city, and mention that you are from the bush it will not be long before a very busy man will lean back in his chair and shrewd, tired eyes will light with happy memories. For him the pressing affairs of the moment have vanished. For him the office walls have fallen down to reveal a gum-tree-lined water-hole or creek, a saltbush plain, or the everlasting aisles in a mulga forest. Once again he is young and strong; again he breathes the air of perfect freedom. He can smell the incense of burning gum leaves. Again he is a bushman, being in the presence of a bushman. He has forgotten that he sold his birthright for a mess of pottage.

> *Mulga:* semi-arid acacia savanna or shrubland that covers a large proportion of the Australian mainland. The term may refer to:
> * *The dominant plant species* Acacia aneura *(Mulga or True Mulga);*
> * *Any of many similar Acacia species which occur, or*
> * *The ecosystem or landscape in which the flora is dominant.*
> *This third usage is probably the most common of the three.*

There are many Australian businessmen and hundreds of Australian city workers who once rode behind a mob of steers, or mustered sheep, or who once searched for gold and dug for opal. They have been caught and enchained by the cities after knowing the freedom of gods. Every year bushmen migrate to the cities; they come, they stay, they are compelled to remain, but in their hearts is always haunting regret.

32. Mulga shrubland

It has been related how the Howies, the Howes and the Cobbolds trekked into the semi-desert and took up great areas of land which they developed into sheep and cattle stations. They gave their lives, they saved and invested their savings in themselves, and they created the confidence of hardheaded bankers. They created two allied industries, the cattle and the wool industries – the greatest of which is the wool industry, and this has been made to carry all Australia's secondary industries.

The Pastoral industry of this country has been the goose that has consistently laid golden eggs, and indeed is still doing so although, alas, the eggs are now smaller. Numerous governments have persistently done their damndest to slay the goose, their desire being based on greed for votes - the votes of small land-seekers and the votes of those engaged in secondary industries which have to be maintained with subsidies.

Returning to Albemarle Station: in Cobbold's day it was about a million and one-third acres in area, and it produced annually some two thousand bales of wool. Today it is less than three quarters of a million acres in area, and it produces less than one thousand bales of wool. The land that it has lost does not produce the other thousand bales of wool.

One man was permanently employed within its boundaries for every twenty thousand acres. So, endeavouring to meet the demands of small men, without sufficient capital but who wanted to become pastoralists, the successive governments of New South Wales re-possessed areas of from twenty to fifty thousand acres on which were settled married men with their families. Assuming that Albemarle's lost half million acres were divided into areas averaging forty thousand acres, this made roughly twelve blocks. On those twelve blocks were placed twelve men and their families - but twenty-five men marched off that land to look for new employment.

Beside this policy of robbing Peter to pay Paul, the poor holders of three small areas were disadvantaged by something far more serious than lack of capital. Forty or fifty thousand acres is barely sufficient to maintain a family in all years; consequently, the holdings were fully stocked, if not overstocked, and there was no reserve of land left to fall back on in dry seasons. Whereas a large run can keep several paddocks empty for just this emergency, the smallholder does not have the space at his disposal to do it. His losses through drought are

98

many times those suffered by the large station, and he goes to the wall; his eaten-out block then becomes vacant and unproductive. In some cases, the blocks go back in that the holder runs a few badly bred cattle, a few poorly bred horses, and earns a living trapping rabbits and in hiring himself to a squatter, in which case his block is as equally unproductive.

Perhaps one small man in ten is successful - but only by buying up his neighbour's land and thereby giving himself a chance to survive the droughts.

For every man given a small pastoral holding, two stockmen are thrown out of employment. There is nothing for them to turn to in the bush. There are no inland towns and cities to which they could go, settle, expand and grow with. Their living having been taken from them, if they want to eat they must migrate to one of the coast cities.

Cobbold and his droving companions, on holiday in Melbourne, quickly found the city irksome and soon felt the call to return to the bush. The discomforts, the hardships, the labour and the pests of the summer were soon forgotten. Like soldiers who have passed through a modern war, they remembered only the bright side of their war with a recalcitrant land.

2.

Late in March 1878 Francis Cobbold arrived back at Mount Margaret Station after a holiday of three months in Melbourne. He was warmly welcomed by the owner, Duncan Campbell - a Tasmanian of Scotch descent, who was young, raw-boned, athletic and genuine. He offered Cobbold employment on his books, which had fallen into arrears owing to an increase in his business operations.

Having brought the station books to date, Cobbold joined in the muster of fat cattle for the Melbourne market, and during these operations he fell ill.

In those days, of course, there were no flying doctors, no ambulances to rush out from hospital centres to bring in sick cases from surrounding stations. Very few of the station owners and managers had even a primitive medicine chest.

At this time, an old man was employed at the out-station of Mount Margaret to perform the duties of hut keeper. Age had placed him beyond an active life. The years had bowed his shoulders, but his figure was still tall and his voice remained refined. He was the alcoholic Doctor Ball, one time cook to the brothers on Williams Station.

Taking Campbell's advice, Francis Cobbold rode to the out-station to consult Doctor Ball. Arrived there, he was feeling desperately ill and, having loosed his horse in the night paddock, he staggered into the kitchen. Ball was most concerned by the visitor's appearance and immediately examined him.

Typhoid! A man named Foley had died of typhoid only six weeks previously. Had Cobbold occupied Foley's room? Yes.

Breeding triumphed over environment and the old gentleman became doctor, nurse and wardsman. He got the sufferer into a bunk. He washed him and made him as comfortable as the circumstances would permit. There was no medicine and no possibility of obtaining any. For seven weeks he nursed the patient, calling to his aid all his old medical skill, dependent only for assistance on those articles commonly found in bush kitchens on which to diet the patient. For seven weeks, towards the close of his life, Ball again was the healer, the professional man - one risen again to his former state from the slough of menial bush labour. Foley died, but Cobbold lived.

Back again with the cattle, the young man was for the second time smitten with misfortune, on this occasion with a virulent attack of sandy blight. There is no greater affliction in the Australian bush. In layman's terms, sandy blight is a severe irritant rash on the inside of the eyelids produced by a combination of sand and flies. The patient is compelled to rub the affected parts, inflammation sets in and, unless treatment is given, temporary and sometimes permanent blindness is the result. Sufferers from even a modified form of sandy blight are forced to bathe their eyes extensively in the morning before the eyelids can become loosened from the glue-like puss which gathers beneath the lids and sticks them firmly together when the patient is asleep.

A semi-blind man is useless in a cattle camp, and Duncan Campbell advised Cobbold to make his way to the Station homestead. There, an eye lotion containing *Lapis Divinus* was made up - a treatment for sandy blight brought from India by Doctor Ball.

Since it was winter, the season was good and there was plenty of water lying in the gilgie holes, the young man set off for the homestead on an old mare whose foal was then at the homestead; this seemed like a sure magnet. Campbell, as indeed any horseman, believed that the mare would make straight for her offspring. However, either the horse forgot her foal, or forgot that it was at the homestead, and instead she headed into rough and timbered country where she had been running for a long time.

It was only twenty miles to the homestead across country and, believing that the mare would head straight there, Cobbold did not trouble to follow the faint track. In any case, he was so blind that he could not see the ground unless he dismounted and stooped low. This he often did to obtain water from a claypan with which to bath his eyes and temporarily reduce the severe itch.

Riding all day at a pace which would not tire the horse, but not so slow that they would not cover the distance to the homestead before night fell, Francis Cobbold was not unduly perturbed when night did fall. When the wind died into the stupendous silence of the bush, however, he could hear no sound of homestead life: no horse and cow bells, no barking dogs, no crowing of cock birds. He had permitted the mare to walk without guidance - in fact he was incapable of guiding her – but if she had made for her foal the homestead should have been reached, even if she had only covered an average of two miles an hour.

It was a particularly unpleasant predicament. At this time of the year, the abundance of water was balanced by the coldness of the nights, as well as the absence of food. He allowed the mare to graze for a couple of hours, keeping close by because if they parted he might never reach her again, even if he heard her neck bell. Fortunately he did have a few matches, so he made a fire and sat by it all night, repeatedly bathing his eyes with warm water heated in his invaluable quart pot. The water eased the itch and reduced the inflammation, but it had no power to cure the rash. If he had had Epsom salts in his possession, some grains of this dissolved in water would have given him partial relief.

Because he had used all his matches, and because he could foresee the possibility of spending yet another night in the open bush, in the morning he found a stick of slow-burning wood and, like any old aboriginal woman when camp is moved, he carried this firestick until it burned low, when he lit another from it. In this way, by carrying successive firesticks and allowing the mare her head, the second day was passed without reaching the homestead - and no longer did the young man believe that she was making for it. It was one of the few instances where a mare forgot the place where she had left her foal.

The second night passed much like the first. So did the third and fourth nights and the third and fourth days resembled the first day. Knowing that the mare must be making for the country where she had been running prior to her work in the mustering camp, Cobbold decided to strike due east, when sooner or later he would reach the Bulloo River or one of its tributaries. Several hours later he came to the bank of Powell's Creek and, recognising it and knowing that somewhere down it was a dam-maker's camp, he turned down along its course and so presently reached safety.

His training at sea and as a surveyor had served him well. Although he had been without food for five days and was growing weaker by the hour he did not panic, for his mind assured him he was not lost, and the constant bathing had improved his sight to the extent that he could see enough to find his way to a particular compass point.

At the dam-maker's camp, the wife of one of the men was cooking at the fire and, without losing time in vain talk, she quickly looked after the semi-blinded man, taking care that he did not over-eat, and making up a bunk for him.

3.

From the dam-maker's camp to the homestead of Mount Margaret was all of fifty miles - that was the estimate agreed upon by the dam makers. It was the distance between two given points, and not the distance by roundabout tracks, but to one with Cobbold's bush sense of direction it was wholly unnecessary to follow roundabout tracks.

He rose in the morning quite refreshed and determined to make his way to the homestead without delay in case his non-arrival had been noted by Campbell and a search for him instigated. The weather was clear. With the sun by day and stars by night, a cross-country journey through timber and over low stony hills would be merely a matter of time and there should be no difficulties in keeping a course. But there was the mare to be considered. She was old and worn out, and more than one day would be required for the journey. With a large packet of sandwiches, and tea and sugar for his quart pot, he bade farewell to the hospitable dam makers and set off.

Of necessity he rode slowly, often walking beside the horse. In the middle of the day he gave her a long spell at a place where there was excellent feed, but despite his attention, when evening arrived she was very tired. The camp he selected was chosen on account of the plentiful dry wood for fire and grass in the vicinity for the horse, and by the time night came he had hobbled and belled the mare and had collected a reserve of firewood handy to the fire. Having eaten, he quickly fell asleep with the saddle for a pillow and the saddlecloth for a mattress.

It was not the cold of the night that awoke him - he was woken by the ringing of church bells. Sitting up and wondering, he heard a post office clock strike eleven times. There was no possibility of mistaking the bell and the clock. The clock ceased to strike after its eleventh note, but the bells continued even when he stood up. As near as he could estimate by the stars – the Three Sisters and the Southern Cross – it was then about eleven o'clock. At the shortest estimate, he was six hundred miles from Brisbane and far more than twice that distance from Sydney where there were church bells and public clocks.

So clear were these sounds, and so alert was he, that he took up the bridle and brought the mare to the camp - guided to her by the tinkling bell strapped to her neck and guided back to the camp by the glow of replenished fire. However, when he left the camp for the horse there were no unusual sounds to be heard. During his absence from the camp he heard nothing unusual. It was a quiet night - and only bushmen know how quiet a night can be. But when he had brought the horse back to the camp and had tied her to a scrub tree, he could hear horses walking and men talking, and the occasional clinking of harness. Horsemen seemed to be riding in close proximity to the camp, so close, in fact, that Cobbold called out repeatedly. The ghostly horsemen ignored him, but continued to ride and talk. Periodically the clock struck the hours, but he did not hear the bells again and these noises continued until day broke.

In association with these phenomena, Cobbold's state of health at that time must be recognised. He had suffered five days of privation during which he had eaten nothing, but he had spent a comfortable night at the dam-maker's camp and he had recouped his strength with wholesome food. Nevertheless, his mind was still enjoying that clarity and acuteness produced by fasting. It was not impaired by the hardship suffered by his body, and the extraordinary sounds heard in that particular place were not due to hallucination.

In support of this contention, the experiences of other men may be drawn on. An elderly stockman related as a joke against himself how one night he heard an orchestra playing several pieces of music when camped near a small lake in Western New South Wales. He could plainly distinguish the individual instruments and, while charmed by the performance, he tried but did not succeed in locating the position of the orchestra.

He believed that hearing this music in the heart of the bush was the effect of a three-weeks' drinking bout from which he had returned just two weeks previously, but in fact he was not likely to be suffering *delirium tremens* after the expiration of two weeks' sobriety.

Something similar occurred to a writer when living alone in an old hut in Northern South Australia. More than once, when he was settling down to sleep on a campbed moved outside the hut on account of the heat, he heard a violin being played. The music was not loud enough to enable him to distinguish the tune, nor could he work out from which direction it came.

Now for a possible explanation - with regard to the violin-playing it was eventually established that, in a station homestead situated some eighteen miles away, the lady of the house often ran her favourite recorded violin solo on the gramophone. It was arranged that this particular record should be played at certain times when the nights were perfectly still, and over a period of several weeks the music was heard outside the hut twice.

It is possible - indeed probable - that Francis Cobbold's surroundings on the night he heard bells and striking clocks and talking horsemen, produced or possessed acoustic properties which reproduced sounds created a long way away, in much the same way as a wireless set will reproduce sounds sent outward by a broadcasting station.

4.

On reaching the homestead, Cobbold secured another horse and continued back to the cattle camp where he assisted in the closing stages of the muster of cattle for the Melbourne market. The beasts having been despatched in charge of the drovers, he then engaged in the muster of the brumby horses – the progeny of horses gone wild - which at this time were rapidly increasing in numbers. Among the type there are animals which are both useful and of great hardiness, despite the in-breeding, and the number mustered on Mount Margaret totalled sixty.

> *Brumbies: the descendants of escaped or lost horses, dating back, in some cases, to those belonging to the nation's early European settlers.*

For sheer cunning the brumby has no equal. He is difficult to master, difficult to drove, and difficult to yard. Once having been yarded and drafted and handled, if let go back to his former wild state he is a thousand times more cunning when a second muster is carried out.

33. Brumbie horses

Duncan Campbell knew of vacant country on the Georgina, beyond the Diamantina, which he wished to acquire and name Bredalbane. He proposed to Francis Cobbold that he should take these sixty brumbies, with the assistance of one man, the four hundred odd miles north-west from Mount Margaret to the new country.

In all his life Cobbold never declined to undertake a task not wholly impossible, and when he agreed to go he had the confidence in himself of the native born bushmen, as well as Campbell's confidence that he would successfully carry out a task requiring sound commonsense and courage. What was taking sixty wild horses four hundred miles into open, unsettled country compared with trading with the savages of Kandavu

Island and those at the head of the Rewa River on Viti Levu? And we have seen with what facility the sailor and the surveyor learned bushcraft.

Every year the area of land taken up by the genuine squatters was extending north and west in a giant arc of a circle, with Brisbane at the centre. Westward, that line had reached the Diamantina River and was passing swiftly still further westward as fast as men could register their applications.

With a man named Jack Morgan, an ex-sailor, as his offsider, the young man set out for Bredalbane with the horses. They rode hacks in excellent condition, and their swags and stores were taken on a packhorse. On the day they left Mount Margaret they yarded the brumbies at Kyabra Station – thirty miles on their way. The next day, Cobbold noted that his companion was unduly pushing the brumbies faster and ever faster. Morgan appeared to be excessively anxious to reach Bredalbane, and at the speed at which he endeavoured to travel, the horses would very quickly be knocked up.

"What's the hurry?" Cobbold inquired, a question he was entitled to put as he was in charge. "Oh, let's get on to the next yards," replied Morgan impatiently. "There are no more yards," he was quietly informed. This made the man figuratively gasp. "What! Four hundred miles and no yards! No horse yards for four hundred miles?" Cobbold shook his head, smiling grimly. "Coo! Then I'm not going any farther," Morgan announced with much emphasis. He caught the packhorse and from it removed his swag. "Four hundred miles and no yards to muster them brumbies into at night ain't no good for me. You can have 'em on your own. I'm walking back." "All right. I thought you were Jack Morgan, but you seem to be Johnnie Walker."

Scowling, Morgan departed leaving Cobbold alone with the wild horses, leaving him with the choice of pushing on with them unaided or returning with them to Mount Margaret. As a choice, however, it was unimportant, because he never considered the alternative of turning back. Alone, he got the horses moving again towards the country which was to be named Bredalbane, and that evening he reached Cooper's Creek where, in a narrow bend backed by a long and deep water-hole, he jammed the horses for the night and camped not beside the fire but at a little distance from it. He was alone, and the blacks might be watching him.

The creek bend was a natural horse yard, and one he had observed the previous year when he had accompanied Howe and his cattle. The following day he pushed along the track taken by Howie and the next morning set out early to round up the horses and continue the journey. Later, this day, he was overtaken by a stockman named Brown and, when it was discovered they were travelling in the same direction, Brown generously offered to accompany Cobbold and to assist him with the brumbies.

When Cobbold reached the selected country without loss of a horse, he found a man named Harding who had been sent on ahead of to erect a dwelling of sorts, for among the conditions to be complied with by a settler was one which stipulated that a dwelling must be erected to prove the settler's intention of living on the land.

Now there were no cattle - and another condition which had to be observed was that at the time of application at least a quarter of the stock the land was capable of carrying must be grazing on the country. It was estimated that every square mile would support twenty beasts. To get over this slight difficulty created by the Land Act of 1869, Cobbold rode twenty miles to Coorabulka Station, recently taken up and in temporary charge of Jack Galvin, to borrow the necessary number of cattle in order that he might make the essential declaration before a Justice of the Peace.

Galvin was obliging and, having driven the cattle to suitable pasture on Bredalbane and placed them in Harding's charge, the next task was to find a Justice of the Peace in order to forward the process of application for the land before he was forestalled by some other land seeker.

Justices of the Peace did not grow on bushes at that time and in that district, but there was one in the person of Sylvester Browne who was, in modern parlance, a live wire. He was born on a pastoral property in Victoria, and by this time he had extensive interests in pastoral properties in New South Wales and in Queensland, as well as in his native colony. Cobbold knew that Browne was about to take up land on the Mulligan River – later, that river's main tributary was to be named Sylvester Creek. He was aware, too, that Browne was headed for

107

his new country, fifty miles west of Bredalbane, and that he had crossed the Georgina sixty miles lower down. Knowing the general direction taken by Browne and his outfit, it was a simple matter for Cobbold to plot a course and keep to it until he crossed Browne's tracks or actually found him camped.

It was late October and the weather was becoming hot. On this count he delayed his start from Bredalbane until the heat of the day had passed. For the first ten miles the going was good; after that he had to cross a succession of sandhills thirty to forty feet high, miniature ranges of sand rising above the scattered dwarf scrub in lines of gleaming light red. It taxed the horses' strength and rapidly tired them, so much so that at one o'clock in the morning he decide to camp until day broke.

Then, to his consternation, he discovered that the water in his canvas water bag had evaporated. The bag was bone dry.

In these circumstances many men would have returned in haste to the nearest known water supply – Bredalbane. Yet Cobbold did not think to do that. At the first sign of dawn, he saddled and set off to locate Sylvester Browne. The sun presently rose in a clear sky, and immediately the temperature began to rise. The slight breeze was felt only on the summits of the sand hills; down in their valleys, by seven o'clock the heat was terrific.

Those who have never been far from water taps and shady verandas will find it hard to visualise the straits to which Cobbold was brought by that dry water bag. It will be difficult fully to appreciate his action in going forward and not back to Bredalbane, there to make a second start in search of Browne, carrying a second supply of water. With the thermometer registering anything above 114° in real shade – and the meagre shade of this stunted scrub was not real shade – and with even a night temperature ranging from 80° to 90°, it required a lot of courage to go on across the apparently endless sand ranges instead of retreating. Woe betide him should his horse stumble and dislodge him from the saddle and gallop away to leave him at the mercy of sand and heat and flies – and the watching eagles.

He did not reach the western edge of the sand belt until eleven o'clock, and from the last sand ridge he was delighted by the sight of a vast sheet of water gleaming beneath the blazing sun. Eagerly the horses trotted down to the lake, eagerly they splashed into its cool shallows. Cobbold was about to dismount

108

and drink and fill his water-bag, when the horses lowered their heads to drink and then flung them upwards with disgusted snorts. Even then not understanding it, the young man dismounted in the water and took some in the palm of his hands. It was more loaded with salt than is the sea - it was Lake Philippi.

At that time it was many miles in circumference, and Cobbold rode round its southern shore to continue his general course. Both he and his horse were suffering severely from thirst, and the heat increased minute by minute. Even so, he did not regret his determination to push on and not go back. He was travelling south-west, and he knew that he must cross Browne's tracks sooner or later, but certainly some time that day. Without water, to halt during the heat hours would spell disaster.

Dame Fortune had played two nasty tricks on him, and now the capricious lady, having tested the young man and finding no flaw in him, decided to make amends. Without warning of any kind, he abruptly came to the edge of a ribbon of country on which water lay in the claypans, sparkling like jewels in the sunlight. A day or two previously, an erratic thunderstorm had dropped rain.

Refreshed, man and horses pressed on west by south until at three o'clock they arrived at the distinct tracks left by Browne's outfit. By following them until sundown, Cobbold at last saw the smoke of the outfit's campfire across a grassy plain. Browne was only two hours ahead of him and was erecting the first tarpaulin shelter on his new station when the young man caught up with him.

Of course, he was given a real bush welcome, and the following morning he departed from Browne and his companions with the application quite in order. On joining Harding and the cattle again at Bredalbane, he obtained fresh horses and at once set off on the long trek back to Mount Margaret Station, for Campbell would have to register the application without the loss of a single moment in case some other party presented their application ahead of him.

CHAPTER ELEVEN

Years 1878 – 1881
Monkira

1.

Duncan Campbell came to think highly of Francis Cobbold. He had watched the young man, he had received demonstrations of his capabilities as a bookkeeper and a surveyor and, while doubtless he knew other men of outstanding mental ability like Doctor Ball, they did not come up to the standard of character attained by Cobbold. The new Colony of Queensland did not want brilliant men who were unable to keep away from the whiskey bottle, but it did need young people, forceful and determined men of sound education, men who permitted nothing to stand in their way of 'getting on with the job'. The day of the military gentleman type of landholder had gone: it was the era of the man who would work as well as direct others in labour, the man who could dress himself and be independent of a woman to darn his socks, one who could cook his own food if and when necessary. The seaside pioneer had had his little day, and now the country wanted men whose lives were regulated by custom and fashion.

So confident was Campbell in his representative in the matter of Bredalbane that he sent a messenger to meet him to take over the all-important declaration that the terms of the application had been carried out, as well as to convey further instructions which were ultimately to carry the young man up one most important rung of the ladder of success.

Through the messenger, Campbell informed Cobbold that Messrs Peppin & Webber had acquired a large area of land on the Diamantina which they called Monkira – after the biggest and the best water-hole on that river. A man named Carne was the first manager and he had then established his headquarters camp at a water-hole called Toonka, situated about 17 miles east of the river. Carne had recently taken over the first mob of cattle and shortly afterwards he had been attacked with sandy blight which necessitated his retirement. Cobbold was offered the position of manager of Monkira, and was required to make his way there at once.

At Monkira, he found himself in charge of a property of about twelve hundred square miles, one thousand cows and a number of calves, and about a dozen horses. The station plant consisted of a tip dray and a draught horse named Punch, a quantity of stores and a few crude tools, and a homestead which had been roughly constructed in a few days by digging a hole in the side of a sand hill and roofing it with cane grass. His staff numbered two: Tom Bolton, the stockman, and Jack Campbell who acted as cook.

At once the new manager discovered these men were in the wrong jobs. The stockman was an ex-sailor and more proficient with a sail maker's palm and needle than the cook, who had been born and reared on a cattle station owned by the son of one of the earliest pioneers. Cobbold made the cook the stockman, and the stockman became the cook - an arrangement satisfactory to everyone concerned.

Then Tom Bolton left, and one day Jack Campbell left. Cobbold hated to part with both these staunch men.

Jack Campbell was a first rate man at his work, who served Cobbold with sincere loyalty. He was that type of bushman now rapidly disappearing, a type unequalled anywhere. Unspoiled by Australian cities, never having known the soul-crushing influence of any city, Campbell lived only for the glory of the freedom he knew. To him, nothing was ever too much trouble, no task was ever considered to be impossible. There was no meanness in him, no littleness of mind or soul. He would share his money with the readiness with which he would share his rations and tobacco. He had no selfish competitive jealousy; his knowledge and experience was at the disposal of anyone. He had only two vices, the vices of all his type. He gave with his hands and mind, himself remaining financially poor but spiritually rich. His generosity was one vice – when examined by the thrifty and the selfish. The second vice was the love of alcohol - and who can blame him for that? No bushman ever will. Months lived in the heat of the interior, perhaps a year or two years' existence on the poorest of food, no convivial company to enjoy, and seldom the sight of – let alone the opportunity to talk to - a woman and receive the blessing of her refining influence. Of course, no bushman would ever blame the Jack Campbells for their love of drink. Weighed on the scales against their virtues, the occasional indulgence in a bout of hard drinking within a wayside hotel is but a speck.

He was a cheery soul, Jack Campbell, notwithstanding his collection of mournful bush songs. At night, when all hands were smoking their last pipe before turning in under the bushman's usual half blanket, he would begin with:

> *One day while out draftin'*
> *He was horned by a cow.*
> *'Alas!' says poor Jack,*
> *'It's all up with me now.*
> *So they laid where the wattle*
> *Casts its fragment shade,*
> *And the tall gum-tree shadows*
> *His peaceful grave.*

Towards the end of Francis Cobbold's first year at Monkira a travelling hawker found his way to the Diamantina. Like the usual hawker, he had on his wagon the usual surreptitious keg of rum. Jack tasted – and was undone. He discovered that he had urgent business to attend to 'inside'. Cobbold was loath to part with him and did his best to keep him in Monkira, but business was business, and Jack departed with his cheque made out for over one hundred pounds. His business was transacted in the bar of the first hotel he reached; it was the business of getting drunk and remaining drunk while the cheque lasted, of eating nothing and drinking nothing but spirits. The cheque held out longer than Campbell did. All that other men got out of life – comfort, amusement and love – Jack got out of the bottle. He lived life as few know it and he laid it down at the close of an orgy of spurious excitement when he was a millionaire and all men were his guests. He was buried in the shade of the fragrant wattle, his dust mixing with the dust of all those other pioneers who have helped to create Australia.

2.

For two years and three months, no rain fell on Monkira. The big Toonka water-hole dried up. Off the river flats the country became a Sahara, with the difference that above the caked mud flats and the wind-rilled sand the tortured scrub trees still clung to life.

Some three hundred square miles of Monkira was crossed by the Diamantina River and its subsidiary channels. In fact, it was often impossible to distinguish the main channel among the intertwining lesser channels, which extend to a width of five miles at Monkira Water-hole, ten miles at Peruka Water-hole, and twenty-five miles in width fifteen miles below the Peruka Water-hole.

Although no rain had fallen on Monkira itself, a heavy rain falling over the river's watershed sent down a flood; when it had passed, the river water-holes were left filled and three hundred square miles of country began to sprout herbage.

Before the flood came sliding down this remarkable river, which more often than not is bone-dry save in the holes, rain had fallen far eastward of the station, necessitating strenuous work keeping the cattle from migrating to it; for of course in those days there was no wire with which to construct boundary fences.

The floodwater coming down when the Toonka Water-hole was dry revealed the unfortunate choice of forming the homestead near it. The flood was due to monsoonal rains three hundred miles to the north, and monsoonal rain is notoriously regular. By this time, Francis Cobbold knew every water channel and every water-hole on Monkira. The finest water supply of all was the Monkira Water-hole, but there was no homestead site safe from floods nearer than the point of an east-west sand hill situated nearly a mile from it.

Five miles to the west of Monkira Water-hole lay the westernmost channel of the river which skirts the foot of a stony ridge, the eastern slope of the ridge falling to a deep hole of permanent water lying in that western-most channel.

Cobbold decided to build the station homestead on the slope of the stony hill above the water-hole and, packing all the gear on the tip dray, he abandoned the crude camp at the Toonka Water-hole. With the gear moved to the chosen site, all was well. He had a dray and old Punch to pull it about. He also had an axe, a handsaw, and a shovel. And that is all he did have in the shape of tools with which to build a house. Worse still, he had no timber, nor were there any trees providing timber of sufficient size and straightness, while along the river channels the occasional bloodwood tree was of no use.

The young station manager used the only material available – mud - and with it he built the walls of a house which he thatched with cane grass, a house which stands to this day unimpaired by time and weather. It forms the kitchen of the modern Monkira homestead - built of wood, with a corrugated iron roof and glass in its windows.

After the house, he dealt with the stockyards. There being no timber suitable for posts and rails, he cut and carted the crooked coolabah and the dwarf bloodwood, and he erected a stake yard which although not as strong as a rail-built yard, served its purpose for many years.

> *Eucalyptus coolabah is a eucalypt of riparian zones and is found throughout Australia from arid inland to coastal regions. The plant is commonly called coolibah or coolabah, the name being a loanword from the Indigenous Australian Yuwaaliyaay word, gulabaa.*

34. *Extensive coolabah woodland established on a floodplain in Northern Australia.*

By this time the western line of settlement extended far beyond Monkira, and sometimes the people who had taken up that western land passed by or stayed overnight on their way to and from 'inside'. But they were few in number, and their visits to civilisation were rare. Drovers passed through with cattle for the new stations. Station men passed through; they saw and mentally noted and talked of improvements carried out by the manager of Monkira. Francis Cobbold was building better than he knew.

With Francis Cobbold the world moved slowly. The cattle settled down, with the advance in numbers of the natural increase that knew no other country.

One day towards the end of the dry period, a storm dropped water in the locality of the Toonka Water-hole, and shortly afterwards a second storm dropped water over country west of the river and ten miles north of the new homestead. When the resultant herbage was sufficiently high for grazing, Cobbold sent George King, a stockman, to Toonka with nineteen of the best horses and, accompanied by a black boy, he took the remaining horses upriver to the country which had benefited from the second storm. He and his boy that night camped ten miles west of the river's western channel; on rising the next morning, they were astonished by a vast sea of water spread eastward from them and above which only the tops of the coolabah trees were visible. One of the greatest floods known on the Diamantina was sliding southward, and it created anxiety in Cobbold's mind for the safety of the homestead he had erected with so much labour. True, it was built at the foot of a stony hill, but had he wisely selected the site above the level of this particular flood, which had come four hundred miles and was still to travel many hundreds of miles before being sucked up by the greedy wilderness of North-eastern South Australia?

Cobbold lost no time riding south to the homestead. The floodwater forced him west until he came to the extremity of the stony ridge, when he rode eastward along its slope, eventually to reach the homestead and find it safe. North, east and west stretched the inland sea. It lapped against the slope below the house. It swept by in a sliding brown mass, whitened here and there by lines of froth beaten into being by the tormented trees, imponderable and irresistible.

However, the relief felt while standing in the doorway of the house and gazing across the mighty water was soon dashed by a non-thinking man's stupid mistake. King, the stockman, returned and reported that when he reached the main channel of the river with the nineteen horses, he found the channel to be running strongly. He could not have been very intelligent, because he put the horses into the river to swim across to the far side. Instead of following them to be sure they would get clear of the river channels, instead of taking them to Toonka as he had been instructed to do, he turned back to the homestead thinking they would find their own way to the small area of ground around Toonka freshened by the recent rain. And they might have done so if he not put them across far to the north of it - on the direct route to their old feeding grounds at Kyabra which therefore became the natural place for them to go.

Despite days of difficult searching, only the carcases of the horses were eventually found - nineteen horses hung up in the tops of trees. Cobbold recognised them all although there was only the hides and hooves left covering the skeletons. Cut off on all sides by the swiftly rising water, they had bunched together and drowned together, to be carried down the stream and caught among the treetops.

It was a grievous loss, but the loss of cattle might have been far heavier. How so many of them that had been in the path of the flood had escaped was a mystery.

3.

About the end of 1881, Francis Cobbold received a letter from the owners of Monkira informing him that the station had been sold to an Adelaide firm, and that one of the purchasers would be soon on the spot to take delivery.

On the heels of the letter came a Mr Chewings all the way from Adelaide. From that city he had ridden one horse and led another loaded with meagre camp equipment and food, and at once a bangtail muster took place. Each mob of cattle was brought to the stake-built yards, and the brush of each long tail was snipped off and a tally maintained. When they went back into the herd and the herd were finally mustered, the bangtails showed that they had already been counted, and it was an easy task to make a tally of those not bangtailed. The final figures were satisfactory to both owners and purchasers.

Chewings was a likeable kind of man, and on seeking Cobbold's opinion of Monkira, he was told bluntly that it was a poor proposition. Subsequently, on his return to Adelaide he sold out his share to an Adelaide consortium and a working partner duly arrived to take possession. Despite the new firm's financial resources, however, it was in the end beaten by a drought, but not before a valuable herd had been got together – to be wiped out with dreadful completeness.

After that catastrophe Monkira was abandoned for many years.

CHAPTER TWELVE

Years 1882 – 1886
Miranda Downs and The Oaks

1.

It would be understandable to think that someone occupying the position of manager at Monkira Station during its early years of existence, one living on the Diamantina River so far out from civilisation, would be like one forgotten. This, however, was not so. Cobbold had taken Monkira in the form of potter's clay and, with vision and enthusiasm, he had fashioned a little kingdom which, save for a setback caused by a long drought, stands today.

To use a well-worn phrase - he had definitely won his spurs. With only two years' experience of the Australian bush to his credit, he had been allotted a task and had carried it out brilliantly. He had brought that task to an excellent finale and had satisfied his employers so well that they offered him the managership of one of their stations on Cooper's Creek or, alternatively, they would provide £10,000 for him to go to Western Australia and there acquire new country and develop it on their behalf.

This offer was received during the handover of Monkira, and it was not the only offer. Cobbold received a second offer of employment which he did not consider, and a third from a firm which had already become famous, a firm commanding large financial resources and controlled by keen brains – Cobb & Co.

When Freeman Cobb retired to America with his fortune, his Melbourne business changed hands several times and steadily extended into other Colonies. In course of time it was taken over by a company directed by James Rutherford and others. In the year 1865, the business extended to Queensland, and within five years their coaches were travelling 28,000 miles every week and were employing 6,000 horses. By 1871, the activities of the firm had become controlled by dual directorates - in Queensland, Cobb & Co was managed by Messrs Rutherford, Witney, Hall and Bradley. Beside the coaching business, Cobb & Co developed the jarrah trade between Western Australia and India and also became large holders of pastoral properties. In 1892, when Cobbold became one of their station managers, they were an important factor in the rapid growth of Australia.

> *The jarrah tree is mostly used for timber. Jarrah wood makes very durable, strong furniture and building materials, such as wharves, bridges and railroad ties. Before modern asphalt the streets of Berlin and London were paved with blocks of jarrah.*

He was instructed to make his way to the Gulf of Carpentaria, and form a station on the Gilbert River where his new employers had acquired land. Two mobs of cows, each of one thousand head, were then on the road to the new station, and Cobbold was further instructed to overtake them and look them over on his journey north.

Meanwhile Mr George Debney, the working partner of the purchasers of Monkira, arrived with his family. From him, Francis Cobbold bought a buggy. With one broken-in buggy horse and several saddle horses running behind, he and his blackboy left the place he had created from nothing and set off up the Diamantina River. He was leaving the semi-desert of the west for the monsoonal sub-tropic of the North.

His first call was made at Davonport Downs, a large property carrying twenty thousand head of cattle and owned by Cobb & Co. It was managed by one of their oldest and most trusted employees, Patrick McGuigan, who presented Cobbold with the gift of a thoroughbred grey horse named Hector. The animal had been broken with the intention of making him a birthday present for a daughter of one of the firm, but unfortunately his mouth had been spoiled and he was unfit for a lady to ride. Hector was to prove his sterling worth to Cobbold, being useful in every way and capable of winning many races in any bush company. The partnership between man and animal continued for fifteen years, and when Hector died of old age his loss was keenly felt.

The end of the next stage of Cobbold's journey was the 'Diamantina Gates' where for the night he was the guest of Hugh Heber Percy, a member of a well-known Shropshire family who was developing the property as a cattle station.

Further up river, Cobbold overtook Sydney Donner travelling with two wagonettes, a mob of horses, and half a dozen men on his way to take possession of Carandotta Station, at the head of the Georgina River, lately purchased by his family. Then on to Werna Station, lying on a tributary of the Diamantina called Werna Creek. This property was being developed as a sheep station by a Mr Mitchell.

It was a great adventure, this undertaking by a young man not yet thirty years old. It was, however, lacking that spice of the gamble underlying the adventurous journey into Queensland from Albemarle. At that time, Cobbold was seeking a career without actually knowing what he wanted; now, he was an experienced cattleman and a confident bushman, and he had risen to the administrative heights of the pastoral industry. His feet were following a career which really had found him, not he it. The years of failure to establish himself were not only behind him but were to prove a sound foundation on which to erect the edifice of his life. They were the years of failure and yet were not wasted years. He had been given his first fine chance through the instrumentality of Duncan Campbell, and now he was being given his second, provided for him through his own success at Monkira.

Having reached the Flinders River at the little township of Richmond, he caught up with the first mob of Cobb & Co's cattle in charge of a drover named Dargin and with whom he travelled for several days. Then, leaving Dargin, he pressed forward down the Flinders River.

The Flinders River skirts the ti-tree forest as far as the Palmer River, a distance of almost four hundred miles. All the country westward of the Flinders is well grassed undulating downs, while except for a narrow fringe of downs land along the east side, the forest trees crowd almost to the river itself.

Francis Cobbold left the Flinders River to take the fat cattle track from Iffley Station to the Palmer. Actually there was no track or road, nothing to follow other than the tracks of travelling cattle, tracks wiped out by every monsoonal rain. He struck the real track again at Croon Creek Telegraph Station on the Carron River, and then, taking a right hand turn, he followed the Georgetown-Normanton road to reach what was known as the head of the Carron. Here he met two men with whom he kept up an acquaintance for many years – F A Brodie, and Land Commissioner Warde. They had been searching for suitable country, and at this meeting with Cobbold were reserved on this one subject. In those days a man kept his business to himself, for it could not be known who might be a rival land seeker.

2.

The Gilbert River starts among the hills dominated by Mount Gilbert situated just south of the middle of the base line of the Cape York Peninsula. The flow of this river is generally in a north-west direction. Part way down its course it is joined by the Einasleigh River, which is almost as large as the parent stream. Then, about one hundred miles from the sea, the river splits into two, and the north branch again divides before the sea is reached. The country which Francis Cobbold was to mould into a cattle station extended five miles back from both sides of the river and sixty miles along it. To these six hundred miles was added a further block of four hundred square miles called Marlow Downs, a total of one thousand square miles.

The last station down the river was that on the southern boundary of what was to become Miranda Downs, and then it was the farthest north. Named Strathmore Station, the manager was Mr Simpson. Cobbold received from him the usual bush welcome, and here he found McGuigan – he who had presented him with Hector, the horse – who had arrived via another route to inspect and report on Miranda Downs for their joint employers.

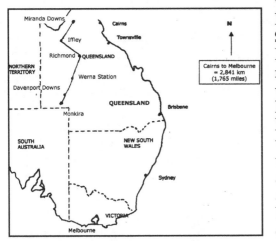

35. *Monkira to Miranda Downs*

McGuigan was older than Cobbold, a man of wider experience and, moreover, one well versed in the tricks of the Diamantina River. When he saw the flood marks visible on the trees skirting the banks of the Gilbert River, and estimated roughly how far those floods had extended back from the main course, he stated his intention of returning an unfavourable report and advising the company not to proceed with the development of Miranda Downs.

McGuigan retraced his steps by the route he had come and in Georgetown, 150 miles upriver, he met quite by chance a man named Charlie Edmunds. Edmunds and his brother Joseph were famous bushmen, trackers and explorers in the Gulf country, and they offered to show McGuigan a thousand square miles of well-watered country for £1,000. McGuigan accepted, accompanying the brothers to the Copperfield River, a tributary of the Einasleigh, where he was shown some country which gave a most favourable impression. Travelling quickly to Townsville, McGuigan took the steamer from that port to Bowen where he applied to the Lands Department for the block and was duly granted the licence to occupy.

In those days of expansion, the land seeker had not the safeguards enjoyed by the gold seeker. A prospector wishing to work gold-bearing country may peg out the area of land defined by regulation and then make his application to work it, and none may get ahead of him. The land seeker was never sure of obtaining the right to occupy chosen land until his application had been granted, and there was always the possibility of rival land seekers getting in ahead of him.

The fact that McGuigan intended to send in an adverse report concerning Miranda Downs did not deter Francis Cobbold from carrying out his job. He could not do anything else without further instructions.

Simpson, the Strathmore manager, said that he did not know what the country was like below Strathmore, and the only way in which Cobbold could find out was to prospect it himself. He set off on this tour with only one blackboy for companion, knowing perfectly well that the blacks were more numerous and dangerous than those in the Diamantina and Cooper's Creek. He saw their tracks but seldom saw them, even on those occasions when he knew they were following him. Miranda Downs extended for sixty miles along the river and went back five miles on both sides. Normally the river is a fine one, wide grass-covered flats running back to the scrub timber. The country was in good fettle, and only the high water marks on the trees were disturbing. Going by these significant signs, the floods must be high, but they could be hardly as devastating as those which sweep down the Diamantina, with its mass of intertwining channels.

When the first mob of Cobb & Co's cattle arrived in Dargin's charge, Cobbold was ready with a site selected for them. He had engaged all of Dargin's men to work for him, and was therefore surprised to find them packed up ready to leave the next morning. Inquiries regarding the reason for this change of mind elicited the reply that they had reconsidered the offer of employment and had decided against it. They would make no explanation in support of this second decision and they stuck to it, even when offered further inducements.

The drover's plant consisted of a dray and horse, several loose horses, a tent, harness, and meagre cooking utensils, all of which belonged to Cobb & Co. This plant was to remain at Miranda Downs. Dargin, however, had not replenished the ration supply over the last 150 miles of his journey so the quantity of rations was extremely low. The refusal of the men to remain and work for him placed Cobbold in the unenviable position of having to hold a thousand head of cattle on strange country with the assistance of only one blackboy, and the position was made yet more serious by the dearth of rations.

All the drovers departed, apparently not caring how Cobbold fared in country with which he was quite unfamiliar. The small quantity of food was eked out by blackfish that the youthful Toby managed to catch in the river, while keeping both eyes well open for crocodiles. However, despite this addition, they could not live solely on blackfish. It had been Cobbold's intention to send two of the drovers with the dray to Normanton for supplies, and now it became essential that either the blackboy or he would have to ride to Creen Creek Telegraph Station and there send a wire to Normanton. Toby was given the choice and elected to remain with the cattle.

There was no track to the Telegraph Station, which lay forty miles distant through the ti-tree forest, but Cobbold had a map of the country and he worked out its position by dead reckoning. Having covered the first five miles across the plain country, he then rode the remaining thirty-five miles through the close-growing willow trees, taller than mallee and almost as useless, and unbroken by plain or natural clearing but crossed by boggy creeks. He reached the telegraph line only half a mile from the station, which was a creditable piece of bushcraft.

From the station he wired to Messrs James Burns & Co at Normanton, and they agreed to despatch at once a load of rations with a bullock team. Christiansen, the lone operator of the wireless station, was good enough to lend him a bag of rice and a small quantity of sugar, and with these welcome necessities he returned to Miranda Downs, to find that Toby had not failed in keeping the cattle.

3.

There now followed weeks of incessant hard riding when no regard could be given to inclement weather. Day after day, Francis Cobbold and his blackboy were employed in constantly beating back the cattle that stubbornly attempted to return to their own country. Without boundary fences, which were to come only with the introduction of German wire, this beating back the cattle had to be done until the original beasts died out.

The rice, tea and sugar, and blackfish did not provide an adequately balanced diet, so Toby was sent to Strathmore where Simpson, the manager, supplied their immediate requirements. Returning with Toby came one of Dargin's drovers who could not have it on his conscience that he had left a white man in such circumstances as those in which Cobbold had been left. Scrafton Browne was his name, and when eventually he retired from the bush to Townsville, he built up a book and paper shop, and became a leading Labour Leader. Beginning life as a chemist's assistant in Bristol, England, Browne always played the game as a true sportsman. His arrival made a deal of difference to Cobbold in the titanic struggle to keep the cattle on Miranda Downs.

Then came two explorers with their respective blackboys. They were Edmund Hungerford and his partner Clark, on their way north into the Cape York Peninsula to search for good cattle country. With others, these men are to be credited with opening up the north and the west of Queensland and the Northern Territory. They did not follow the paths blazed by Leichhardt, Gregory and Kennedy. They blazed their own trails and their business was not to record observations interesting to Governments and Geographical Societies, but to make money by discovery of grazing country and gold bearing areas. They were just as important as those whose names have been handed down

123

to posterity as Australian explorers, and often they were much more successful.

When he thought it time that the second mob of cattle was due, Francis Cobbold rode across to Creen Creek Telegraph Station, where he received mail instructions to divert this second mob to the new country on the Copperfield River which McGuigan had taken up on behalf of the firm. There was, too, advice that a third mob of cattle was behind the second mob.

By this time Cobbold was familiar with almost every acre of Miranda Downs, and he had reached the conclusion that the property did not deserve the damning report on it made by McGuigan. That he decided to allow the second mob to proceed to Miranda Downs and to divert the third mob to the new country, despite the instructions received from his principals, is a little revelation of his character at this period. It proved that he was unafraid of accepting responsibility. It proved, too, his growing confidence in himself. And further, it proved that he was destined to become no mere manager to follow blindly the orders of employers hundreds of miles distant.

The result of this decision was that he met James Burns, the boss drover in charge of the second mob, directed him to proceed to Miranda Downs and then, getting in touch with the boss drover of the third mob, directed that he take his cattle to the new country, which eventually was to be named The Oaks.

Burns delivered the cattle comprising the second mob in excellent condition. His assistant was a man named Smith, and together they were fine bushmen and of a very fine type of Australian. It was partly due to them that their men consented to stay and work for Cobbold, and this altered completely the conditions under which he and Toby had laboured so continuously.

Burns and Smith formed a partnership and set off on an exploration trip over all the vacant country as far as the Archer River. With labour at his disposal, Cobbold detailed two men to assist in building a house and a set of stockyards, to be followed by the erection of a rough rail fence to enclose a horse paddock.

When Burns and Smith returned, Cobbold accompanied them on a prospect down the Gilbert River, north-west of Miranda Downs. They followed the left bank of the river, and unknowingly followed an anabranch in mistake for the main channel. They discovered that the anabranch was larger than the parent stream, and in it were many deep and splendid water-holes of certain permanence. The anabranch entered the sea south of the mouth of the Gilbert and it was named Smithburn after Burns and Smith.

When it was considered that Harry Oakes, with the third mob of cattle, should have reached the new country, Cobbold followed him. Finding Oakes to be another Burns, he received much assistance in settling the cattle. Together they chose a site for the homestead and named the station from the line of Australian oak trees growing near. The site was only twelve miles from the Townsville-Georgetown track, along which passed much of the supplies for the newly opened Etheridge Gold Diggers, supplies transported on wagons drawn by horses.

Francis Cobbold confidently tackled the task of creating two big cattle stations at the same time. At his back were the capital and the men, and from the wilderness he fashioned two properties which retain to this day much of the work he directed.

He experienced little trouble with the blacks. By this time they had come to respect the white man's firearms, and they were too wild to live round about the homesteads and out-stations. They were seldom seen, but their tracks proved that they were about, while one incident established that they visited the homesteads after dark. A carcass gallows had been erected next to Miranda Downs. This structure consists of a heavy winding roller set on top of two stout supports, and the roller lifts the carcass of a slaughtered beast clear off the ground by means of a rope. Instead of the angled iron handle of a windlass, two cross poles are attached to one end of the roller like the arms of a windmill; these enable the worker to revolve the roller by pulling downward on the ends of the cross poles. Finally, when the carcass is clear of the ground, the pole end pointing to the ground is lashed to the upright.

One evening when a beast was killed for meat, the carcass as usual was hauled up on the gallows and dressed, to be left overnight for the air to cool it and set the beef.

Hanging a carcass like this was unfamiliar to the natives. Here was a chance for them to obtain plenty of meat without the labour entailed in running down a beast and spearing it in the open; when the homestead people had retired for the night they

125

sneaked in and gathered round the gallows, hacking off pieces of the meat. They were much like cunning rats nibbling at the bait of a trap, but they were less sophisticated than rats. It was not long before all the meat was removed from the carcass as far up as they could reach, and one fellow, more intelligent than his companions, reasoned that the rope lashing the pole end to the support maintained the carcass at its aggravating height. With his tomahawk, he slashed at the holding rope until it was severed. The weight of the carcass then jerked the forked cross poles round at terrific speed, when without doubt the perpetrator would have been ripped up and killed. That was not definitely known, of course, because his friends removed his remains. On the cross poles was found the evidence of the tragedy, and never again did the blacks touch hanging beef.

4.

The Townsville-Georgetown track runs parallel with the Einasleigh River, and twenty miles below the Oaks, at the junction of the Copperfield River with the Einasleigh, was country named Carpentaria Downs, the head station being 25 miles up river. Before Cobbold took over The Oaks, Carpentaria Downs had been taken over by the Barker family. Frederick Barker settled down there and began the erection of a homestead beside the Carpentaria Downs lagoon.

At the same time as Cobbold was creating The Oaks, Frederick Barker and his brother, who occupied a station named Rosella Downs some forty miles away, began an examination of the boundaries of Carpentaria Downs coincident with the visit of a surveyor who was running traverses of the river. It seems probably that the Barkers gleaned significant information from the surveyor regarding their boundary adjacent to The Oaks, for they arrived one morning at The Oaks and without preamble the elder brother said:

"Cobbold – you are on our country."

"Oh – how do you make that out?" Cobbold inquired. "Come into the house and see our leases to occupy and the plans of this run."

Cobbold produced the documents, and the Barkers produced theirs. An examination caused Cobbold uneasiness. He had seen such a lot of overlapping when he was working with the Victorian Surveys.

126

Having no firm ground beneath him for argument, he promised the Barkers to look into the matter without loss of time and, riding to the nearest telegraph station 40 miles distant, he communicated with his principals. They instructed him to take all the steps necessary to unravel the tangle.

He left for Townsville at once, and from there took the steamer for Bowen in which place he thought was situated the Lands Office. At Bowen, however, he was informed that because of the demand for land raised by the diggers and others at the new Palmer Goldfields, Commissioner Jackson had removed to Cooktown.

Cobbold went to Cooktown, and eventually discovered that a lot of the country comprising Carpentaria Downs had been acquired many years previously as Barkley Downs, afterwards taken up under another name and again surrendered. It made the Barkers' title to most of Carpentaria Downs extremely doubtful, and placed in Cobbold's hands a weapon with which to fight them for the land under his jurisdiction which they claimed belonged to them.

The bombshell he exploded beneath their feet was far more powerful than the one they had exploded beneath his. A lot of heated talk followed. His proofs were demanded, and when they saw them they realised that they were cornered.

"Fighting this case, gentlemen, won't get us anywhere," Francis Cobbold urged. "Let us compromise. Let us find out which of the titles are valid and which are not. Let us apply for the unexpired terms of leases affecting us, and have them offered at auction. Let us reach an agreement to give both parties a fair division of what has to be acquired. As I said, to fight the case would be stupid."

Frederick Barker glanced at his brother. Then: "That's sense, Cobbold. We agree to try to agree with you," he said.

Thus the matter was finally settled between them. The Barkers and Francis Cobbold remained neighbours for several years and friends for fifty years.

5.

These years demanded everlasting labour from Francis Cobbold. The climate, so detrimental to many, suited him perfectly. He had found his career and he had found himself, and this great new country of Southern Queensland was an ideal background for the descendant of that long line of businessmen and born organisers, the Ipswich Cobbolds.

9 generations of Ipswich Cobbolds brewed good beer for 266 years.

As manager of two cattle stations placed 220 miles apart, he was obliged to spend three or four months alternately on each property. The wire had arrived with which men were building paddock fences. There were the splendid herds of first class shorthorn cattle to muster and draft, and their progeny to brand. There were always further improvements to be planned and carried out.

The journeys between the two stations were undertaken on horseback. Cobbold rode light and always refused to overtax his mount, and thus the only gear taken beside the saddle and bridle was the saddlecloth, quart pot, a small quantity of rations, and a pair of hobbles. His clothes consisted of a felt hat, a cotton shirt, a pair of white moleskin trousers, and the usual elastic-sided boots. As Georgetown lay midway between the stations, he replenished his tucker bag when passing through.

On one occasion when travelling to The Oaks, it was exceedingly hot. He had got beyond Georgetown, had passed across the Newcastle Range, and was riding through the ti-tree forest, in which he was forced to cross the winding Stockman's Creek no less than five times in ten miles. It was his intention to camp at a certain place, but falling darkness found him still in the saddle. When night had finally banished the day, a sudden and severe thunderstorm burst upon him.

There was nothing left for him to do but to go on. To camp before he had made the last crossing over the creek might mean delay, for it was one of those in which floodwater roars down with astonishing abruptness. As it was, when he did make the last crossing, the water was up to the saddle flaps.

As sometimes happens in this part of Australia, such a storm following a hot day let the mercury out of the thermometer. From a hot, humid evening, it became a bitterly cold night within the space of a few seconds. The wind roared across the tops of the scrub trees and, added to the evaporation going on with his light clothes, Cobbold was quickly chilled to the bone. So cold did he become that he almost gave up. To make a fire was impossible, for even if it had been full daylight he could not have found dry wood.

128

Subconsciously he had noted a big paperbark tree growing in the creek at the last crossing, and his conscious mind now recalled it. It offered the wherewithal with which to make a fire, but it stood in the middle of the creek, and the night was totally black. When he made the attempt to locate the tree, Cobbold realised that it was his only chance, for without a fire he would without doubt perish.

Good luck, plus judgment, rewarded him. The water was warm to his chilled body when he waded into the creek. It rose above his waist when he found the tree, and with his pocket knife he cut away the outer strips of the bark, which are like the pages of a book and as thick as the ordinary novel. From the inner side he cut as much as he could cram under his felt hat to keep dry.

Back again on the creek bank, he fired the bark. The flame lit up the surrounding bush and revealed dead sticks, which he hastily threw upon it. And then, when the heat was striking on his disrobed body and the water in the quart pot was coming to the boil, he realised how closely he had been to death. He recalled a black fellow who, when taking a note from the Toonka Water-hole to the Monkira homestead, had been caught by such a storm as this and had perished miserably.

About the time of this incident, the forest country between Iffley Station and Creen Creek had been taken up by Mr W C Brown, who had built his homestead about twenty miles south of the Creen Creek Telegraph Station. Men were erecting fences for him when one of them, sinking a posthole, struck gold.

A rush took place, and in an incredibly short space of time a town arose. Hotels were built, and banks were established. A Gold Warden/Magistrate was appointed. By 1886, the new gold diggings provided feverish activity. A large area of promising reefs was opened and one - the Highland Mary Reef - was for a time a good producer. Francis Cobbold brought a share in it which returned him several hundreds of pounds.

One day Mr Kellaway, the manager of the bank of New South Wales in Croydon, asked Cobbold if he had met the new warden and, learning that he had not, offered to take him along to introduce him. Together they walked to the office of the Gold Warden/Police Magistrate.

The new Warden was none other than J C Pilbrow who had gone to grow cotton on Sandwich Island in the New Hebrides with Cobbold and young Wetherall. Shortly afterwards, Pilbrow was transferred to another field, where he died.

CHAPTER THIRTEEN

Years 1886 - 1890
O'Brien, Cobbold and Co

1.

Years before Francis Cobbold arrived in Queensland, a partnership had begun of three men which was remarkable in several ways and particularly for the loyalty displayed by each towards the others. It was to be a partnership without equal outside the pages of a novel. It was one that endured for life – and indeed beyond life, as the will of one of them proves. Throughout its entire course, it was never marred by bickering or sharp practice.

Patrick O'Brien, an Irish farmer, drove a small mob of cattle into the hill country at the head of the Gilbert and Einasleigh Rivers. He took up a block of land on the Gilbert River which he named Green Hills. A young man at that time, O'Brien was of striking appearance, being tall and handsome and magnificently proportioned. Dark brown eyes looked out at this new and virgin country from beneath a wide, smooth forehead. His heart was without personal rancour, and free from nationalist prejudices. He was generous, sympathetic yet firm, and extraordinarily observant; he possessed that rare human gift of intuitively picking a man out of the ruck and accepting or rejecting a proposition without knowing the intricate business details. O'Brien was a silent thinker, never allowing his right hand to know what his left was doing.

The second member of the partnership was William Steele, a good-looking Scotsman. When gold was discovered in the ranges, he arrived with many other prospectors to knock about among the hills with the miners, and to be fairly successful. A good talker and a keen reader, Steele had received a sound business education in his uncle's mercantile house in Glasgow.

The third member was Edward Hunt, a stocky, solid, unassuming Englishman. A carpenter by trade, he had built and opened a general store on the Gilbert River diggings where the miners, coming to appreciate his sterling qualities, entrusted their gold to his keeping. There were, of course, no banks and to despatch gold by teamster's wagon to Townsville was risky.

131

Hunt secured the gold left in his care in a cumbersome but efficient safe kept in the store.

One Saturday night, when a dance was held at the principal hotel attended by everyone in the town except for Hunt and his assistant, a man knocked vigorously on the store door. By that time, Hunt and his assistant had retired to their beds set up within the store itself, and when the former demanded to know what the visitor wanted, he was asked to supply some trivial thing. Hunt thereupon opened the door, to be confronted with the business end of a rifle above which glinted the baleful eye of a notorious criminal who the white men called Peg-Leg Sam and the blacks named Waddy Mundoi - meaning wooden leg.

"Back!" ordered the ruffian, "no tricks now. I'll drop the one of you who attempts to be funny."

Menaced by the weapon, Hunt and his assistant could do nothing but obey. They backed off before Peg-Leg Sam, who followed them in then slammed and barred the door.

"What are you after? I haven't much money here," Hunt said.

"I'll have wot ye've got. And I'll have all the gold in yer safe, too," announced the bandit.

Hunt's lips became thin. His eyes narrowed. "You'll not get the gold," he said firmly. "The gold is not mine. It belongs to the miners, as doubtless you know. No, you'll not get that."

"Oh won't I? You hand over the key to the safe, quick, or I'll put you out. I'm going to have that gold if I have to put you both out. The safe's too heavy to take away and burst open. Come on now, the key." The unswerving rifle was aimed at a point between and above Hunt's eyes, the ruffian's grubby finger touching the trigger.

"I'll see you in hell first, Sam," stated the adamant storekeeper.

"Think friend! Life's sweet. You'll not lose the gold 'cos it ain't yours to lose," snarled the angry Sam.

"Give him the key, Mr Hunt! Give him the key!" implored the frantic assistant, realising that, if Sam murdered his employer, he too would be killed as the only witness. The poor man fell on his knees to plead further with Hunt.

"You'll not get the key, Sam," Hunt repeated, and the dogged determination on his face convinced the ruffian that threats to shoot would not gain entry to the safe, while killing two men would give him no advantage and inevitably lead to a hangman's noose. With a string of oaths, he snatched up an axe and dealt a blow to the handle of the safe's door, so smashing the mechanism of the lock that even with a key it was impossible to open it.

Edward Hunt roared with laughter. "Now you've done it, Sam, my lad. The key is no good to you now even if I give it to you – which I don't intend doing. You can't carry away the safe, but you can take my advice and carry yourself away."

Mouthing threats, Peg-Leg Sam unbarred the door and vanished. Those within the store heard him mount his horse and ride furiously into the night, the only loss sustained by Hunt being the damage done his ponderous safe.

The grateful miners subscribed to a testimonial, but Hunt steadily refused to accept it, maintaining that he wanted no reward for merely keeping a trust.

Meanwhile, O'Brien had opened a butcher's shop in which to cut out his surplus cattle for sale to the increasing number of miners who were finding gold among the hills and constantly opening up newly-discovered reefs. Three partners - two Cumberland men and an Irishman named Murphy - found a reef from which samples looked promising. Extraction of the gold from the reef quartz required money for crushing machinery, however, and the three men did not have sufficient to purchase the necessary plant and have it carted to the field. It was then that O'Brien, Hunt, and Steele got together and formed an association that was then known on the goldfields of Australia as 'dividing mates'. In simple language, this meant all for one and one for all until one of them married. Not until one had his own family establishment did he have a separate estate.

In the beginning, this arrangement had little legal binding, and it depended entirely on confidence and trust. Later on, of course, a proper deed of partnership was drawn up between O'Brien, Hunt and Steele so that in the event of one dying the other two would be legally protected.

They approached the discoverers of the reef, called the Cumberland Mine, and offered to buy into it with the money necessary for a crushing plant. The offer was accepted, and the first crushing proved the undoubted value of the reef. With visions of great wealth, the three original partners were jubilant, Murphy wanting to get out immediately. The 'dividing mates' offered him ten thousand pounds for his share, and this he accepted on the condition that the money would be placed to his credit in a bank, and that the bank should transfer it to the Bank of England in London. This was duly done and Murphy departed.

After the next big crushing, the other two Cumberland men decided to quit - either they could not visualise the amount of gold
still to be won, or they were overwhelmed by the sum of ten thousand pounds paid to Murphy. Steele, the businessman of the 'dividing mates' partnership, raised the money, and so they three became sole owners of a mine which was to prove a great gold producer.

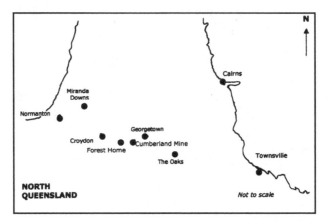

36. *North Queensland showing the Cumberland Mine*

North of O'Brien's station, Green Hills, was property owned by the Edmunds family called Forest Home. The partners bought out the Edmunds' and ran the two properties as one, thereby forming a fine cattle station. In the other direction, too, they expanded their joint businesses: O'Brien being the pastoral manager in general, Steele being the business manager of the combine, and Hunt managing the Cumberland Mine.

In time they became the kings of the Etheridge Goldfield. If they differed in opinion, they never failed to arrive at an amicable agreement. Perfect harmony controlled the partnership. They became closer than brothers and between them grew a spiritual affinity seen sometimes among twins or

134

triplets. This was how things were when Francis Cobbold became Cobb & Co manager of Miranda Downs and The Oaks.

2.

The people of Georgetown, including the three kings of the goldfield, saw little of Francis Cobbold when riding through the township on his way between Miranda Downs to the Oaks. Any business he had to transact in Georgetown was completed expeditiously. When earlier Forest Home managers accepted every excuse to visit the township and stay there as long as possible, Cobbold found no excuse to delay there.

In fact, he had no inclination either to gossip or to drink, these being the only attractions offered by Georgetown. His salary for managing two huge stations was just two hundred pounds a year, and yet he was managing to save money.

When he sold bulls to the three partners on behalf of his employers, the bargaining was keen and he always obtained a fair price. At this time there was demand for dairy cows, the emerging townships requiring milk, and on several occasions Cobbold was asked to sell cows in the normal way of business. When it was known generally that he would not sell Cobb & Co's breeding cows, offers were made to buy them on the quiet. So safe from detection would such dealing be that a lesser man might well have succumbed to the temptation to augment his income, but tradition, breeding and education were the three unbreakable bars making betrayal of his trust impossible for Francis Cobbold. It was not a matter on which to spend a moment of time. He became known as a square man, and he was respected as much on that count as on his keen bargaining with men like O'Brien, Steele and Hunt, and others with whom he legitimately traded on behalf of his employers.

When he was on Monkira he built better than he knew, and it was the same here. In 1886, when on his way to the Oaks from Miranda Downs, he called on the operator in charge of the Gilbert Telegraph Station, whom he knew too well to offend by not calling and accepting a drink of tea. During the conversation, the operator mentioned he had heard that O'Brien and his partners had sold the Cumberland Mine for £185,000; Cobbold found the item interesting as local gossip.

Arriving at the small township named after the famous mine, he was met by William Steele, who possessed a comfortable house there. Steele insisted that Cobbold stay with him that night, and as there was a good paddock for his horses near the house, Cobbold gladly accepted the invitation. Dinner over, Steele said in his easy, fluent style: "I suppose you have heard that we have sold the Cumberland Mine for £185,000?"

"Yes," admitted the guest. "I did hear a rumour to that effect, but thinking it only a rumour, I did not take much notice of it."

"Rumour for once does not lie," Steele went on. "O'Brien has gone to Townsville, and Hunt is on his way to England to finalise the transaction." Steele now became concise and emphatic. "We are leaving the district where we three came together and prospered. O'Brien is in treaty for the purchase of Carpentaria Downs which, as you know, adjoins The Oaks. How would those two properties fit together, do you think? Would your people sell us The Oaks?"

Still not dreaming of the ultimate reason for Steele's invitation to stay the night, and thinking that this project of joining The Oaks with Carpentaria Downs was the object, Cobbold replied frankly. He assured his host that The Oaks naturally fitted in with the Carpentaria Downs, which was well watered, while The Oaks was less favoured. Should the two properties be joined and worked as one, they would be bounded on the west side by the Newcastle Range, and on the east by the Basalt Tableland.

"I feel almost sure that my principals would sell The Oaks," he proceeded. "When McGuigan took up The Oaks, he thought he had got a thousand square miles, but actually he got much less than that. I repeatedly pointed out to my people that there is in consequence not much room for development. With The Oaks joined to Carpentaria Downs, the resultant property should be a fine one."

"Humph! " Steele pondered. "If we buy Carpentaria Downs, which is almost certain, The Oaks would be worth more to us than to anyone else, would it not?"

"Yes it would," Cobbold agreed, and then gave a shrewd thrust. "But why give more?"

"Yes why?" echoed Steele, regarding his guest approvingly!

They discussed this proposition of joining the two properties, as well as the economic working of the whole, and then Steele fired his big gun. He said: "How would it suit you to come into our partnership, and to take over the management of all our pastoral properties?"

Francis Cobbold regarded Steele with understandable astonishment. Here were three locally famous men, three dividing mates who had become like one family. Their resources were pooled. They owned stations and businesses, and had just closed an offer for their mine stated to be £185,000. Yet it was less the financial magnitude of their standing that so astonished Cobbold than the undoubted compliment extended to him by being asked to join them.

William Steele's business acumen was largely responsible for the success of an extraordinary partnership; Francis Cobbold was a mere station manager whose savings amounted to only five hundred pounds. Had Steele not been so earnest, Cobbold should well have been excused for thinking that the offer was in the nature of a joke - and one made in extremely bad taste!

But how could he go in with big capitalists, how could he, with his small resources?

"It is a matter that can be arranged," Steele countered.

"Well, before I give you a decision, I must know the sentiments of your partners," Cobbold prevaricated.

Steele waved his right hand as though to dismiss the idea that he would forward such a proposition without having conferred with his two partners. "We have decided the matter," he said briskly. "I speak for we three. We have watched you, you understand. As I told you, we wish to leave the district, and we know no one better than you in whom we can place implicit trust."

They discussed the terms of the proposed partnership extension and Cobbold could find nothing to fault. He declined, however, to sign the ultimate deed of partnership until he had severed his association with Cobb & Co. Furthermore, as their representative, he could not take any part in the negotiations for The Oaks other than to advise his principals that Steele and his partners were offering it.

3.

Francis Cobbold wrote to Cobb & Co putting them in touch with William Steele. Both sides being aware of his valuation of The Oaks, the sale was quickly effected. This left Cobbold clear to tender his resignation, and to James Rutherford, the chief of the Queensland branch of the great firm, he wrote:

"The Oaks having now been sold to Messrs O'Brien and Co, I am offered by them a partnership to manage their pastoral properties and therefore I beg to tender my resignation. I will, however, carry on here until you send someone to take my place."

To this Rutherford replied: "There is no necessity for us to send a man up there to you. I leave it to you to appoint whom you like."

Here was an undoubted compliment. Cobb & Co thought so highly of their manager, were so sure of his strict integrity, that they considered it unnecessary to conduct an audit and to undertake a formal handover. In effect Rutherford had said 'Appoint whom you like. We shall be quite satisfied with your choice of a successor to manage Miranda Downs.'

Cobbold offered the appointment to C F Power of Wallebadah. Power accepted it and proved the confidence placed in him by giving entire satisfaction for some fourteen years. When the property was then purchased by O'Brien, Cobbold & Co, he continued in their service until, with several other properties, Miranda Downs was sold.

When Francis Cobbold joined the 'dividing mates' the pastoral properties belonging to the re-organised firm were valued at £110,000. In this the four partners held equal shares. It was arranged that FE should put in and give promissory notes for the balance of his share of £27,500. One clause of the partnership deed read that it was to last for twenty years, subject to termination by any member of it at the end of five, ten or fifteen years. Another significant clause read 'Each partner shall be just and faithful to the others and to the partnership'. It was a clause carried out not only in the letter but in the spirit of the agreement. The partnership was destined to remain unbroken during the lifetime of them all, FE surviving the original three by eighteen years.

Carpentaria Downs was purchased for £25,000, and The Oaks was added to it. FE made his headquarters at Carpentaria Downs, where he built the house which stands to this day. He had entered a partnership which, to anyone not knowing the original members of it, might seem hazardous when consideration is given to the particular terms relative to him; he, however, never doubted the integrity of the partners, nor they his, and he never subsequently found cause to regret the step he took.

FE - as Francis Cobbold became known among his partners - now found his position vastly superior to that which he had held with Cobb & Co. As their manager, his activities in improving their properties had been restricted by the ideas and the desires of principals who lived hundreds of miles away, and who had seen neither the properties in the far north of Queensland nor their manager, and who had far more important and valuable properties near to their hands. As a partner in a firm who knew every acre within the boundaries of their leases, FE enjoyed a power which was limited only by the agreement of his partners to any proposition for improvement he cared to lay before them - such was their confidence in him that only rarely did they hesitate to give their consent.

He found that the former owners had made no attempt to develop the capabilities of Carpentaria Downs by the construction of working improvements to save time and money. His partners agreed with his ideas, made the capital available, and so he began this developmental work with energy.

The combined runs had a double frontage to the Copperfield River, which had a wide sandy bottom with good water-holes at intervals. There was, too, a double frontage to the Einasleigh River. Thus both the Copperfield and the Einasleigh ran through the property, the two rivers meeting twenty-five miles below the homestead Cobbold had built and close by several fine water-holes in the latter stream. Like the great majority of Australian rivers, these two running through the Carpentaria Downs are not flowing streams all the year round. They are fed with neither mountain snow nor springs. They carry the rain dropped on the Gilbert watershed to the Gulf of Carpentaria - water which surges down their courses to leave the naturally scooped holes in the bends full to the brim.

FE was fortunate in having agreeable neighbours. To the south was John Fulford, the managing partner of Lyndhurst Station, his partner being Henry Barnes of Dyraaba Station, New South Wales. Also to the south lay Spring Creek Station run by Thomas Collins. Lyndhurst was a beautiful station of about 900 square miles, while Spring Creek was even better, considering its relatively small size of 200 square miles. They were the best big and best small stations on the whole of the Basalt Tableland. The first carried about 25,000 cattle, the second about 9,000.

Having built all the working and herding yards on Carpentaria Downs and its outstation, FE approached his southern neighbours with the proposition that they join him in the cost of creating boundary fences and thus eliminate a great deal of unnecessary stock work. They agreed and the fences were built.

In addition, there was the supervision of Forest Home to be maintained. The Etheridge Goldfields areas of about 5,000 square miles had been proclaimed; a big portion of Forest Home came into this proclaimed area and was by the far the largest station. Many small towns had come into being in addition to Georgetown and with these towns arose difficulties which eventually had to be faced.

Forest Home Station was originally held under the Pastoral Leases Act of 1869 (Queensland) and, when a large part of it was 'declared' because it came within a goldfield area, it was removed from the jurisdiction of the Lands Department and came under that of the Mines Department. This departmental transfer did not deprive the lessees of Forest Home of their pastoral rights; however, under a special act it gave power to everyone holding a miner's right to take up a Miners' Homestead Lease of forty acres anywhere they wished on a goldfield area on payment of two pounds per annum.

The Lands Department, of course, was interested in Forest Home as a pastoral property, but when the greater part of it automatically became the concern of the Mines Department, it was no longer considered as a pastoral property but as a mining property. Where the Lands Department had been sympathetic, the Mines Department was indifferent to its continuance as a cattle station.

The creation of the Miners' Homestead Leases, on a goldfield area which included pastoral runs, naturally became a source of bitterness with the pastoralists. This was not because of the little areas of forty acres taken from them, but because of the localities of the areas selected by the miners and others who, while not bona fide miners, were still eligible to select areas which naturally included valuable water-holes. To permit a miner to take up forty acres on which to build himself a house

140

was absurd. To permit him to select his forty acres anywhere he desired was a further absurdity. The area was much too large for a home and much too small to support two cows for milking in a normal season. Water-holes most essential to the large stock owners were suddenly cut off without compensation; it was the loss of these water-holes which produced the inevitable friction.

It must be understood that the pastoralists held the land under lease from the Government. The Government retained the right of resumption when the lease expired and the Government created the right of resumption by Act of Parliament. The land was not outright freehold, as it should have been; the main disadvantage of the leasehold system to the country was that the occupiers of the land would not improve it beyond their immediate requirements for the period of the lease. Who could blame them? They would have been foolish to spend money in improvements of permanent value when their tenure was so insecure.

> **Resumption:** <u>Law</u>   *The action on the part of the Crown or other authority of reassuming possession of lands, rights etc which have been bestowed on others. (Shorter Oxford English Dictionary)*

Government action in closer settlement has been marked by two glaring errors which were detrimental to the country as a whole without fully benefiting those people it was desired to establish on the land. Invariably, the areas which were sliced off large properties were split into holdings too small to maintain the settlers with reasonable prospects of permanency. The original owners of the leased land suffered loss through resumption, while the newcomers did not gain financial success commensurate with the loss suffered by the former. (The other method of closer settlement, especially that relative to returned soldiers, has been even more peculiar. The various state Governments compensated owners of freehold farmland on which to settle returned soldiers - buying out one set of farmers to found another set.)

Later, it will be shown how Forest Home suffered from the Miners' Homestead Leases system, and the worry it caused FE and his partners. They had to fight for common justice in the courts, at grave risk of losing their titles to the land for which they were paying rent and on which they had spent thousands of pounds in improvements.

4.

The wide district of the southern Gulf country, of which the Gilbert and the Etheridge goldfields were the centre, was a colony within a colony. Here, Brisbane, the capital city of Queensland, was as remote as Melbourne. There was no sympathy with the city folk and the farmers of the south-east and the south. Men were nearer in spirit to Great Britain than to the new populous centres of Australia. They took pride in the fact that they belonged to the Gilbert and Etheridge and not to Queensland. If only the rainfall had been more equitable to the land, if only the land had been kinder to man and beast, there would have grown up within Queensland - in the far north at any rate - a race of men as proud and as rich in tradition as the old Virginians of America.

There was no poverty and no unemployment. Men were winning gold by their own efforts, and earning high wages in the mines controlled by shareholders. The pastoralists were becoming affluent, since the herds were rapidly increasing on all stations. The wire had come - and corrugated iron. Men were earning big cheques erecting fences - not a mile or two but hundreds of miles. There were always vacancies among the drovers and the stockmen. It was an era when men were physically hard, spiritually generous, and proud of their handiwork. The seasons were bounteous, money was plentiful - and on top of the crest rode Francis Cobbold.

Despite his multifarious duties and keen attention to the thousand and one problems always demanding his attention, he found time for a little recreation. With other station owners and managers within the radius of seventy miles, he attended the Annual Picnic Race Meeting. The first was held at Junction Creek Telegraph Station in 1883 when horses were run by Frederick Barker of Carpentaria Downs, Auriel Barker of Rossella Plains, George Collins of Spring Creek, Brodie of Dags, Firth from Mount Surprise, Harry Williams of Springfield, and Cobbold of The Oaks, who ran his grey gelding Hector.

Hector won the first race in which he was entered. The following year the meeting was held at Carpentaria Downs where, in addition to those just named, came Fulford of

Lyndhurst Station. Hector acquitted himself with great credit, running many races and winning often. At each of the succeeding meetings, the original patrons never failed to turn up and were joined by other neighbouring owners and managers.

Some of these men were to go to the wall in the great financial crash, the basic causes of which even then were being laid by politicians. Others were to retire to the Old Country and still others were destined to accept a big share in the public life of Queensland. Through their own courage and pertinacity they had made themselves the aristocracy of a district as large as England and Wales. While the feudal lords of Europe had raised themselves by the might of their arms and royal favour, these men raised themselves above their fellows by grit and determination to make good in a harsh land.

They took to horse racing as ducks to water - it could hardly have been otherwise with men who spent the day, and often the night, on the back of a horse. Their horses were good and hardy; animals run at the Picnic Races were all untrained and 'off the grass', but they had speed and stamina. Bush horses to this day are superior to the hand-fed horses of the farms and cities.

CHAPTER FOURTEEN

Years 1890 – 1895
Stormy Waters

37.   *Frank Cobbold, 1890*

1.

After the drought of 1884-1886 the seasons changed, becoming more pleasant every year until the climax of 1890, which proved to be a year of amazing bounty. It augured well for FE's future success but he, like hundreds of thousands throughout Australia, could not foresee the dark shadow which was to fall on the country three years later.

Having established himself in a comfortable home on Carpentaria Downs, FE married Bessie, the eldest daughter of his neighbours, John and Margaret Fulford of Lyndhurst. At the Lyndhurst homestead, they were married before a gathering of a few relatives and friends, and as he had been working continuously for twelve years, FE made the occasion of his honeymoon a long holiday spent visiting his sister in Melbourne.

> *Bessie was born in 1870 in Grafton, New South Wales. Her father came originally from North Devon. He was born in 1840 and married Bessie's mother Margaret Hindmarsh, who was also his cousin, in 1868.*

*38. Copy of the certificate of marriage between
Frank Cobbold and Elizabeth Fulford, 13th June 1889*

Australia has always suffered growing pains, a fact it is easy to forget in these years when everyone ceaselessly searches for new markets to absorb surplus products. Like other stations, the two properties controlled by FE were not producing at full capacity. In 1890, the properties taken together were carrying 57,000 cattle while there were no less than 13,000 branded calves.

A meat canning works had been started ten miles south of Townsville, but this could not hope to absorb the production of the fast-growing herds of Northern Queensland. A few years previously, a meat works had been set up at Poole Island, but a

145

cyclone destroyed it before production could start. A new concern was formed, called the Queensland Meat Export & Agency Company, which built works at Townsville, Brisbane and Sydney for freezing as well as for canning and extraction.

O'Brien, Cobbold & Co communicated with Brisbane Station Agents, from whom they received particulars of numerous properties for sale. Having decided to purchase one of them, FE started a mob of two thousand cattle southward while he himself travelled to Townsville, where he took the steamer to Brisbane and train to Charleville.

Thirty miles to the south of Charleville, and between four and five hundred miles west of Brisbane, lies a station named Riversleigh. Its situation was ideally suitable for what was required of it: namely, to receive and fatten cattle from the Gulf Country, and then send fat cattle by rail either to Brisbane or Sydney, or by southern trucks down the rivers to Melbourne or Adelaide when prices and conditions warranted. Further to this, Charleville was a good stock centre visited by many of the big stock dealers.

After careful inspection of Riversleigh, FE closed for the purchase, walk in walk out, for £6,000 – two thousand mixed

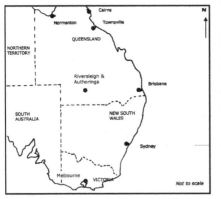

cattle being then on the station. The two thousand bullocks despatched from Carpentaria Downs duly arrived, and it was then considered essential that further stock must be moved south from both Carpentaria Downs and Forest Home if disaster was to be avoided – there was a grave danger of being caught overstocked when the next dry period arrived.

39. The location of Riversleigh and Authoringa Stations

Droughts in Australia are always local in scope, although the locality may be as large as a European country. Every locality is sure to suffer its turn of dry seasons, the general rule being the succession of several dry years culminating in one or two years with rain. The small man, or selector, must always be fully stocked in order to live and he, like the big squatter, is faced

146

with the danger of being overstocked at the end of a good-years period and at the beginning of a dry-years period. It is a danger fairly generally recognised, but it is much more serious for the selector than it is for the squatter, who endeavours to keep several of his paddocks resting. The selector cannot afford to have any of his little land areas non-productive; he cannot afford to have any of his small paddocks resting.

To be overstocked at the beginning of a dry-years period means that all the stock will quickly suffer severely from the limited supply of feed and water, when half the number on the same area would pull through a drought more successfully. During a succession of good years it is not an easy matter to prevent overstocking, as good years are productive of a high birth rate and a lower death rate among all animals. As this role extends to all parts of the country blessed with good years, everyone has stock to sell, is in fact anxious to sell to escape overstocking, and consequently the market is flooded and prices are low. Often it is economically impossible to sell, the market prices not balancing the outlay expended on drovers' wages, rail and freight, and auctioneers' charges. Instead of receiving a cheque for the mob of prize beasts, the unfortunate owner is presented with a bill for immediate payment.

FE saw that if his firm did not extend their opportunities it would be in danger of sustaining heavy losses. The properties he controlled were too far from city markets to be always successful in getting fat bullocks to them; the city markets were the only reasonably sure markets, while the local market offered by the meat and boiling down works was wholly inadequate.

They must go on – or go under. There could be no standing still.

Besides being in a favourable situation from which to despatch stock to the city markets, Riversleigh is also favoured in lying inside the Great Australian Artesian Basin which covers a little more than 600,000 square miles, half of which is Queensland. The water in this basin is strongly alkaline and unsuitable for irrigation. By letting it drain away through long channels so that most of the alkaline may be deposited, the water can be used in station homestead gardens and is admirably suited for stock. Some wells tapping this subterranean supply at first yielded over one million gallons every twenty four hours.

A previous owner of Riversleigh, Mr Mellwains, had intended to put down a bore and had selected the site. On this same site FE decided to have the bore put down by contract labour, a Canadian well-borer undertaking the work. The site had been selected because the fall of the earth's surface seemed favourable; obviously, it would not pay to sink a bore a thousand feet or more when the subsequent gush of water from the bore casing ran into a neighbour's property. Having examined the site, FE agreed with others that it seemed to command a slope in the desired direction - the choice of direction being governed by the length of the channel made possible at the minimum of cost to excavate it.

The teams had started out with the well-boring plant when FE experienced a qualm of uneasiness. Supposing that the surface fall from the intended bore was not favourable? Suppose the water from the proposed bore ran away in a direction opposite to that desired? One may easily think that a particular area of land is flat; it is so easy to be convinced that another area of land slopes to a particular compass point – and then be quite wrong. It is so easy in the interior of Australia to fall victim to an optical illusion which has given rise to the statement that in Australia water runs uphill. It does not.

In this case, as in the past, FE left nothing to chance. He drove to Charleville at high speed, where he wired to Brisbane for a Gravatt's Dumpy Level and Staff. Meeting the inward train the next day, he collected the level and hurried to the bore site in time to prevent the well-boring plant being unloaded.

The instrument showed the earth fall to be in the opposite direction to that thought; an imperceptible rise would have cost the price of several levels in the added cost of deepening a channel sufficiently to get water over it.

FE surveyed miles of bore drains with Connors, the manager, giving him sufficient instruction in the use of the level to survey drains for other bores to be sunk subsequently. Two thousand pounds were spent in wages and materials for improvements on Forest Home and Carpentaria Downs, while nearly a thousand pounds were paid in drovers' wages.

With Riversleigh in their possession, FE and his partners now controlled a halfway house - a rest-camp which provided a fattening area for cattle from their northern stations.

Nevertheless, time quickly proved that Riversleigh was not large enough for the purpose for which it had been purchased. Then Authoringa, a property of about six hundred square miles adjoining Riversleigh, came on to the market and this could provide the opportunity for expansion. So many difficulties had yet to be overcome at the freezing works before the export of beef could be carried on a big scale, and meanwhile they could not absorb the products of the northern cattle runs. Losses by the several works were at times so heavy that the companies had to give up buying on their own account, and were able only to freeze and ship at owner's expenses.

The price asked for Authoringa was £12,000 based on the number of cattle it carried – two thousand. Pastoral properties held on lease from a government were and are bought and sold on the number of stock carried at the time, with all improvements thrown in. Yet times were hard and prices were low, not only for cattle but for sheep and wool as well.

FE hesitated. Then he decided to buy if he could purchase the property at a reasonable price – a price based perhaps not on the real value but the actual value at the moment. He offered the representative of the company £10,000 cash, which was accepted subject to approval by his company. On arriving at Brisbane, FE was informed that the company had ratified their manager's acceptance and, now in command of Riversleigh and Authoringa, he possessed an overflow for his cattle within easy distance of important markets. This overflow would definitely remove the menace of overstocking on Forest Home and Carpentaria Downs.

Early in 1893, he started three thousand bullocks on the long trek southward. They were divided into three mobs, one destined for Authoringa, and two much further south to Wodonga, on the Victorian side of the Murray, where there was a market for store cattle. Each of the three mobs was in the charge of a boss drover, assisted by three stockmen, a camp cook and a horse boy.

No matter where he happened to be, FE kept in touch with the three boss drovers, they telegraphing to him at every town they reached. By this means he was able to arrange their expenses by placing credits in one or other of the banks in town ahead of them, the accounts to be operated by cheque forms carried by the boss drovers.

Then, when the cattle were half way down Queensland, the first hammer blow of ruin fell on thousands of people without warning. The Queensland National Bank closed its doors. After it, one after another of the big banking companies abruptly discontinued business until only the Bank of New South Wales, the Union Bank, and the Australasian Bank remained open. Following the collapse of the land boom in Victoria, the big bank smash of 1893 had come.

And on the outback tracks, FE had eighteen men in his employ in charge of three thousand bullocks. The men would want their wages - and certainly the drovers would need money to buy rations for themselves and their assistants and water for the bullocks. The accounts he had been so careful to arrange with the banks were frozen. The doors of nearly all the banks were shut.

2.

It could be thought that any nation which had experienced the tragic plight of a financial depression would create adequate safeguards to ensure it would never happen again. Men, however, are no different in the mass than they are individually. They are forever seeking money they do not earn, and they never spend money wisely unless they have accumulated it shilling by shilling at much cost and sacrifice.

The financial system ruling during the early years of Australian settlement was sound enough, being fashioned on the precepts laid down in England but, unlike England, there were no safeguards in Australia to prevent the financial systems from becoming sufficiently elastic to admit practices little short of criminal.

When reading of the World Trade Depression beginning in 1930, when listening to the economists and their fantastic theories and palliatives, one finds it difficult to believe that there have been several such depressions during Australia's short history. Without proper thought, we are apt to regard the present financial depression as the very first of its kind which has fallen on men, when actually there have been many at various times from which we should have learned how to avoid making the same mistakes. There have been financial breakdowns in Australia three times during the 1840s, one in the

150

1850s, another in the 1860s, yet another in the 1890s, one in 1907, and the last from 1930. People are incorrigible.

3.

With his drovers bereft of resources with which to pay their men and purchase supplies, FE determined to follow up the three mobs of cattle. From time to time he had remitted funds to country banks, but these had been locked up as soon as received. The situation was almost desperate, for the drovers were bound by the Travelling Stock Act to keep moving at not less than nine miles a day. They would be hurried from pillar to post; their men would be in a condition of insubordination and prepared to abandon the cattle.

FE hurried to Townsville, rushed to Brisbane and on to Sydney. There he met Sir James Burns, the head of Burns Philp & Co. Sir James knew the four partners well and had known the original three for twenty years. They held a large number of shares in his company, and had disposed of much of their merchandise through it.

"Hullo, FE! How are you weathering the storm?" enquired Sir James.

"Bad enough, but we might be in a much worse position," replied FE, and then explained his difficulties regarding his drovers.

"Don't let it worry you overmuch," urged Sir James Burns. "I'll see that you have all the money you want."

Here was a man who offered to let FE have all the money he wanted when nearly all the banks in Australia were shut and when people held banknotes which were worth less than their proper value! It proves the solid ground which supported the firm of O'Brien, Cobbold & Co.

By this time Sir George Dibbs, the Premier, had guaranteed the note issue of the Bank of New South Wales with all the resources of the Colony, so FE made arrangements with this greatest of the Australian banks for remittance of funds - at the same time taking a bag full of sovereigns.

He then set off by train and coach to locate his drovers, the first of whom he found near Forbes. The drover was decidedly relieved to see him, especially as FE had sufficient funds for immediate necessities. The distribution of a few sovereigns put new heart into the men as bank notes were now regarded by the wage-earning class with grave suspicion, a suspicion justified when store and hotelkeepers declined to accept them.

The second mob of cattle was at considerable distance from the first, so FE bought a sulky and a fine black horse and harness, all for £30. He drove by road down the Bland River, past Norangarell Station, and so to Wagga where he caught up with the second mob and smoothed ruffled tempers with a few more sovereigns.

This mob of cattle had been destined for the fat store cattle market at Wodonga, but in the interim the market had utterly collapsed; he had no alternative but to turn them back.

The reader will appreciate the difficulties which have to be met by the owner of cattle on the road. After these had left for the market at great distance, that market collapsed. Every day the value of the beasts was going down by the addition of extra droving expenses, and in addition they were losing condition through the constant travelling along stock routes used by other mobs of cattle and sheep. They would have to be disposed of somehow, somewhere, otherwise they would become a liability, not an asset.

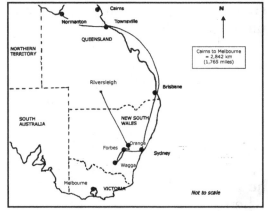

40. *The journey to retrieve cattle during the bank crash*

The horse and sulky were of great value to FE in this emergency. With it, he got in touch with the stock agents in the various towns on route. These men he found most helpful and willing to give information about likely buyers, large and small, and so before getting back to Forbes he had sold a thousand of the bullocks in lots of from fifty to two hundred. The remaining thousand followed him through Forbes, through Orange, to Bugoura where sufficient well-grazed, well-watered country was rented for six months to hold the bullocks. Having settled them, FE drove back to Forbes where he sold the horse and sulky for what he had given for it.

On 3rd January 1891, FE wrote the following account to his father, Arthur Thomas Cobbold:

O'BRIEN, COBBOLD & CO.,   Carpentaria Downs,
Telegraphic Address: Via Pentland
GEORGETOWN   North Queensland
                                                    3rd January 1891

My dear Father.

I have only three days returned from a ten weeks trip through the colony of New South Wales trying to sell the bullocks we sent from here last April and May.
    Last October I got telegrams from South that things were going to be very bad for the cattle owners in Southern markets and I hastened down by horse from here to Pentland thence train to Townsville thence steamer to Brisbane thence train through Sydney and on to Wagga Wagga where I caught the cattle before they reached Wodonga to have been sacrificed at auction as the markets by then had completely collapsed. I bought a light buggy and one horse and turning the cattle back with their heads again pointing to Queensland drove slowly ahead trying to sell privately to the neighbouring graziers or just grass to keep them on until markets recovered their tone. After travelling 150 miles this way I managed to sell 600 bullocks at £2/10/5 on the average. I was then able to rent 14,000 acres of good grass land at £42 per month for the remainder of the bullocks; 1421 head. Besides my direct journey I scoured the country for fifty miles on each side of me as I travelled looking for buyers.
    After I left the 1421 cattle in the rented paddocks I started on my return home and visited Riversleigh on the journey back where I stayed a week, we have 1000 bullocks there those that went down last New Year but I cannot get a buyer for them even at as low a price as £2/10/. a head.   And now to make matters worse

*frozen beef in the home markets appear to have
fallen to a price below what we can actually
send it home for.   It has already ruined a
great many people Graziers dealers and others &
I fancy it must come to a general smash up
amongst those whose only resources are cattle.*

*I have just been long enough at home to
write up all my arrears of work by constant
application and tomorrow morning I have to
start for Forest Home where I purpose remaining
for a month as I have now a lot of arrears of
work to perform up there.*

*Bessie is very well and wishes me to say
she receives the papers you send her very
regularly. We see very little of each other I
have to travel so much and she not strong
enough to go with me.*

*The socks mother is knitting for me please
send to Townsville c/o Burns Philp & Co*

*No one seems to be able to give a
reasonable conjecture of what is going to
happen to the cattle owners, the increase goes
on at such an enormous rate - here we have
branded 5196 and at Forest Home over 7000
calves for the year and at Riversleigh about
700 making nearly 13,000 altogether and where
we are to get the population to consume the
increase is a mystery. At present I can see no
way out of it, my liabilities press on me on
every hand our cattle unsold in N.S.Wales and
apparently no sale for our bullocks here is a
very bad look out with no funds to meet current
expenses.*

*I write this in great haste trusting
Mother & yourself are well.   Bessie writes with
me in love to all*
                    Your affect son
                         Frank Cobbold

Eventually people began to recover from the shock of the
financial debacle. Some of the stronger banks re-opened their
doors, others came out with re-construction schemes then they

too opened for business. Their shareholders, of course, were the main sufferers, the depositors and those with current accounts faring much better. As far as FE's firm was concerned, it did not lose a penny although it was some time before its deposits were returned in full.

4.

A wise choice of bankers had enable O'Brien, Cobbold & Co to emerge from the financial debacle in 1893 without direct loss but, like everyone else in Australia, they suffered through the resultant market stagnation and the reduction of values. Nevertheless, the following year found the firm well established and financially sound.

Towards the end of 1895, FE and his partners acquired a property called Waterview, near the coast of North Queensland. Despite the condition of the markets and the ruling prices, FE still maintained that not to advance was to stagnate, and that there is no sounder principle in business than to buy when the market is low. When the majority of men are considered to be – and many believe themselves to be – too old at forty, at this age FE was just getting into his stride after a long and arduous apprenticeship which had covered several professions. At a time when men were figuratively gasping after being nearly drowned by the financial deluge, at a time when men were becoming over-cautious and timid, he advised an extension of operations, and such was their faith in him that his partners never hesitated to support his propositions. He said: "Let us buy Riversleigh". They agreed.

He said: "Let us buy Authoringa to join to Riversleigh". They agreed.

He said again: "Let us purchase Waterview. We must go on or go under". They again agreed.

The silent O'Brien saw that FE was right regarding the danger of being caught overstocked at the end of the good years. The shrewd William Steele knew that FE was right in buying properties when the property market was at a low ebb. Hunt, the downright, the stolid, the tenacious Hunt, clearly recognised the business genius of the latest and the youngest partner, and knew he was right on both counts.

From an apprentice on a sailing ship in 1867, from a novice in a Melbourne warehouse in 1868, from a rover among the South Sea Islands, from a surveyor in Victoria and a bookkeeper in New South Wales, and from a stockman in South-Western Queensland - now, in 1895, FE controlled five great pastoral properties on which ran thousands of cattle in addition to branded and unbranded calves. He was spending over five thousand pounds a year in wages and materials for improvements and more than two thousand a year in rent of the leases. Even in this year of depression the estimated value of the combined properties amounted to £61,000.

Financial debacles can be avoided; drought cannot be avoided. The introduction of foreign pests and diseases can today more easily be prevented than in 1893, when early that year teamster's bullocks carried the cattle tick into Northern Queensland from Fort Darwin.

Swiftly the tick affected all the herds grazing on the North Queensland cattle country. The loss of stock became appalling, estimated to be from forty to sixty per cent of the total number of beasts. In 1897, when FE despatched one thousand fat bullocks to Townsville in three mobs only 330 arrived, the balance having perished on the road from tick fever. Of 2,200 fat cows in the cow paddock at Carpentaria Downs, a muster disclosed the loss of 1,600. The small herd of Devons were almost wiped out, only eleven surviving from more than forty. The firm's losses in cattle amounted to nearly sixteen thousand, while the total estimated values of the properties fell to £55,000.

The tick fever, coming on top of the bank smashes and the stagnate markets, ruined many cattle owners, men by whose grit and perseverance the cattle industry had been founded. Reviewing his own position, recalling the promissory notes still outstanding, FE considered it time to take stock of his own resources. With great reluctance, he informed his partners of his desire to retire from the firm. To this they strongly and emphatically objected. None of them could be allowed to retire unless and until all avenues to stop such a move had been examined without success!

"The position is this," FE persisted. "I still owe the partners a great deal of money which I never had to put into it. As you know, the sum is in the form of promissory notes. While I am prepared to carry on, even to lose the little I have, I am not prepared to go on and lose what I have not got – money

156

represented by the promissory notes – and money which it is very doubtful I would ever be in the position to refund."

Even when the position was plainly put to them, the partners would not listen to the proposal for such a break. They suggested that, as the promissory notes appeared to worry FE, they should be wiped out and that FE should come in with a much smaller share to be paid for in cash – if he would not have it in any other way. It was not necessary, of course, but FE could satisfy his scruples by any method he wished so long as it did not mean breaking the partnership.

Frank Cobbold then bought a share in the pastoral properties for two thousand pounds cash and it was agreed, indeed urged on him, that he continue as the general manager at the same salary. So he achieved a position which eliminated that grave risk of losing what he had never actually possessed, and might have entangled him in debt that would have ridden him for the rest of his life.

We can now more fully appreciate the generosity displayed by the three dividing mates when they offered to take FE into their partnership, worth £110,000 for £500 cash and promissory notes for £27,000. We can also more fully appreciate their shrewdness when inviting FE to join them, their shrewdness in picking a man from the ruck of station managers and pastoralists. Their confidence in him had been such that they were content to live in semi-retirement, and their confidence remained as strong as ever to the point of conceding everything he desired. Happy the man who can command such confidence.

Not long after this readjustment, William Steele died.

5.

Financial nerves also suffered from the bank smashes and, like many other people, FE was determined not to be caught again without funds. From the bank in Georgetown, he drew one hundred good English sovereigns, and locked them securely within the office safe at Carpentaria Downs.

As the mailman arrived every Saturday evening to stay overnight and to proceed the next morning, FE habitually rose early on Sunday morning to complete his outward correspondence. One Sunday morning he had occasion to open the safe to get postage stamps, and a moment later when the breakfast gong was sounded, he hurriedly slammed shut the safe door and omitted to lock it and withdraw the key. When he returned after breakfast, the key was gone and the safe locked.

The closest search failed to produce the missing key. FE was convinced that he had not locked the safe. Questioning the domestic staff shed no light on the mystery, and reflection raised reluctant suspicions against the Chinese cook. He was the only person who was able to enter the office silently while the household was at breakfast, but he had been with FE for three years during which time his service had been blameless; he could not be openly accused.

There was therefore a little problem. Had the person who took the safe key also taken the sovereigns? Or had he locked the safe and taken the key, intending that it be thought that the key had been mislaid and then, at a more favourable opportunity, taking the gold? Had he taken the key after locking the safe to delay discovery of the theft of the sovereigns? Obviously the problem would not be solved until the safe was opened.

A week elapsed before the duplicate key held in the bank in Georgetown was procured to open the safe, when it was found that the sovereigns were intact. Before that key was obtained, however, FE had brought several bullock chains to the office which he wound round the safe and locked together with a padlock. After the second key was obtained, the safe was still not a safe with the original key in someone's possession, and so the annoying task of removing the chains to take valuables from the safe, and replacing them again, was continued.

Several months later, on his return from a long visit to Forest Home, FE walked into his office to find the missing key laid on the blotter on his desk.

The bookkeeper, Thomas Wish, showed as much astonishment as his employer. He could throw no light on the return of the key, and vowed that he had been in the office half an hour before when the key was certainly not on the blotter.

It remained an unsolved mystery. No one but FE had known that the sovereigns were within the safe and, as has been stressed, sovereigns were rare tokens of currency in a country where bank cheques predominated. It seemed, however, that it could well have been the Chinese cook who was the thief who stole the key. Without doubt the clanking bullock chains annoyed him as much as FE was annoyed by having constantly to remove and replace them.

CHAPTER FIFTEEN

Year 1897
'A Cantankerous Old Man'

1.

The object of the Queensland Legislature when passing the Miners' Homestead Lease Act, was to provide a person engaged in gold mining or prospecting with an area of land on a Proclaimed Goldfield of sufficient dimensions to permit him to erect a house, grow vegetables for his family, and keep a cow for milking. That was the object: the object was not to allow the holder of a Miners' Homestead Lease to accumulate a herd of cattle and for the beasts to roam on land for which other people were paying high rent.

The objective of the Act is perfectly clear – however, the act did not state clearly that the holder of a Miners' Homestead Lease must not accumulate a herd of cattle which could not possibly find sustenance on forty acres and which would have to consume herbage and water paid for by another person. It was therefore necessary for Francis Cobbold and his partners to take the matter of such a theft to a court of law and there request a learned judge to interpret the direction of those who conceived the Act.

The pastoral property controlled by FE, part of which came within a Goldfield Area, was known as Forest Home. When the dividing mateship was formed between O'Brien, Hunt, and Steele, Forest Home was purchased from the Edmunds and to it was added Green Hills Station belonging to O'Brien. Green Hills became the out-station of Forest Home, and although this formation permitted the two properties to be worked as one and thought of as one by O'Brien, Cobbold & Co, it was not regarded as one by the Lands Department, which continued to look on the component parts as separate, with each block of land falling under one lease.

In the beginning, the pastoral holdings were acquired under the 1869 Lands Act. They were taken up in areas of 25, 50, and 100 square miles, this being the minimum and the maximum area that could be taken in one lease. Under certain conditions of stocking, a Licence to Occupy was granted for one year, after which – the conditions having been complied with – a Promise of Lease was granted for twenty-one years.

The blocks fronting the Gilbert River, with its valuable water-holes, were the first applied for, and for most of these a Promise of Lease was granted. Before all the blocks had been taken up, however, gold had been found and an area of about 5,000 square miles was proclaimed a Goldfield Area. Many blocks of land came under the jurisdiction of the Mines Department; this body was only interested in the goldbearing country which bore a very small proportion to the whole. The Mines Department apparently did not object to the Lands Department – for revenue purposes – issuing Licences to Occupy bearing the endorsement "… and this land, being within a Proclaimed Goldfield's area, no Promise of Lease will be given, but the Licence to Occupy will be granted for one year only, renewable from year to year, subject to giving up possession when required without compensation."

It later transpired that this 'issue of a Licence renewable from year to year' was *ultra vires*, but the land was remote, the Department wanted revenue and since the Parliaments were otherwise occupied it was not thought necessary to amend the Land Acts. Nevertheless, this Licence to Occupy from year to year, although a bad title, was better than none, and so from time to time areas were acquired under this new Endorsed Licence.

Although the Goldfield Proclamation covered many of the blocks that had been granted for twenty-one years on Promise of Lease, these were never in dispute. For the purpose of the actions at law in which FE was compelled to engage, they were never called in question. The trouble lay with those blocks taken up later and held under the Endorsed Licence which, as stated, held no Promise of Lease and therefore no security of tenure.

When the Etheridge Goldfield was proclaimed, much of the area cut into Forest Home, which included Green Hills station. Over a part of Forest Home and Green Hills, some of the mining residents had taken up 40-acre blocks under the Miners' Homestead Lease Act, and the selections of these blocks naturally took in valuable watering places. Further to this loss of water rights, there was no redress other than through a court of law to prevent the holders of the 40-acre blocks from running

160

their herds on property for which they paid no rent, and from boxing their cattle with the station herds, causing the pastoralists to spend money on wages to stockmen to separate them.

The inevitable outcome was that the station men became bitterly opposed to a number of goldfield people. Among the mining population, numbering roughly two thousand, were teamsters with their hundreds of working bullocks and horses and dairymen with their cows; the land for which O'Brien, Cobbold & Co were paying rent became little more than a Town Common. In fact, many of the people regarded the land as common property even though they were not paying rent and rates for it.

Cattle stealing became rampant, and only a series of successful prosecutions reduced it. Stealing cattle was made easy by the governing authority permitting any person of twenty-one years and over to own a registered brand. Horses and bullock teamsters of necessity had to own a brand for the identification of their stock, but men could easily procured a registered brand for which there was no legitimate use.

The ease with which a dishonest person could carry on criminal practices is well illustrated by the case of a stockman named Brown, who left his employment with O'Brien, Cobbold & Co at Forest Home. He drew his cheque at the beginning of the wet season, when stock work is traditionally at low ebb, and informed the manager that he intended to prospect for gold while the wet period continued.

He became the registered owner of a brand and he set to work cutting out of the Forest Home herd all those mickie and heifer calves weaned by their mothers that had been missed or had been considered too young to be branded at the last round up. Branding these youngsters with his own brand, this clever gentleman left them to roam again with the main herd.

At the end of the wet season, when the manager and his men checked the cattle again, they were astonished to find so many youngsters bearing an unfamiliar brand. Investigation revealed that the brand was the registered property of the stockman who had left ostensibly to go prospecting, a man who had no land and owned no cattle herd.

Bob Neary, the manager, became alarmed by the number of beasts branded with the strange cipher, the letters of which formed the stockman's initials, and reported the fact to FE. Then

Brown coolly rode to the station homestead and gave notice of his desire to muster all his stock. It should be recalled that this occurred in the 1890s, and that an allegedly responsible government controlled the country. It was so serious a theft that FE travelled to Townsville where he talked to the firm's solicitor and sought advice. Having heard the problem, the solicitor said:

"What evidence have you to support your connection that this man has branded your unbranded cattle? It is only an assertion."

"Very well," temporised FE, "But where are the mothers of all these calves bearing Brown's brand?" (Naturally the mothers belonged to and bore the brand of O'Brien, Cobbold & Co.)

"That's beside the mark," replied the solicitor. "Brown hasn't to prove anything. The onus is on you to prove that he put his brand on your cattle. How can you prove that when the mothers have weaned the youngsters and now would have nothing to do with them? There is no law to meet the case."

"But if a suspected thief is found in possession of rich booty, hasn't he to prove how he came possessed of it?"

"It does not apply in this case. The fact that Brown doesn't own land and has never owned cattle would not prove that he now owns your cattle because you have no proof that they are yours. They may be running on your property – so are other cattle and horses not yours, stock to which you lay no claim."

Unable to obtain common justice through the processes of the law, FE returned to Forest Home determined to put into practice other measures. The pirate proceeded to muster the cattle and cut those bearing his brand. These he temporarily confined within hastily and roughly built bush yards. During the night, however, his yarded beasts somehow broke out. As he had to erect several of these yards, he could not mount guard over them all, and it was indeed strange that no sooner had he mustered and yarded some of 'his' cattle than they broke out again.

Dame Fortune seemed to spurn poor Brown. When he attempted to muster at one end of the run, FE's stockmen were sure to be driving the cattle to the other end. When he had cut out a mob of branded youngsters, he was always met by a station stockman droving a mob of cows – when the cows and the calves would joyfully box together.

With others like him, the pirate was obtaining financial assistance from certain 'birds of a feather' who, while not taking an active part, were not only willing but anxious to be involved in what they thought were lucrative pickings. It was thought that the young cattle on Forest Home could be stealthily branded and then, when old enough, could be mustered and sold to butchers or dairymen. There were others operating this racket including a man name Tressidor. In time however, due to the vigilance of FE's stockmen who made mustering of the youngsters so difficult, the backers became anxious about their money represented by stores and liquor. One storekeeper said to FE: "That Tressidor owes me eighty pounds. He owes money to others, too. How could I go about getting payment? He's got a few cattle on enclosed pasture and, of course, his brand."

"Bankrupt him," FE sternly replied. "You know as well as anyone that these fellows don't rightfully own these beasts running about with their brands on them. By backing them, you are encouraging scoundrels."

The storekeeper went on with the business of getting his money, and eventually all FE's cattle that Tressidor had managed to brand and muster off Forest Home were put up at auction, together with his registered brand. No one bid although there was a full attendance. All were hostile to the pastoralists and the storekeeper who had bought about this sale of goods belonging to such an upright and innocent man as Tressidor. Poor Tressidor, to be trodden on by blasted capitalists!

The auctioneer was vainly endeavouring to obtain a bid when FE strode into the circle and snapped out: "Eighty pounds!"

Before the crowd could recover, he had turned and walked out.

His own cattle branded by Tressidor were now his because with them came the registered brand. And, too, all the youngsters on Forest Home bearing Tressidor's brand, and which Tressidor had been unable to muster, were now safe from him or any other duffer. Brown was wiped out in a similar fashion. Tressidor flung his saddle and bridle on to the back of a bullock wagon and thus left the district - broke.

2.

In Northern Queensland, as in all other vast grazing districts in Australia, trespass in itself is not regarded as serious. It is the advantages which can be taken by unscrupulous trespassers and the damage they can cause - and which is so difficult to prove and assess - which is so serious.

With his partners, FE discussed means to combat the menace. They pointed out that it would be necessary to tread softly as their titles to Forest Home were, to say the least, unorthodox.

FE said that "We have either to prove our titles to Forest Home and stop this trespassing, or walk out of the place with our thirty-five thousand head of cattle and sell them in the southern stock markets for what they will fetch. It is not a matter in which a compromise can be reached because both sides of this little war are not honest. The worst trespasser of the lot, the man who is behind most of the trouble is Thomas Macnamara. Let us tackle him. If we win, we remain and carry on. If we lose, we must realise on our stock and look elsewhere for country not so blighted. To stand still is impossible. To stand still will lead people to think that we do not believe in the validity of our titles. Why, they will come calmly to drive off our branded cattle. We've got to go on or go under."

"Very well," agreed his partners. "We'll go on."

With the decision made, FE travelled to the Lands Office in Brisbane where he obtained a certified plan of the whole of Forest Home. Time was then spent in locating accurately the boundaries of the principal aggressors in relation to those of the property. This accomplished, FE opened fire.

3.

Back in 1891, Thomas Macnamara and his eldest son had bought between them a hundred head of cattle. They placed them on two blocks, each of forty acres, which they had taken up under the Miners' Homestead Lease Act on the lower end of Forest Home, and they each obtained a registered brand. They then built themselves a home and established a cattle run. Anyone familiar with land in Australia will appreciate the absurdity of starting a herd of cattle on eighty acres.

The block of country on which these Homestead Leases were taken up was called Box Hill No 2 run, held by O'Brien,

164

Cobbold & Co under lease under the Pastoral Leases Act of 1869, but now contained within the boundaries of the Etheridge Goldfields Reserve. The Macnamaras lived there for several years, unmolested and in fancied security under Section 64 of that Act.

In August 1894 O'Brien, Cobbold & Co instructed Messrs Boer and Gorton of Croydon to issue a writ against T Macnamara Senior for £200 damages and trespass, and the action was tried the following November at the District Court sittings in Georgetown before Judge Noel and a jury of four.

The purpose of the action was not to remove the Macnamaras from their forty-acre blocks but to stop their herd of cattle grazing off those blocks of land for which FE and his partners were paying rent. In order to remove the herd from their country, it was necessary for FE to raise the legality of the Homestead Leases.

The Defendant's counsel maintained that, since O'Brien, Cobbold & Co's runs were within the boundaries of the Etheridge Goldfield Reserve, grazing rights were enjoyed by all the residents of the Goldfield, and he quoted 64 of the 1869 Pastoral Leases Act.

In summing up, His Honor said that the Defendant's counsel had endeavoured to throw doubt on the validity of the Plaintiff's title, but it was evident to him that even a defective title was better than no title at all. The Plaintiff had occupied the land for many years and had always paid the rent.

The amount of damages awarded O'Brien, Cobbold & Co was £15 as the trespass was clearly proved.

Whether Thomas Macnamara Senior was badly advised, or whether it was the outcome of ignorance and obstinacy, is difficult to determine. He had a certain following among the rougher elements of the goldfield and they may have urged him on to pick the chestnuts from the fire. He relinquished his Homestead Lease block on Box Hill No 2 run and moved thirty miles or more up the Gilbert River to Green Hills No 8 run, which lay within the boundaries of the newly-proclaimed Green Hills Goldfield Reserve. There he took up a 40-acre Miners' Homestead Lease, but he refused to shift his cattle from the Box Hill country, which were grazing with FE's cattle on FE's land.

In 1896, writs were issued for the second time for trespass against both Macnamara and his eldest son Thomas, each for £200. The trespass was clearly proved, and although in the first action the Macnamaras may have had grounds for believing they had grazing rights in common with the occupier, at the time of the second action they could have had none. His Honor said: "It seems to me that the elder defendant is a cantankerous old man and one who fancies himself as a bush lawyer. They, the plaintiffs, chose to sue for damages and they are entitled to them. In the first case of trespass where there are extenuating circumstances they, the jury, may find nominal damages, but in cases of repeated and persistent and continuous trespass punishing damages should be awarded."

The jury's verdict, however, showed where their sympathy lay, and revealed very clearly the strong antipathy towards the pastoralists. They found damages against the elder Macnamara for £7. The judge awarded the plaintiffs £15.15s.0d. Against the junior defendant, the jury awarded damages for £1, and in this instance the judge could not see his way clear to add costs as the two actions were heard as one.

4.

Physically and mentally, Macnamara Senior was the antithesis of Patrick O'Brien. When O'Brien arrived in Australia, he left behind him the troubles of Ireland. Macnamara, however, was too little to be able to divest himself of the hatred of England and the English, a hatred which had shrivelled his mean little soul and warped his outlook on life. There are many such in Australia and elsewhere, but mercifully there are many more of O'Brien's type of Irishmen who have enriched Australia with their presence and have honoured the Emerald Isle.

Before this trouble, O'Brien had retired to Townsville. It was Francis Cobbold who was the active partner managing the firm's pastoral properties. FE was O'Brien, Cobbold & Co to hundreds of men on the goldfields, and it is probable that, had he been of Irish nationality instead of English (and of that class of Englishman regarded by Macnamara as the enemies of Ireland) Macnamara would not have continued a struggle which was not only long but hopeless.

He was a small, bearded, soured old man full of prejudices, an unfortunate victim to an inferiority complex, ruled by unreasoning hatreds, and possessed of just that degree of primary education which led him to think that he was a clever, clear-headed man in a community of fools. His children, who were born in Australia, had not inherited their father's prejudices and bitterness, but he held the whip over them partly through kinsmanship and partly with his chequebook.

When the Macnamaras lost the second action the son, Thomas, said he would muster and remove his cattle from Box Hill No 2 run as soon as rain fell. He was prepared to do the right thing, but in the end he was over-ruled by his father who moved the stock to his forty acre holding on Green Hills No 8 run, also on Forest Home country. Then this petty little man transferred the stock and his registered brand to his daughter Mary and his second son Martin, thinking that by this act he could defy O'Brien, Cobbold & Co, and continue his absurd aggressive tactics.

Despite having spent years in free Australia, the poor man could not visualise its freedom and its scope. He was mentally enslaved by the potato patches of his homeland. He continued to be – in his warped mind – the downtrodden tenant oppressed by the landlord. He had a little money, he had a herd of cattle, and he had assistants in the persons of his sons, and by going north into the vast area of still vacant country he could have taken up hundred of square miles of land and with reasonable foresight and frugality have made himself a pastoralist as others had done before him and after him. That course, however, did not appeal to a nature which must hate and which craves to possess something created by somebody else at much cost.

He had him, this accursed Englishman, where he wanted him! He would show the Goldfield's people how to beat this Englishman and all the big squatters. In the Goldfield's district, there was never a man so resourceful, so cunning, so wide-awake as Thomas Macnamara. He was the people's natural leader. He would lead them to freedom, et cetera, et cetera. We all know the type. They have their little day and their followers.

O'Brien, Cobbold & Co posted notices in December 1896 requiring the Macnamaras to remove their stock on pain of impounding or suffering such further action at law as, in the opinion of the proprietors of Forest Home, circumstances might warrant. The Macnamaras figuratively put their fingers to their noses.

In July 1897 the manager of Forest Home, now Thomas Simpson, received instructions to start from the out-station of Green Hills and muster all the stock to the head station at Forest Home, picking up during the operation all the Macnamaras' cattle and driving them to the pound at Croydon.

The muster began on August 3rd and went on till August 5th. It produced only one hundred of the Macnamaras' cattle, and a second muster was ordered to take place on August 12th and to continue to August 14th. A further number of eighty cattle belonging to the Macnamaras were taken in this dragnet, making a total of 180 which were driven to the pound at Croydon.

At Croydon, the droving expenses and the pound fees amounted to 17s 3d per head which had to be paid before the beasts were released and, as the amount per head was more than half the value of each beast, the Macnamaras let them go by default, and brought an action against O'Brien, Cobbold & Co for damages.

Mr Boer appeared for the Macnamaras and Mr Ross for O'Brien, Cobbold & Co. Judge Noel, who had heard the two previous cases, again sat on the bench - it can easily be imagined that Judge Noel was now heartily sick and tired of the Macnamaras.

In opening the case for the plaintiffs, Mr Boer said that this was an action for damages for tort or injury done in illegally taking possession of and driving about 180 of his clients' cattle to Croydon pound. The plaintiffs between them were the owners of two hundred cattle more or less, which they depastured on their father's Goldfield Homestead Lease on the Green Hills Goldfield and which defendants illegally took possession of and drove to Croydon pound.

His Honor: "How many acres did you say the Homestead Lease was?"

Mr Boer: "Forty acres, your Honor."

His Honor: "Dear me! Two hundred cattle on forty acres, did you say?"

Mr Boer: "Well, off and on Homestead Lease, your Honor."

Counsel for the plaintiffs said he would first proceed with Mary Ellen and Martin Macnamaras' case, and would accept a verdict in the case of Thomas Macnamara Junior according to the decision given in the first case.

Mr Ross, for the defendants, agreed to let the first case decide both, but as the action proceeded complications arose which precluded the possibility of carrying out this agreement. The first witness for the prosecution was Mary Ellen Macnamara.

She said that she was the owner of a hundred cattle more or less. The cattle had previously been her father's property but she took possession under a Bill of Sale, the consideration being £305 she lent her father. She took her young brother Martin in as a working partner.

His Honor: "How did you come by three hundred and five pounds?"

Witness: "I obtained that money from the sale of six horses."

His Honor: "Did you, indeed! I wish my daughter was as good a woman at business."

Witness went on to say that in August she missed cattle and had been told that they had been taken to Forest Home for impounding later. On August 12th she saw George Kelly, the manager of Green Hills, drive three of her cows and one belonging to her brother Thomas from off her father's Homestead Lease. She and her mother witnessed this from the veranda of their house. Witness described the cows and the brands they bore.

Thomas Macnamara Senior gave corroboration of the previous witness's statement regarding the sale and transfer of his stock. He confirmed the dates of the two musters on Forest Home and said that on the 14th August he rode to the Forest Home head station accompanied by his son Martin, where he saw 180 cattle belonging to his son and daughter being herded. He asked the manager what damages were on the cattle and Simpson said there were no damages, the cattle were going to Croydon. Witness said to Simpson "All right, take them."

Mr Ross produced the plan of Forest Home runs which FE had gone to the Lands Office, Brisbane, to secure. Mr Boer then offered objection to the plan on the ground that it had not been certified by the Surveyor General.

On being called, FE stated how he obtained the plan, which had been certified as correct by the Lands Department.

Mr Boer: "Did you see the plan certified?"

FE: "No. I did not actually see that. But the certifying signature was on the plan when it was handed to me."

Mr Boer then said he doubted it was a certified plan. It did not bear the signature of the Surveyor General. Mr Ross looked blankly at FE; FE thought quickly. The case for the defendants appeared as though it would collapse. "Say that a plan can be certified by the Surveyor General or by one of his deputies," he whispered.

Mr Ross said it, and the judge referred to his books.

His Honor: "That is so, Mr Boer."

Mr Boer: "Very well, your Honor. We all know the signature of the Surveyor General, but who here could swear that the signature on the plan is that of the person represented to be a deputy for the Surveyor General? I have never seen it before."

Again Mr Ross looked blankly at FE. Again FE thought quickly. "Ask for time," FE again whispered to Mr Ross.

Mr Ross asked for time to bring someone to the court who could identify the signature on the plan. Mr Boer objected. His Honor looked at the clock, noted that it was five minutes to twelve, and adjourned the court for two hours.

FE hurried outside and jumped on to the first good saddle horse he found in the street. He knew a man who might be able to swear to that signature, a certain Thomas Geraghty who was a Government Surveyor then working near the Durham Mine eight miles away. If Geraghty did not know the signature, no one would.

FE rode hard and straight. When he arrived at the Durham, he learned that the surveyor was out in the bush at work. Into the bush he rode and, following the vague directions, was lucky enough to hit on Geraghty having his lunch with his party. Did Geraghty know such and such a signature? Too right, he did! Then he must come to the court, be at the court by two o'clock. FE then had to procure a horse for Geraghty by hunting for one in the bush, and with no time to spare he got the surveyor to the court.

Geraghty was the next witness called. He swore that the signature on the trace plan put before him was that of an official

170

in the office of the Surveyor General. He had often seen the signature on plans and documents in the course of his departmental work.

Mr Boer again raised the objection to the plan on the ground that it had not been certified by the Surveyor General in whose custody the originals were. Mr Ross contended that a deputy of the Surveyor General could certify the plan. In this instance the deputy had been the chief draughtsman at the Lands Office. His Honor referred to his books and then said: "I have found here a section applicable to this case. It says, the copy of any original documents, which may be tendered in evidence, must be certified to by a responsible person in the office where the original document is kept, and bear upon its face the impressed stamp of the office and the date when issued. This appears to me to have been complied with."

Mr Boer: "I submit, you Honor, that that only applies to Joint Stock Companies and Banking Corporations."

His Honor: "I don't think so. I admit the plan. You can appeal if you like."

William Jack, an employee of O'Brien, Cobbold & Co, then related how he had assisted in the general muster, and William White swore that he was in the employ of the Macnamaras and described how he had been bringing home the milkers on foot. When he missed four of them, he rode down to the creek where he had found Kelly and a man named Crossley. He asked Crossley if he had seen any old milkers, and Crossley answered in the negative. Questioned further, he said that he had been herding eight cows. He believed that Kelly had taken the four missing cows. The others might have wandered off.

When he was called, Martin Macnamara said he was fifteen years of age and that his sister had taken him in as a working partner. They depastured their cattle on their father's selection and on the surrounding Goldfield.

Mr Boer in addressing the Court said that several offences were disclosed by the evidence. Taking the cattle off the selection was one. Another was forcibly taking them out of the possession of White. The third offence was impounding the cattle temporarily in the yard at the Forest Home under section 37 of the Impounding Act without giving the statutory notice within twenty-four hours. Fourthly, the holding of the cattle from the third to the fourteenth of August in contravention of Section 37 of the Impounding Act, which expressly lays down that the stock may be temporarily detained in other places than a pound, but can only be so detained subject to the impounder giving the owner notice of such detention within 24 hours and, failing the owner releasing them within twenty-four hours, driving them to the nearest pound. Another offence committed by the defendants was the refusal of the defendants' manager to allow Thomas Macnamara Senior to release the stock when he went there prepared to do so; and sixth, and lastly, that the Macnamaras by virtue of their Miner's Rights and Goldfield Homesteads, had the right of commonage on the Goldfield.

Mr Ross pointed out that Martin Macnamara, being an infant, could not sue as a party to a contract. With this, His Honor concurred.

After further argument as to whether a non suit should also be entered against Mary Ellen Macnamara on the ground that one party being non-suited the other could not sue for the whole, his Honor ruled that one part could sue.

Mr Ross then pointed out that Thomas Macnamara Senior held the Homestead and Miner's Rights but owned no stock. Mary Ellen and Martin Macnamara owned the stock but held no Miner's and Homestead Rights, and therefore had no claim to commonage on a Goldfield. With reference to breaches of 37 of the Impounding Act his learned friend opposite was barking up the wrong tree. He would show that his clients acted in accordance with Section 36 of the Impounding Act, which section they obeyed within reasonable limits taking into consideration the size of the run and the distance to the Croydon pound.

Mr Boer: "I call your Honor's attention to Section 37 where the giving of notice of the Impounding is compulsory; also the driving of the cattle to the pound within four days. I hold that Sections 36 and 37 should be read and taken together."

His Honor: "No. The Sections are totally opposite in principle and construction. There are two separate courses and by adopting one or the other the defendants are within legal limits. I find their proceedings under Section 36 of the Impounding Act to be in order and rule that taking into consideration the size of the run, they proceeded in accordance with the Act. It would be absurd to suppose that when framing the Act the Legislature intended that each day's muster of cattle should be separately driven to the Croydon pound more than sixty miles away."

Mr Boer: "That I contend was the intention, your Honor."

His Honor (curtly): "Then they should have said so. I do not make the law. I am here only to administer the law and I do so as I find it."

Mr Boer: "Then, your Honor, they might as well hold the cattle six months as twelve days."

His Honor: "No. As a fact, I should rule that to be unreasonable. Acting as the jury in this case, I hold twelve days to be fair and reasonable under the circumstances disclosed."

His Honor ruled that as White did not see the cattle taken, and as there was no evidence that the musterers saw White, there was no risk of a breach of the peace and, therefore, there was no offence. With reference to the allegation of the refusal of Simpson to allow the cattle to be released, there was no evidence of the tender of any fees. As a fact, when Simpson told Macnamara he was going to take his cattle to the pound, Macnamara said "All right! Take them." This did not amount to a refusal to release. Mr Ross had pointed out that Mary Ellen and Martin Macnamara held no rights under the Goldfield's Regulations, and had no rights of depasturing on Goldfields Commons. His Honor found that the impounding had been carried out in accordance with the law, excepting with regard to three beasts belonging to the plaintiffs which, if not actually taken off the selection, were taken so near as to engender a reasonable belief that they might have been actually within the boundaries when taken. Kelly and Crossley had been called on behalf of defendants and they admitted they were within half a mile of the selection and, as they could not take accurate measurements, might they not carelessly have approached so near as to have been actually within the boundaries of the Homestead Lease? He, therefore, found for the plaintiffs for three beasts at two pounds and ten shillings each, and he would reserve the question of costs until he had heard the case of Thomas Macnamara Junior as he failed to see how both cases could be tried together because T Macnamara Junior, as the possessor of a Goldfield's Homestead on Box Hill No 2 run, which had once been within a Goldfield's area, MIGHT possess commonage rights on the Green Hills Goldfield in accordance with Section 4 of the Goldfields Act Amendment Act of 1895. That was provided the defendants could not prove a title to the land. It would be incumbent on the defendants to prove title before they could upset the case of T Macnamara Junior.

Mr Boer: "This I am prepared to show your Honor they cannot do."

His Honor: "Then I hope I have done no injustice in the first case though it would appear by your showing that I have. If defendants cannot prove title they have no right to impound, but if you apply I will grant leave to come again."

Mr Boer: "I apply for leave to come again to ask for a new trial."

Leave was granted.

Mr Ross: "We can prove a clear title, your Honor."

His Honor: "Then you must prove it up to the hilt."

Mr Ross, in opening for the defence said: "We admit the impounding. We admit the Macnamaras' title of each to their forty-acre Goldfield Homestead Lease, and to the right of depasturing on a Goldfield's common. But I am prepared to prove my clients' title to the lands from where the impounding took place as the rights of commonage cannot extend to those lands."

FE was then called. He said that he was a partner in the defendant firm. He produced a tracing of the run, and the Promises of Leases, and the Occupation Leases. He produced, too, the rent list showing the names of the runs in the name of his firm. His firm had paid the rent regularly and had paid for it in the present year. He had given the instructions for the impounding to be put into effect.

Mr Boer examined the documents produced by FE with studious care. When he stood up to speak to the judge there was a glint of triumph in his eyes. He said: "Your Honor, I call your attention to these titles. The defendants have no leases, only the promises of leases."

For the second time, Mr Ross regarded FE blankly. He appeared about to sit down as though the case was already lost. But FE was not done yet. He had not studied those documents night after night, and thought about them day after day for so many years not to know by heart every word and the exact meaning of every clause. Mr Ross listened intently to his whispered urging, then turned to the judge.

174

Mr Ross: "I maintain, your Honor, that the Promise of Lease is as valid as the Lease."

His Honor, after having examined the documents: "It says here: No instrument of lease will be issued for this run (runs) but the Promise of Lease shall be equivalent to the lease itself except as against the Crown."

Mr Boer made one more attempt. He called Mr Simpson, the manager of Forest Home, and asked him why he did not inform Thomas Macnamara Junior when he met him at Macdonaldtown that his cattle were being mustered at Forest Home for the purpose of impounding.

Simpson: "His Honor said it down in this Court last year that the giving of a trespasser notice of a muster might be taken to mean the usual notice given by pastoralists to one another and, therefore, might be construed to mean a tacit consent of the proprietor to the trespass. After that, I had instructions to give no notices of muster to trespassers."

His Honor, in giving judgement, said that this was the most difficult case it was ever his misfortune to try during his experience as a judge, and he hoped he would never have to adjudicate on such a complicated case again. It bristled with traps and pitfalls, but he could not put from his mind two previous trials before him in that same Court in which the same parties figured. He used the words 'same parties' because he was convinced that Thomas Macnamara Senior was the real party to the sections. He was a wrong-headed and persistent old man who would not take no for an answer. Although he had been told twice already in that Court that he was an obstinate trespasser, and that the law would vindicate the right, he still persisted in coming to him in that Court for redress. For his (his Honor's) part, he had no sympathy for him in his loss, and wished he would take his troubles elsewhere and not trouble him again. So far as the actual impounding went, he ruled that as a whole, it had been properly carried out and was perfectly legal and justifiable. The defendants had a clear and good title to the lands, and were justified in the course they took. They gave their instructions to impound in proper form and in compliance with the law, but these instructions seem to have been negligently carried out by the defendants' servants in respect to three beasts owned by Mary and Martin Macnamara, and one beast owned by Thomas Macnamara Junior. He ordered that the defendants pay two pounds and ten shillings for each of these beasts.

Although he felt quite sure that Macnamara Senior was really the party to the actions, he had given special care to this trial because apparently his two previous decisions did not satisfy Macnamara, who was a most persistent trespasser and could not be brought to believe that he had not a perfect right to apply other people's land to his own uses. No doubt it was in great measure due to ignorance, and he thought it a pity that he, Macnamara, was not better advised by someone who could read. In the case of T Macnamara Junior, he would allow no costs. In the case of Mary Ellen and Martin Macnamara, the question he had to consider was, if a jury had found damages for seven pounds and ten shillings, would he, as the judge, have granted costs. He did not think he would. Therefore, no costs allowed in either case. He felt that he was right, because this was an action for damages for injury done to the extent of four hundred pounds of which the plaintiffs recovered but ten pounds which really meant they had failed in their action.

This trial at law finally settled Thomas Macnamara and those who had followed his lead. There was nothing further that they could do in the face of Judge Noel's scathing comments. FE gave them all ample time to clear out their cattle with as little loss as possible, and for some time afterwards there was peace – peace after twenty years' of warring with trespassers and cattle duffers.

CHAPTER SIXTEEN

Years 1898 – 1901
Cobbold & Co

1.

After having been married only eight years, Francis Cobbold suffered the first major sorrow of his life. It was a double sorrow, for both his wife and his father died on the same day.

> *Bessie died of uterine cancer on 10th October 1898 at the age of only 28. She was buried at Carpentaria Downs Station.*
>
> *FE's father, Arthur Thomas Cobbold, died at his home – The Elms, near Sudbury. He had enjoyed good health generally and had taken a walk to Sudbury and back the week before his death, aged 83. He was buried at Sudbury Cemetery.*

This bereavement seemed to be the prelude to a period of great anxiety, for it fell at the beginning of a dry-years period which was to affect severely hundreds of pastoralists and thousands of farmers from the Gulf of Carpentaria southward to the outskirts of Melbourne and Adelaide. After the first shock of personal loss had eased, perhaps there was less anxiety for FE than that experienced by his fellows. He had foreseen the inevitable coming of the dry-years period and had prepared for it by the purchase of Riversleigh and Authoringa to relieve the firm's northern stations of their surplus stock. Certainly his wise policy in buying those places was now to be amply justified.

The dry-years period began in 1895 and reached a climax in 1902, when a drought ended that had gripped the eastern half of Australia for seven years. There was not a blade of grass nor a single bush from Central Queensland almost to Melbourne. When the apparently endless drought at last ended, the farmers south of the Murray River were feeding their surviving horses on the straw which had served for seven years as thatch for their barns. The sheep died in their tens of thousands and the cattle in their thousands. Once-affluent squatters handed over their properties to the finance houses and walked away; farmers who had struggled and become quite successful abandoned their farms to the storekeepers who had stood by them while it was

177

financially possible. Only the far north of Queensland suffered less in comparison.

After the tick fever swept across North Queensland, a line was drawn across the State in an effort to isolate the infected herds from those in the southern districts. Eventually, however, the northern herds became immune and, when the drought almost wiped out the southern herds, the imaginary line was abandoned and many of the southern cattlemen bought northern stations to replenish their herds from them. However, the combination of the tick and the drought meant that many fine pastoral properties came into the property market with no stock on them whatsoever. The prices asked for them were just a fraction of their nominal value, but, even so, there were few buyers. Lolworth, one of the best properties on the Basalt Tableland and about five hundred square miles in area, well-watered and well-improved, was on the market for nearly a year at £500 before a buyer was found for it. Its value should have been at least £10,000.

So severe were the drought losses that the cattlemen appealed to the government for relief. However, instead of the government saying, in effect and without loss of time: "While this drought lasts and until the expiration of one year following it, you will not be forced to pay rent and taxes," it procrastinated and spent money on the inevitable Commission to examine the alleged disabilities. The Commissioners took six months to enjoy the scenery and take 'evidence' at the townships, which were surrounded by the bones of dead cattle. In receipt of the usual high salaries, the Commissioners declined to hurry or expedite their report, and it was six months before the government received it. It then needed six months to consider it, and as the cattlemen had not sought assistance or relief until they were desperate, by the end of the twelve months many of the patients were figuratively very dead.

At the end of 1899, when the cattle industry was at low ebb, FE conferred with his partners and pointed out to them the uselessness of trying to sell anything. Although the drought had severely reduced the cattle herds, the price of beef remained low. Many another man would have advised shutting up shop and selling everything for what might be obtained, then retiring to a city and opening a small business or some such with the city folk whose wages continued to increase. Not so FE. He again pointed out that when the prices were low it was time to buy, and not till prices were high was it time to sell.

William Steele was dead. He had often said: "I have never made a will, and I don't intend to. The Government will distribute my estate as fairly as I can myself."

He died intestate. The Court appointed O'Brien and Hunt with Mrs Steele as guardians of the children, and the Steele interests in the partnership were left undisturbed. Mrs Steele knew her late husband's partners too well not to trust them fully.

When FE urged buying, O'Brien and Hunt gave him carte blanche, and he went out into the Burke Division in north-west Queensland and bought two adjoining properties for £1,500. They were Riversleigh and Lilydale, and on them were eighteen hundred cattle.

In 1900 FE paid these properties another visit, covering the hundreds of miles driving a buckboard, with a blackboy riding behind and bringing along the change horses. On the return journey he stayed overnight at Normanton; while glancing through an old copy of The Sydney Morning Herald after dinner he saw a property notice announcing the sale by auction of Miranda Downs, with 12,000 head of cattle. Miranda Downs! Who knew Miranda Downs better than he, who had created it out of nothing but wilderness? He knew every yard of the river frontage, every water-hole, almost every tree?

The date of the auction was announced in the paper and was then very close. The auction was to be held in Sydney and, as there was no-one who could deputise to offer bids for him, he needed to travel there quickly. He did not know the reserve price placed on the property, and to fix the limit of his offer would be unwise in the tense state of the market. Besides, the finance would have to be arranged, and the proposition discussed with his partners.

That night he worked out the stages of the long journey to Townsville and in the morning he sent off a bunch of telegrams, one of which was addressed to his partners announcing to them that he was on his way with a most attractive proposition.

Then began one of the fastest passages across Northern Queensland ever accomplished with horses – up the Carron Creek to the Gilbert Telegraph Station, across to Forest Home, then to Carpentaria Downs and over the highlands and across the lowlands to the coastal port. FE travelled all of every day and most of every night.

Reaching Townsville, he was met by O'Brien and Hunt. There was just an hour or so before the southbound boat left. The matter of the purchase of Miranda Downs was put to the partners, but there was not time to discuss it fully. They agreed to the purchase. Money would be required. They hurried to their old friend A T Halloran, the manager of the Bank of New South Wales, and he arranged a credit of £18,000.

FE reached Sydney on the day before the auction. He talked to George Maiden, of Goldsborough Mort & Co, and told him frankly that he had come from the Gulf of Carpentaria to buy Miranda Downs and that, if it was knocked down to him, he was disposed to take it on a walk in walk out basis without any muster of cattle. He was prepared to pay cash in return for a delivery note to be telegraphed to the manager at the station but, from the day of the auction, he and his partners were to be the owners. There was no misunderstanding about the genuineness of FE's intentions.

One bid was wired from Cairns by an alleged buyer; in the room were only two other buyers. Miranda Downs was knocked down to FE for £12,300. He then wired to Power – the man he had nominated as his successor when he left Cobb & Co – re-appointing him manager *pro tem*.

This is an illustration of the manner in which FE nearly always conducted a business transaction. His experience taught him that, if there is a genuine seller and a genuine buyer, the simpler the negotiations and agreements, the less room there is for dispute.

FE's partners expressed pleasure with the purchase of Miranda Downs, and they agreed that pastoral affairs must soon take a turn for the better if the country was not to smash altogether. Their confidence in FE was justified - and his confidence in himself and in the country was justified, too. Within eight weeks of the purchase, he sold off one thousand bullocks from Miranda Downs for £5,000 cash, for delivery as soon as the monsoonal rains were over so that the beasts could travel to the meatworks. Then he sold off a small cast of bullocks from Lilydale and Riversleigh for £1,500.

2.

On the death of William Steele, the Court had appointed O'Brien and Hunt as the trustees of the children's estate. Their charter precluded them from risking the children's interests in speculative dealing in stock and stations, so with the purchase of Miranda Downs a new company was formed consisting of FE, O'Brien and Hunt. It was called Cobbold and Company to distinguish if from O'Brien, Cobbold & Co.

FE was now putting his all - his capital and his brains and his untiring energy - into the pastoral industry, while his partners led more or less retired lives in Townsville and were putting only a portion of their considerable fortunes into these two companies. The fact that FE was making money for his partners did not count with him at all. They had presented him with an opening to a career much wider than that of a station manager, and the terms connected with that opening had been generous. Throughout his business career and subsequent to forming this new company with himself at the head, FE had entered into several partnerships, all of which were successful and none of which permitted any man to say that he lost money through being associated with FE. Several years later, when he met an old partner who had withdrawn from a firm FE directed, he was to be informed regretfully: "I've never done any good since I cut away from you."

Despite the droughts and the tick fever, despite the insecurity of land tenure in Australia, despite the rising rentals and increasing taxation, FE's faith in Australia in general and Queensland in particular never flagged. Australia had made a remarkable recovery from the financial debacle of 1893, and it only wanted another good years period to bring in another long period of prosperity. Even a drought gives blessings, for it kills indigenous and imported pests, and it rests the land. Following a drought, the first good rain transfigures the country as completely and as rapidly as Aladdin's genie could do it – arid deserts bloom like an English lawn within a month, and change the aspect of saltbush and bluebush and the scrub trees from shrivelled leather to succulent food for animals. From the gaunt spectres of sheep and cattle, emerge beasts fat and polished like those to be seen at an agricultural show.

Australia's greatest wonder is that, in spite of the natural calamities opposed to it, the Pastoral industry has managed to survive the constant, ceaseless attacks made on it by politicians who think only of placating the city voters. Australia would be even greater than it is if only the politicians would permit it.

When they voted in favour of the federation of the six colonies, the people were promised an Utopia - and an Utopia they could have had. They were promised a united country under one Parliament and that federation would assure free trade between the six colonies. In fact, it resulted in duplication of government and government services, and restrictive taxation on Inter-State trading. To take a motorcar or truck from one State into another, the owner has to comply with formalities as strict as those in the case of entering one country from another in Europe.

The pastoral industry - that immense bulwark against poverty, and rock-like insurance against adversity - came to be bled to nurture tin pot industries in the seaboard capital cities. Australia is a natural pastoral country and one in which secondary industries are unnatural and unnecessary; its distance from world centres, and its contiguity to Asia with its low standards of living, prohibit the exportation of the products of secondary industries. But the people herded into cities like ants demanded soft living, and the pastoral population was greatly outnumbered by city voters. So in order to protect the city voters, prohibitive import duties were placed on goods exported to those very countries who had always taken Australia's wool, meat, butter and fruit.

Francis Cobbold was not directly concerned with wool. At the beginning of Federation, he knew that the export of beef and mutton would undoubtedly grow with the improvement of transport facilities across the world. The local markets were steadily growing, and would continue to do so through increasing population. In 1881, the population of Australia stood at two and one quarter millions, and in 1891 it was more than three and three quarter millions.

To FE, a visit to Miranda Downs was like going home. He conferred with Power, the manager, as to the future policy of governing the property in the name of Cobbold and Company, and then he went on to pay a flying visit to Lilydale and Riversleigh.

His road lay through a large block of country fronting the southern shore of the Gulf of Carpentaria, a block extending thirty miles from north to south and sixty miles east to west. On this great area of some two thousand square miles were scattered about eleven thousand cattle. It was named Inverleigh, and was owned by Mrs Colless, a widow who resided in Sydney. She was represented by Mr George Maiden of Goldsborough Mort & Co, who had auctioned Miranda Downs.

Originally, Inverleigh had been the central station of three, Tempe Downs being on the east, and Punch Bowl to the west. The pioneers who had formed these three stations were before their time and, when they met with adverse circumstance, they had been forced to abandon the country. For the most part, this was ultimately forfeited for non-payment of rent.

At the time Inverleigh interested FE, one of the Punch Bowl blocks was occupied by a man engaged in the somewhat peculiar trade of brumby hunting; while another block on Punch Bowl had been taken up under an Occupation Lease by a man named Neilson. There were also other small settlers towards and on the Leichhardt River which formed the western boundary of the entire block of country. The state of settlement on the three original stations of Inverleigh was roughly similar to Forest Home, with its restrictive Miners' Homestead Leases, although the circumstances and the class of settlers were vastly different. Inverleigh held scattered blocks of country over a total area of 782 square miles, of which 327 square miles were held under shortly-expiring tenure under the 1869 Act. The balance of 455 square miles was held under occupation Leases under Annual Tenancy. Except for a cottage, kitchen and men's hut, and a few horse paddocks and yards, there were no improvements. The place was stagnant, and the scattered settlers were unambitious and without capital. The annual rent of the secured area was £414.

With Inverleigh there was one serious drawback and many minor ones. The property was the most badly-watered in the Gulf country - but a careful examination revealed to FE that, with the expenditure of money and the removal of the struggling settlers by arrangement, the property could be developed into a fine, compact, and yet immense block of country. The tenure circumstances being as they were, it would be most unwise to spend much money, but there was always the possibility that the Lands Department would consent to be shown that security of tenure of Inverleigh would be of certain benefit to the country – and to itself.

Returning to Croydon, FE talked to F A Brodie, the stock and station agent, and commissioned him to wire to Maiden asking for the offer of Inverleigh on behalf of the new firm of Cobbold & Co. Brodie knew that the property was for sale and FE knew that the cattle were then being mustered.

Owing to the poor mail communication between Croydon and Carpentaria Downs, some time elapsed before FE received Maiden's reply. It read: "Inverleigh not now available."

At this time FE's sister in Melbourne was married to the Hon William Cain MLC, who wrote a letter to FE, which he received shortly after the receipt of Maiden's reply telegram. The letter read.

> Her first husband, William Dickson, having died in March 1876, FE's sister Sarah Jane made a trip to England where she married – on 18th April 1877 – the Hon William Cain, who had been born at Rusher Abbey in the Isle of Man in 1831.
> He was a Harbour and Railway Engineer as well as an investing Pastoralist, who became Mayor of Melbourne 1886-87. He was a member of the Legislative Council for the Province of Melbourne from 1903 to 1911.

"I returned from Sydney on Wednesday last where I saw Mr Maiden who, just as I was leaving, informed me that he had that day received instructions to sell a cattle property in the Gulf country at what he considered a bargain – Inverleigh, 13,000 cattle less 10% at 30s 0d and horses at £4 less 10%. It would be a walk in walk out purchase, no muster. I requested him to send particulars to you, then I would write and wire you asking your advice as to this purchase, in which I would be interested conditionally that you thought it a bargain and would take one-fourth interest in it with me. It might suit you and your partners to take a larger interest, say one-half. I do not think it will be offered at auction."

FE at once wired: "Lose no time. Will join you in the purchase."

O'Brien and Hunt expressed appreciation of the offer but declined on the ground that as it appeared to be a family matter they might better keep outside. FE then agreed to take one quarter share as he felt so certain that, having once got rid of the squatters, and provided there could be obtained a reliable tenure for a long period, the place could be developed into a large and valuable cattle station. The purchase price of Inverleigh was £18,000 – one third cash, and the balance by instalments.

Inverleigh was less an estate than the ruins of one. The little squatters scattered on it were doing no good for themselves and were a hindrance to the big squatter. They had, of course, taken up those abandoned blocks with the best watering places, and their selection left the major property irregular in shape and consequently difficult to work. The creeks and the few short rivers emptying into the Gulf of Carpentaria, together with their water-holes and lagoons, were only of use for six or seven months of the year. When they dried up, all the cattle had to converge on just two permanent water-holes or trespass on neighbouring runs.

Obviously the stock-carrying capacity of Inverleigh was limited by its permanent water supplies and, after a thorough inspection of the whole of the property and the advice of Brown, the manager, FE took up nine further blocks of land each having a few months' water supply, thus increasing the area of Inverleigh by 310 square miles at an additional rental of £108 15s 0d per annum.

Having now secured 1,092 square miles at an annual rental of £522 15s 0d, the first objective was to buy out the little squatters, and the second objective was to obtain reasonable security of tenure over the whole area of the three original stations on such terms as would justify the owners spending money on development.

The first objective was easy to accomplish compared to the second. With the first, FE had to deal with plain men; with the second he had to deal with the Official Mind, and the Mind groped and prevaricated, bullied and hesitated. The case had been presented to the Official Mind in plain business English, and the Official Mind resented being asked to think and to act. For so many years Inverleigh had rotted. It was far away in Western Australia or Java or somewhere. Why could not this Cobbold person go and hang himself and let Inverleigh continue to rot? The Official Mind was bored to death with both Inverleigh and FE. Already a file devoted to it was a yard deep.

Then FE appeared at the Lands Office in Brisbane. By appointment, he reached the presence of the Minister. Mr

Shannon, the Under Secretary, placed on the Minister's desk the yard-deep file of documents relating to Inverleigh; he then withdrew.

In concise and vivid language, FE drew for the Minister a word picture of Inverleigh. He sketched the scope of the land, and the insecurity of tenure given by the terms of the leases. Inverleigh included within its boundaries seven hundred square miles of coast country which was, and would remain, a waterless desert one month after rain unless, and until, bores were put down. He showed how the expenditure of much money could turn those hundreds of square miles into safe grazing for cattle.

"Yet how can we spend money when we possess no security of tenure; when within a year or two large slices of the country may be taken from us?" was the climax of his argument.

The Minister was not really the representative of the Official Mind. He was a politician and moreover, a man of understanding. Before he took up his duties as a Minister of the Crown, without doubt he called a spade a spade. On the margin of the topmost document of the Inverleigh file he wrote:

"Lease granted for thirty years at an annual rental of eight shillings per square mile."

Perhaps he inwardly delighted in the prospect of the jolt he was going to give the Official Mind, who regarded him as a mere rubber stamp! He rang his bell and called for the Under Secretary. Shannon was handed the file, and his attention was drawn to the memo written on the margin of the topmost document. The Official Mind gave no sign of being jolted when it walked to the door and passed outside. FE chatted to the Minister for a few minutes before politely taking his leave.

In the corridor lurked the Official Mind, waiting to pounce on the person who had caused the jolt to Its Lofty Dignity. It was boiling with rage. It was become almost ordinary, almost human. It actually called a spade a spade, and doubtless never forgave Itself!

"This is a job!" shouted Shannon, and if the Minister had his ear against the door, he must have chuckled.

"Job, Mr Shannon!" echoed FE calmly. "Why you have got us by the wool for thirty years. We have to pay £900 in rent every year for the first ten years when we have been paying £300 a year. We are committed to spend £6,000 on exploration for artesian water. A job, did you say? Whatever benefit we get by expenditure of our capital and the use of our brains, your department will receive a mighty big share of it. Good day!"

Yes, the Official Mind received a jolt despite its armour of rules and regulations and Acts and amendments. If only it could be made to understand that its purpose is to oil the wheels of enterprise and not to clog them with grit!

3.

Towards the end of 1901, FE married Beatrice, the daughter of John and Mary Child. The year had been one of strenuous effort, entailing incessant travelling with little rest between long journeys. The major turning points of his life had arrived, and he was now laying the firm foundations of success, which would be consolidated when the next good-years period arrived.

Queensland			6361186
MARRIAGE CERTIFICATE			REGISTRATION NUMBER 1902/ 2160

	Bridegroom	Bride
When and where married	23 December 1901 St.Joseph's Presbytery, Townsville	
Name and surname	Francis Edward Cobbold	Beatrice Child
Marital status	Widower	Spinster
Birthplace	Ipswich, Suffolk, England	Townsville, Queensland
Occupation	Grazier	-
Age	48 Years	31 Years
Usual residential address	Carpentaria Downs	Townsville
Parents		
Father's name and surname	Arthur Thomas Cobbold	John Child
Mothers name and maiden surname	Sarah Elleston	Mary Wood
Father's occupation (if recorded)	Gentlemen	Grazier
Rites used	Roman Catholic	
Names of witnesses to marriage	J.C. Ball / Alice M. Ball	
Name of celebrant and authorisation number (if applicable)	W. Walsh	
Registrar		
Name	W. Rillie	
Date of registration	7 January 1902	
Place (or district) of registration	Townsville	
Notes (if any)		

I, David John Mackie, Registrar-General, certify that the above is a true copy of particulars recorded in a Register kept in the General Registry at Brisbane

Dated: 27 November 2007   Registrar-General

N.B. Not Valid Unless Bearing the Authorised Seal and Signature of the Registrar-General

41.
Copy of the certificate of marriage between Frank Cobbold and Beatrice Child, 23rd December 1901

> *Beatrice – always known as Bea – was born in Townsville on the last day of the year 1869. She was the only girl amongst six children, her late father coming originally from Shropshire. She married FE two days before Christmas in 1901 at St Joseph's Presbytery according to Roman Catholic rights.*

Towards the close of 1902, when on his way to Sydney, Edward Hunt died on the train. His body was brought back to Brisbane for burial. In life, he had always been true and faithful to the partnership and his partners. Death added proof of his steadfastness. He had made the Union Trustee Company of Australia his executors and trustees with an expressed desire in his will that they were not to interfere with his partners, or take any part in the management of any concern in which he was interested as a partner with Patrick O'Brien and Francis Edward Cobbold.

He prefaced this wish with the words: "I desire that …"

He had made certain people in England beneficiaries, and they wanted their money. The trustees pointed out that the business in which the deceased had been, and the remaining partners were, engaged was too risky to be approved by trustees managing the estate of Edward Steele's children. FE appreciated the trustees' scruples, although as the two firms had so far weathered the droughts and the pests there was now little prospect of failure. There appeared no getting round that preamble – "I desire that …"

However, in order to assure clarity of meaning it seems to be necessary to discard the King's English in favour of some other medium, not only with Acts of Parliament but also with wills and other documents.

Hunt wrote: "I desire that my financial interest remain undisturbed in the partnership." The ordinary man, blessed with an ordinary brain and in command of ordinary English, would be quite sure in his mind that when Hunt wrote "I desire that …" he meant that he desired a certain thing to happen, that he wanted it to happen, that it was his earnest wish that it should happen. According to the lawyers, he did not wish, want, or desire anything of the kind. Had he wished, wanted, and desired it, he would have written the words "I direct that …" And because he chose to write the word 'desire', what everyone knew he earnestly desired should be avoided, came about. All the pastoral properties owned by O'Brien, Cobbold & Co, and Cobbold & Co were to be thrown on the market because Hunt's trustees thought the businesses were too risky, and the lawyers said that word 'desire' was the negative of 'direct'.

After all the arrangements had been completed for offering Forest Home, Carpentaria Downs, Miranda Downs, Magoura and Riversleigh and Lilydale at auction, the trustees shied off flooding the pastoral property market with all these stations when times were so bad. They called for a conference between themselves and the surviving partners, and at this conference an amount was fixed by which O'Brien, Mrs Steele, and FE could purchase the late Edward Hunt's interests in the O'Brien, Cobbold & Co partnership.

Among these three it was arranged that they each acquire an equal share in the firm of O'Brien, Cobbold & Co and that FE and O'Brien would take equal shares in the firm of Cobbold & Co.

To finalise this readjustment, FE required money. O'Brien knew this, and he then had the opportunity of taking a bigger share in Hunt's interests without doing injury to FE. However, the spirit of the original dividing mateship continued strong. Hunt's loyalty was a bright light and Steele had known that his partners were financially strong enough to bear his loss. When FE mentioned to O'Brien the probable difficulty he would have in finding the money to purchase his share of Hunt's interests, O'Brien said almost off-handedly:

"Why not go along and see Halloran at the bank?"

Halloran has already been mentioned in this work. He was an exceptionally fine man both physically and mentally, and besides being the manager of the Townsville branch of the Bank of New South Wales, he was the Bank's Northern Inspector. He stood to receive FE in his parlour, six feet in height, a brown fist stroking the long auburn beard. Like other shrewd men, Halloran had long since summed up Francis Cobbold, and it is highly likely that on this occasion the generous O'Brien had forewarned him of the visit. Carefully refraining from giving his visitor an inkling of what might have passed between O'Brien and himself, however, he listened to FE's business for a while before exclaiming:

"Money! You want money! Oh, you can come here and get all the money you want!"

To the man in the street this might sound fantastic. It is an interview of which he might dream, with himself in FE's place. Yet it is less fantastic than it might appear to those outside banking circles. A banker will say that of every ten clients who promise to fulfil their obligations, only one steadily does so. FE was the one in ten. He had never failed in a promise to the bank, was told almost impatiently that he could have all the money he wanted - and was told so in a manner leaving no possible ground for doubt.

CHAPTER SEVENTEEN

Years 1901 - 1905
Changing Scenes

1.

1902 was the final year of the worst drought ever experienced by the Pastoral Industry in Australia. South from the monsoonal belt of North Queensland, the cattle herds and the sheep flocks that had taken years to build up were almost wiped out.

Authoringa and Riversleigh stations suffered seven bad years in succession and, having sold all the stock for which buyers could be found, and with the remainder so reduced that it was unprofitable to carry on without completely restocking, FE sold these two stations to a company at a loss – the only loss he experienced during forty years of buying and selling pastoral properties.

In September 1901, when both he and O'Brien were in Brisbane on business, FE noticed an advertisement of the sale by auction of a big tract of country called Magoura. Magoura joined Inverleigh on the east, and it comprised one thousand square miles of leasehold and 640 acres of freehold land, with 12,000 cattle. The auction was to be held in Brisbane a fortnight later.

On several occasions FE had passed through this property on his way to and from Inverleigh, but he was not sufficiently familiar with it to offer without first inspecting. With O'Brien in agreement, FE therefore left immediately for Townsville. There he talked to Halloran about finance, and Halloran expressed his confidence that FE would not risk purchase of the property unless he was perfectly satisfied with its prospects of becoming profitable, and assured him that funds would be available for a cash purchase.

Covering the five hundred miles to Magoura on horseback, FE at once conducted his inspections, and on the day the sale was held in Brisbane, he rode twenty miles into Normanton in time to telegraph the Bank of New South Wales to commission an agent to bid up to £18,000. There were no opposing bids, however, so when the auctioneer announced the reserve as £14,000, the agent closed for the property at that figure, walk in walk out. At the same time, FE sold bullocks to the value of £1,800 before he left, thus reducing the cost of the purchase to £12,200.

Early in 1902, FE heard that the Queensland Meat Export & Agency Company had decided to buy cattle stations as the prices demanded by the cattle owners were thought to be excessive. He therefore approached the Directors of the company, who said that they were considering four properties on offer by the Bank of New South Wales with 65,000 cattle at £2 10s 0d per head. FE offered his group of four stations with 65,000 cattle at the same figure, the offer to be for ten weeks. Robert Stewart, the manager of the Company's Townsville works, was sent out to inspect, and in the middle of March 1903 FE again went to Brisbane to learn the Directors' decision.

The Chairman was Sir Robert Philip, and at the end of a meeting lasting all day the Directors agreed to purchase FE's group of properties, conditionally on his taking the management until the end of the year to enable them to become acquainted with the working of the properties before finally taking them over.

This FE agreed to do.

All that was now left of the two partnerships were the two properties on the Gregory River - Riversleigh and Lilydale. With their small herds of cattle, these no longer interested either O'Brien or FE, and a purchaser was found for them in Sir Robert Philp who required a cheap property for one of his sons. So the two firms - O'Brien, Cobbold & Co and Cobbold & Co - dissolved after seventeen years. It was an association of which any man could be proud of being a member, an association unmarred by jealousy and meanness, suspicion and distrust. Steele had first dropped out, and then Edward Hunt, but only when death had claimed them. Now, by mutual consent and not with regret, O'Brien and FE parted, O'Brien to retire to Sydney, FE to go north again for a while.

Selling these six properties, and the consequent breaking up of a smooth-running partnership, could not have been accomplished without heartache. FE had created Miranda Downs. From its very crude state, he had made Carpentaria Downs too, and a man does not relinquish something he has created without experiencing sadness. For the term of his management of the properties for the Queensland Meat Export & Agency Company, FE lived at his home on Carpentaria

Downs, and without doubt he will have had pangs of regret that soon he would be leaving it for the last time.

An Australian cattle or sheep station has its definite personality. While to an outsider it appears to be a limitless extent of land without form and feature, and exactly like any other tract of land in the interior of Australia, even adjoining stations are as different as two bay colts, two Hereford bulls, or two wether sheep of any breed. In the first place, their sizes and shapes are as different as any two men and, in the second place, their topographical differences are glaring although on both there may be the same kind of scrub, the same lie of sandhills and the same tree-lined creeks. Almost despite himself, the stockman who has worked on a great cattle or sheep station takes pride in it forever.

42. The homestead at Carpentaria Downs

Towards the end of 1903 the Directors of the Queensland Meat Export & Agency Company wrote asking him to submit a name for their approval as his successor at Carpentaria Downs. Thinking of all the men who had worked under him as managers, he selected H C Wilson, the then manager of Forest Home. There was no man superior to Wilson in the management of a big cattle herd on an enormous area of country, and subsequent history again justified FE as it had done in relation to his selection of Power as his successor at Miranda Downs.

193

There is some doubt as to why Upfield felt that FE's recommendation of H C Wilson as his successor at Carpentaria Downs was justified. Some ten or so years after FE handed over, a member of Wilson's household, one Nellie Duffy, was savagely murdered in a case which made headline news. Whilst the crime was never solved, the most detailed examination of the facts by Stephanie Bennett in her book 'The Murder of Nellie Duffy' most certainly did not cover H C Wilson in glory. Ironically, Nellie Duffy was buried next to FE's first wife, Bessie.

Near to the severance of his connection with the Queensland Meat Export & Agency Company there was a pleasant surprise - his many friends in the district, including other owners and managers, residents of Georgetown, and the employees of the several stations, presented him with a handsome set of branching candelabra.

FE's last official act was to resign his commission as a Justice of the Peace, having served for a period of nearly twenty years.

This important end to an era of ceaseless activity left Francis Cobbold at what was to him a loose end. He was now over fifty years old. He had led a strenuous life remarkably barren of leisure, but it had been a life of continuous physical training. Now, physically and mentally, he was as fit as a man half his age. He had come out of the two partnerships rather well – he was clear of the bank and in command of ample funds.

To retire from the pastoral industry was for FE quite impossible. The wanderlust in him was as strong at fifty as it had been at twenty. To stagnate in a suburban villa and potter about in a garden, or even to retire to Sydney and take up yachting, was unthinkable. He had to 'go on or go under', and there was no impediment to hinder him from going on.

There was Inverleigh. Inverleigh wanted a man of his peculiar genius to raise it out of its state of rawness into something like a well-oiled efficient machine. Money was not, and never had been, the ultimate goal with FE; his tastes were inexpensive and called for little money. FE offered to buy another quarter share in Inverleigh from his brother-in-law, which then gave him an equal interest and, by agreement, a predominant position in its management.

194

2.

FE determined to take a long holiday before getting down to the serious task of improving and consolidating Inverleigh. With Mrs Cobbold, he left Australia on a world tour about the time that war broke out between Russia and Japan.

They visited New Zealand first and then America, where in San Francisco he experienced the uncanny feelings rendered by an earthquake. From America, they drifted south to Mexico, thinking of the possibility of staying in that country for a period if opportunities for investment offered sufficient inducement.

The country of the province of Chihuahua appeared to him to be good pastoral land not unlike some parts of South-Western Queensland. However, when they were well into Mexico he was less pleased by the land, which was inhabited by a mixed breed of small cultivators surrounding numerous small towns and poor villages. The people seemed to depend almost wholly on irrigation.

There were plenty of properties on offer at prices equivalent to one to four shillings an acre in English money. One of these was 1,5000,000 acres in area and named La Santana Hacienda. It carried 4,644 horses, 1,225 mules, 13,586 cattle, 16,007 sheep and 9,133 goats, besides a population of three hundred natives scattered over the estate. FE could have managed the natives, but the goats were not to his liking.

He found that plenty of country in Mexico could be bought cheaply on a freehold title, but the conditions did not approximate to those ruling in Queensland. FE therefore gave up the idea of investing in Mexico – which turned out to be fortunate in view of the subsequent chaotic state of the country following the fall of President Diaz.

It was only natural that the meat industry of Chicago would interest and attract him. Reaching this great midwest city, Mr Malkow conducted him over the huge Swifts Meatworks; it was the same Mr Malkow who, later still, came to Queensland and started Swifts' Meat Freezing and Preserving Works at Brisbane. Swifts impressed the visitor with their wonderful organisation.

Then on to New York and across the Atlantic to London. FE went 'home' to pay visits to his relatives and the friends of his boyhood, and to re-visit the scenes on which were based his very early memories. The weeks passed in quiet enjoyment of remaking contact with the beginnings of his life, but the Gordian knot had been cut, and he realised that no longer was he an Englishman in the sense that he belonged to England. The people he met were kindly and charming and warm, but he did not feel one of them in the same way that he was part of the people of Queensland. He was home in England, and yet England now was not really home. Home lay south of the equator; it was that country to which he had freely given his life, that country in which, and with which, he had grown up. He met his relatives as strangers in all but name.

No, retirement in either Australia or England was impossible for the restless soul of this man. Ahead of him there was so much more to be done; the rest of life and its freedom in Queensland and in New South Wales was too strong ever to permit him to vegetate.

Before returning to Australia, he decided to visit South America, where several close relatives lived in Buenos Ayres. Since Mrs Cobbold wanted to remain in England for a longer period FE sailed without her, after having - on the advice of his bank's stockbrokers - invested £10,000 in equal amounts in Mexican Central Railway Gold Bonds, Shawinigan (Canadian) Water & Power, Rio Janeiro Trams, New York Telephones, and Balgrano Trams (Buenos Ayres). If he had put this total amount into rubber, he would have made a profit of about one hundred thousand pounds in two years. As it was, he received dividends at five per cent for ten years, when he disposed of the investments in four of the concerns at par. The Mexican Bonds returned interest up to 1914. Since then nothing has come from them, and today they have no quotable value.

Senor Chevalier Boutell was an English cousin from Suffolk and a man of considerable standing in Argentina. He was the General Manager of the River Plate Trust Loan & Agency Company, and of the Mortgage Company of the River Plate. He was Chairman of the Bolsa de Comercia – the General Bourse of the Argentina – and the local director of a dozen important companies, including those

Frank Hepburn Chevallier Boutell (1949-1921) was the brother-in-law of Nathanael Fromanteel Cobbold (1839-1886), the 6th son of John Chevallier Cobbold (1791-1882), FE's uncle.

having control of a railway, a tramway, and an electric light concern.

Boutell was the open sesame to the best in Argentina. A member of the Jockey Club for many years – the leading institution of its kind in Argentina, with an entrance fee of £450 – Boutell invited FE to make this place his headquarters from which he undertook several memorable trips into the interior and met many of the leading bankers, financiers, and estancieros,

FE was conducted up the River Uruguay as far as Concordia, the second most important city in Entre Rios - which means 'between rivers', the Province being bounded on one side by the River Uruguay and on the other by the Parana. Senor Boutell escorted his guest over the Entre Rios Railway of which he was the local director. Leaving the railway at the City of Parana, FE was then introduced to the Governor of the Province and visited San Jacinto, an estancio of twelve square leagues which, because of its proximity to Buenos Ayres, was worth nearly two million English pounds. Here FE saw the celebrated racehorses 'Ormond' and 'Flying Fox', for which their owner had paid respectively 25,000 and 26,000 guineas.

The stability of a country is largely dependent on its laws governing property rights. The leasehold system of Australia comes into sharp and unfavourable relief when examined together with the freehold system of Argentina. In the latter country, the chaos existing in the pastoral areas of Australia is entirely absent. The landowners know exactly where they stand and are unfettered by the uncertainty of the future.

When it came to discussing pastoral business in Argentina, FE found conditions vastly different. Had he called at the offices of any big pastoral company in Australia with £30,000 to invest, he would not have been lost sight of until he had been sold something. Not so in Argentina. Senor Boutell explained that although they had very large sums lent out on mortgages on pastoral and agricultural properties, they had not a single property to offer for sale on their books.

In the 1860s, FE's two brothers, Thomas and Octavius, had migrated to Argentina where they prospered. Thomas died in 1920, and Octavius in 1932 at the age of seventy-eight. Two other brothers went to Argentina and they did well, Walter dying in 1920, and Frederick dying towards the end of last century. The latter's widow and daughters returned to England to live, but Walter's children - Walter, Norman, James and Marcus - clung to the country of their father's adoption.

The names of the first two, and that of Rowland T Cobbold are inserted among the 528 names on the Roll of Honour, 1914-1918. James and Marcus served for the duration of the Great War and returned. All these Cobbolds volunteered in Argentina, except Walter Frederick who was in Queensland in 1914 managing Radcliffe Station. Joining the Australian Expeditionary Forces as an artilleryman, he gained his commission in the 28th Infantry Regiment, and was killed in action 11th June 1918.

Upfield is not entirely correct here – FE's brothers Walter Joseph, John Clifford and Frederick George went to the Argentine in 1868. Thomas followed in 1895 and Octavius also emigrated much later. Walter died in 1927, John disappeared and Fred died unexpectedly in December 1900. Thomas may well have died in 1920, but Octavius's death was about 1929.

B.McK.   2nd December, 1918.

DESPATCHED

Dear Sir,

        With reference to the report of the regrettable loss of your son, the late Lieutenant W. F. Cobbold, 28th Battalion, I am now in receipt of advice which shows that he was Killed in Action on 10th June, 1918, by machine gun bullet, during attack near Marlancourt, France.   He was buried in Franvillers Military Cemetery (Albert-Amiens Road).

        The utmost care and attention is being devoted where possible to the graves of our soldiers.   It is understood that photographs are being taken as soon as is possible and these will be transmitted to next-of-kin when available.

        These additional details are furnished by direction, it being the policy of the Department to forward all information received in connection with deaths of members of the Australian Imperial Force.

                              Yours faithfully,

                                        Major.
                              Officer i/c Base Records.

W. J. Cobbold, Esq.,
   Estacion Soldengaray
      F.C. Sud,
         BUENOS AYRES,
            South America.

43. *Letter notifying his family of Walter's death in action*

Rowland T(ownshend) Cobbold was born in 1892, the eldest son of Alfred Townshend Cobbold (1852-1934) and Alice Bessie Nunn (1859-1928). He was working in Argentina when war was declared and he returned home to volunteer immediately. A letter from his mother to his sister says '... Rowland was killed East of Ypres; he was forward observing officer for his Battery in the attack – all his telephone wires were broken by shell fire and he was killed while trying to establish communication by lamp with his Battery. He was hit in the head by shrapnel and so death would be instantaneous.'

3.

On his return to Australia, FE was at once plunged into the vortex of business when he was told of the threat of an action for damages by the Queensland Meat Export & Agency Company for defective titles of the Forest Home cattle station.

During his absence, the Company that had bought the four properties from O'Brien, Cobbold & Co had applied to the Lands Department for leave to surrender the Forest Home titles in exchange for new ones. The Lands Act of 1902 had been amended in 1904 as promised, and now the Department refused the Company's request on the ground that certain concessions regarding rent which had been granted by a previous Minister were *ultra vires* and, until these back rents were paid, no fresh titles would be given.

The solicitors pointed out that the Contract of Sale was for all O'Brien, Cobbold & Co's rights, title, and interest in the lands, that that was all they could give, and that the titles they transferred were all they had ever held. On submitting a case to Counsel however, the solicitors were informed that, notwithstanding all this, the titles were bad and good grounds for an action for damages existed.

This state of affairs regarding Forest Home was by no means singular in scope or unique to Forest Home. Annual Licences for a large part of Forest Home run had been renewed six times, and early in 1890 the Crown had made a demand for double rent as in the case of Promises of Lease. FE had resisted this on many grounds, and the correspondence with the Lands Department, together with many personal interviews with Under Secretaries, continued until May 1896 when the justice of his contentions was submitted and all correspondence minuted by the Minister. The excess rents demanded and paid each year under protest were remitted.

FE's solicitors wrote to the Under Secretary for the Department of Public Lands as follows: "Sir, we understand from our clients, Messrs Cobbold and O'Brien, that you have been in communication with the Queensland Meat Export & Agency Company Limited, with respect to certain alleged arrears on the runs as per margin, the payment of which you stated to them is necessary before any action under the 1902 Act can proceed.

"Our clients have considerable correspondence with you covering a period (six years) in respect of these and other runs, and this correspondence shows that the Minister for Lands admitted their contention, viz, that the provisions of the Pastoral Leases Act of 1860 whereby rents were increased during successive seven year periods of lease should not apply to annual tenancies which were subject to the provisions of the Goldfields Act.

"The runs being situated in the Etheridge Goldfield Reserve could only be held under annual tenancy and, as previously mentioned, the correspondence shows it was admitted that annual tenancies which were subject to the provisions of the Goldfields Act were not subject to section 20 of the Pastoral Leases Act of 1869.

"Our clients were under the impression that the question of increased rentals had been finally settled in 1896, as from that time up to the time the Queensland Meat Export & Agency Co. Limited became the purchasers (1.1.03) they had paid rent on above runs at 5s 0d per square mile, and same had always been accepted without any question as to arrears. In fact the rent lists from 1896 to 1903 do not show that any arrears were due on these runs. It was only after the election to take advantage of the provisions of the 1902 Act that the alleged arrears appeared in the rent lists, viz that from 1904-5."

It was an awkward position because the firm of O'Brien, Cobbold & Co had ceased to exist and the only recourse left to the Government was to refuse conversion of the titles or renew them when they expired. The Company's only recourse was an action at law against the principals of the firm from whom they brought the property.

FE urged a conference to find a way out. The Directors of the Queensland Meat Export & Agency Company were certainly not keen to engage in the hazard of a lawsuit, but they honestly felt they were suffering damage. After many interviews with Government officials, a compromise was found by which all surrendered something, and the Company received the renewals of their leases. The Attorney for the William Steele Estate wrote to FE expressing pleasure at the manner in which he had smoothed out what might have become grave trouble.

"I thank you," he wrote, "for your letter of the 17th instant, and am grateful to you for fixing things so well under the circumstances."

The settlement of this affair afforded FE opportunity to give his attention to Inverleigh.

CHAPTER EIGHTEEN

Years 1905 - 1911
Inverleigh

1.

At the beginning of this century, the titles and the extension of the titles granted under the Act of 1896 - and many of those granted under the Act of 1884 and the Amendment Act of 1886 - were close to expiration. Consequently, the 1902 Land Amendment Act was placed on the Statute Book; this was an act offering the pastoralists the opportunity of acquiring new leases.

The big drought which broke in 1902, however, had left the majority of them in a lamentable condition. In Queensland, the total number of sheep fell from over fifteen millions to about seven millions, and the cattle total had been reduced from over five million to little more than half that number. The terrific effort to keep the stock alive had produced enormous liabilities and, after the long delay in considering the reports of the Commissioners who had travelled the State seeking information, the Government brought in and passed an Act which professed to be a Relief Act (1902).

The Act fell far short of what the pastoralists had hoped for, what they expected, and what they considered they were justly entitled to. The provisions made in former acts which limited increases of rent, as well as the right of appeal to the Supreme Court on questions of fact, were eliminated. The right of appeal, especially, had proved again and again a sure protection against impositions of unfair rents.

The lessees did not rush to take advantage of the opportunity to secure new leases offered by this 1902 Act. After discussing the position from every angle, FE and William Cain, the owners of Inverleigh, decided not to come in under it. It had become a widespread belief, existing to this day, that the pastoralists were accumulating ample fortunes with great ease. Without doubt, there are periods when the pastoralists do make handsome profits, like the shopkeepers who make additional profits just before Christmas and Easter, but the irrefutable fact is that overall the bad years equal the good years, and that during the bad years pastoral leases are severe. A taxing authority is always eager to take advantage of prosperity to increase its impositions, but it also shows remarkable reluctance to ease or remove them when prosperity has given place to drought and adversity. Knowing this by bitter experience, knowing too that many more men have a fortune investing in the pastoral industry than those who have made one out of it, the pastoralists naturally hesitated before taking a single step.

The so-called Relief Act was an iron fist in a silken glove.

It proved the Crown, as a landlord, to be an unconscionable usurer. It revealed its desire to have absolute freedom to raise rents and therefore retain absolute power over its tenants. It sought the position of being able to remove a tenant if it did not like the manner in which the tenant parted his hair, by raising the rent of his lease to a point at which it was impossible to pay. It wanted the power to force him off the land without compensating him for the improvements he had carried out and, above all, it wanted to leave the tenant without the right to appeal for the type of justice which is permitted to thieves and vagabonds.

Even so, there was a small group of Queensland pastoralists who thought the Act to be a sound one. One day FE sat at lunch at Scott's Hotel in Melbourne with the Hon William McCulloch, Andrew McIlwaith, Agar Wynne, and his partner in Inverleigh, William Cain. McCulloch asked FE for his opinion of the 1902 Act and FE replied frankly that no one was going to place himself at the mercy of a government by accepting a lease before knowing what the rent was going to be. McCulloch, the owner of Langlo Downs Station, then said with emphasis:

"You'll get no better terms!"

"Well, if I can get no better terms, I will not apply," was FE's equally emphatic statement.

Later, when FE met other pastoral friends, they were astonished by his attitude to the Act, saying it was the best they could hope to get in the circumstances.

On the eve of taking his long holiday abroad, FE decided to leave the matter of this Act in reference to Inverleigh until his return to Australia, by which date he felt sure several important amendments would have been passed. Again he forecast rightly.

2.

A glance at the map of Queensland will draw attention to the immense bight of water called the Gulf of Carpentaria. Fronting sixty miles of the southernmost tip of the Gulf lies Inverleigh, which FE consolidated, improved and organised into a great cattle station - despite the indifferences, if not the active opposition, of a government department. By negotiating the purchase of the leases of several small blocks of land, and by six years of negotiations with the Government for the secure tenure, he brought more than two thousand square miles within the boundaries of Inverleigh. When he had advised the purchase of a much-disjointed Inverleigh from Mrs Colless for £18,000, it carried only 11,000 head of cattle.

The only natural boundaries of this huge property were the Gulf of Carpentaria on its northern front for sixty miles and the Leichhardt River on its western front for a distance of twenty-five miles from its mouth. On the south-west, Inverleigh adjoined Wernadinga run; on the south, Neumayer Valley and Donors Hills Stations; and on the east, Magoura Station which was afterwards purchased by FE and his old partner, Patrick O'Brien.

For a large area fronting the Gulf of Carpentaria, Inverleigh was the worst watered stretch of country within FE's experience, the only really permanent supplies being in the water-holes at the head station on Station Creek, and in a large water-hole on Armstrong Creek, of which Inverleigh owned half and Magoura owned the other half. Several creeks carried water off Inverleigh to the sea, and one, Station Creek, flowed right through the property from the boundary to the south of it.

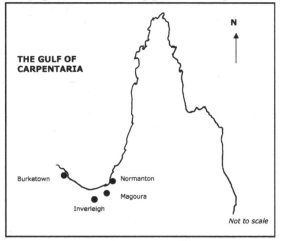

44. *Location of Inverleigh*

Not one of these creeks contained a permanent flow of water. During the monsoon season they did carry water, and at the end of the season their holes and small lagoons contained water for six or seven months. However, unless early summer rain fell to fill the natural clay pans when these dried up about

October, the cattle had either to crowd on the two permanent water-holes or trespass on adjoining runs. As it was clearly impossible for these two permanent supplies to carry the whole of the Inverleigh cattle for any definite period, a great many of them moved across the south-western border into Wernadinga country, where there was a chain of splendid lagoons.

The stock-carrying capacity of a station is much more limited by its water supplies than it is by its food growths. At Inverleigh, FE quickly discovered that its water supplies were severely limiting the number of cattle it carried - a number far below its normal capacity relative to its size and class of country. Almost every year, seven hundred square miles adjacent to the coast was useless for several months because there was no water.

This was the situation when FE joined the Hon William Cain in its purchase from Mrs Colless. At the time the Amending Act of 1905 was passed, the area had been increased by taking over the leases of several small settlers and FE was continuing the struggle with the Lands Department to obtain some security of tenure in order that he might spend money on vital improvements with reasonable safety and prospects of getting it back.

3.

Towards the end of 1903, the manager of Inverleigh thought he had found a good site on the Poingdestra Creek for the construction of an earth dam. A supply of water at this spot would permit a number of cattle to graze on country otherwise prohibited to them during the dry seasons, and FE gave authority for this work to be put in hand. The Chief Engineer of the Chillagos Railways, Mr Frew, recommended a man named Savage who was an experienced dam maker, and he was sent to do the building. On examining the proposed site for the dam, Savage agreed with the manager's opinion.

The dam was built. Then a flood came down the creek and swept away the middle section of the wall, proving that to build a wall of sufficient strength to withstand the rush of water could only be done at uneconomic expense. The manager's request for £500 with which to repair the break was refused, and FE now realised that there was nothing for it but to sink for artesian water – work which would be too costly and too adventurous to be put in hand until greater security of tenure had been obtained from the Lands Department.

Then an important tribunal came into being affecting the Pastoral Industry of Queensland. In accordance with the provisions of the Queensland Land Act of 1902, the Land Court became engaged in the classification of the many holders; in 1904 its work was completed and the lessees were given six months to decide whether or not they would surrender existing leases and take advantage of the 1902 Act.

However, by May of that year the lessees had shown no general desire to come in under the Act. Before the six months was up, the then Premier, Mr Arthur Morgan, realised the fairness of the lessees' contentions and intimated that he would agree to the demand for the continuance of the 50 per cent limitation, which would be embodied in an Act of Parliament. The promised Act was passed in 1905, and under its provisions the lessees were allowed an extension of time up to March 1906 to lodge notice of their desire to come under the Act.

FE now made an application to come in under the new Act, following it up with a request for security of tenure to enable him and his partner to invest substantial sums of money in fencing large areas and conserving water by artesian wells or other means.

The surface dam on the Poingdestra Creek having proved a failure, and the great cost of sinking bores for artesian water not to be undertaken lightly, FE spent five months on a careful survey of the whole of Inverleigh.

In addition to good sales of fat bullocks, he had sold a thousand heifers at £3 per head to Mr Barnes of Lyndhurst, so he and his partner found themselves comfortably off for funds.

At this time FE was well into middle age, able to retire to the comforts and ease offered by a city if he wished and yet he was still enthusiastically giving his mind and his body to the development of this huge cattle station. The Official Mind was doing its darndest to hinder him, while the heat and the flying pests were sufficient to daunt a much younger man. On account of its physical demands, this labour of bringing over two thousand square miles under the microscope, as it were, was no mean task. It was accomplished on horseback, and on the high seat of a jolting backboard. It was the general order to camp

206

anywhere he happened to be when the sun set, and then sufficient food had to be cooked for the next day and notes written on the observations and calculations made the same day.

His objective now was the discovery of suitable sites for the construction of surface dams, weirs, or any natural feature that could be adapted to the conservation of water. He gave particular attention to the lower reaches of the several creeks that emptied into the Gulf, conducting a search for rock bottoms and conglomerate banks. He found these special conditions on the Station Creek at a place where the bed of the creek was of rock for its entire width of ten chains and the banks were of 'pudding stone'.

> Puddingstone is a conglomerate rock made up of a mixture of different, irregular sized grains and pebbles held together by a finer matrix, usually formed from quartz sand. Its name is said to derive from a resemblance to Christmas pudding.

The one permanent water hole was in a rocky hole on a conglomerate platform; the homestead was built here. The plateau ended about a quarter of a mile below the homestead and the creek dropped abruptly about thirty feet, and so this part was called The Falls. From here, the creek ran with an imperceptible fall for the ten miles to the sea. The rush of water in flood times had scoured out a succession of big water-holes, which in a favourable year would last until the monsoon rains made their appearance. Before these reliable rains fell in about early November, however, the south-east trade winds died away, being succeeded by the north monsoonal winds which forced the salty water of the Gulf up into the creeks, destroying the fresh water as far up as The Falls. So this water supply was destroyed when it was most wanted.

Years passed, devoted to other interests as well as to Inverleigh, before FE began the project of building a weir at the site selected on Station Creek below The Falls. Its length was to be one eighth of a mile, and its height was to be six feet in the centre, its deepest part. Mr Henderson, a government hydraulic engineer, was kind enough to work out the composition and the dimensions of the weir, and this valuable assistance, added to FE's surveying knowledge, augured well for success of the plan.

FE purchased the necessary cement and, with Brickey and the cement, he left Brisbane for Normanton on the *Menace*. Brickey was a convivial soul who regarded this trip to North Australia in the nature of a holiday tour and, when they were being conveyed on the tender upriver to Normanton, he fell in with two gentlemen as convivial as himself.

The three had a roaring time that night in one of the hotels, and the next morning Brickey was absent, either through a fat head or because he conspired to get out of his contract and return to Brisbane, completing an enjoyable holiday at FE's expense. Next morning, however, FE climbed into the station buggy and drove off to Inverleigh alone; he was inconsiderate enough to take with him the man's belongings and, what was of even greater importance, the return half of the steamer ticket. A poorer and wiser Brickey eventually turned up on the coach.

Meanwhile the bullock teams became busy carting cement, sand and stone to the site of the weir. For a few days Brickey lay up recovering from the effects of the drink, but eventually he went to work and steadily the building of the weir progressed. During the work, the Governor - His Excellency Lord Chelmsford - accompanied by the Minister for the Lands, other dignitaries and their many attendants visited the station. The Vice Regal party was touring the Outback and was warmly welcomed at Inverleigh.

Later, when walking down Station Creek looking for wild duck, the party arrived at the weir building. FE accompanied them with an old aboriginal in attendance to retrieve the birds brought down. At the weir, FE explained that its purpose was to keep back a much greater volume of fresh water and to prevent the salt water from the Gulf forcing its way above it to spoil the water imprisoned. His Excellency remarked, referring to the partly built wall: "It is a very fragile looking thing!"

And the old aboriginal put in: "Big feller water come down, poof! Altogether go bung."

But it never did 'go bung'. The wall was half built when the first of the usual floods came down over The Falls, and it withstood the pressure of water against it. The wall was completed during the following year and the weir stands efficient to this day, adding a valuable addition of fresh water to the station's meagre supplies.

4.

The Great Artesian Basin is roughly triangular in shape, its northern point reaching the southern tip of the Gulf of Carpentaria – taking in Inverleigh and the several stations south of it – while the points of the base line lie deep in New South Wales and South Australia. To the west of the Basin is the Great Plateau, which covers more than half the continent, and on the east of it runs the coastal mountain belt extending from Cape Yorke Peninsula to Southern Victoria.

At the far northern point of the Great Artesian Basin, the soil is of geologically recent formation. Being at the edge of the Basin, this part is higher than the centre; many people considered it to lie outside the Basin altogether, while others thought it was too far above artesian water to make raising it to the surface a practicable proposition.

When at long last FE's persistence overcame the endless obstructions offered by the Lands Department, and the Minister had granted him and his partners a lease of Inverleigh for thirty years at the annual rental of 8s 0d per square mile, he determined to proceed at once with the boring for artesian water. FE's partner was acquainted with a Doctor Brown, whose brother was a well-borer in Queensland known as Lightning Brown on account of the rapidity with which he sank wells. Knowing that Mr Brown had been working in shallow ground, which did not call for heavy plant, FE was doubtful of his success, since bores on Inverleigh would certainly have to be sunk to a great depth before water could be reached. He had watched the sinking of three bores on Authoringa and Riversleigh, the deepest of which was 3,300 feet, and he realised that was more advanced than Mr Lightning Brown or any other bore-sinker operating on Inverleigh. However, Lightning Brown signed a contract to sink one bore early the following year.

Returning to Inverleigh in March, FE anxiously awaited the arrival of Mr Lightning Brown, and when April and May passed and Mr Brown failed to put in an appearance, he set the telegraph wires at work. It was then that he learned that Mr Brown had started on horseback with the intention of visiting the site of the proposed bore before sending for his plant. On his way, he had discovered that the further north he travelled the deeper would be the boring. Sensing that the depth would be over 2,000 feet, with extraordinary casualness he turned back

209

and omitted to inform FE or his partner of his decision to abandon the contract.

So six months were wasted, and further valuable time passed before a contract was signed with the Inter-Colonial Boring Company. It put down the first bore on the Poingdestra Creek, striking water at a depth of 2,260 feet and providing a gush of 850,000 gallons of water every twenty-four hours which flowed down along the creek bed for twelve miles before spreading out over a flat plain.

The Number Two Bore was put down on Station Creek about 20 miles south of the weir. Water was struck at a depth of 1,793 feet, giving a flow of about a quarter of a million gallons every twenty-four hours. The Number Three Bore was sunk at a site about thirty miles westerly of the lower end of Poingdestra Creek and produced three quarters of a million gallons every twenty-four hours.

These three bores and the weir provided ample water for stock on the whole of the coastal area which formerly had been an arid desert during the rainless periods. FE had faithfully carried out his promise to the Minister for Lands in return for security of tenure.

5.

Wernadinga Station fronted the east bank of the Leichhardt River, with Inverleigh on its north and north-east boundaries and Neumayer Valley Station on its south-east and south boundaries. Running through it and roughly parallel with the river is Lagoon Creek in which lay the chain of splendid water-holes.

Originally, Wernadinga was part of Neumayer Valley Station, but during the hungry 1890s the owners of the big run were compelled to surrender an area of 360 square miles, and hope that no one with sufficient capital or enterprise would occupy it because it was their intention to re-apply for it when their fortunes mended.

For several years the herds on both Inverleigh and Neumayer Valley were edged over to this abandoned country for the dry season on account of the permanent water supply in the lagoons. It was an amicable arrangement which suited the owners of the two big properties and neither paid rent for it.

210

Neither of these big properties had a water supply to equal it, and its only fault lay in its position.

In the same district were two brothers named Williams who owned the lease of a badly-watered block of country carrying a small herd of a few hundred cattle. Cruising about in search of more favoured country to take up, they happened on the abandoned block, and some time later read the notice stating its availability to any applicant wishing to apply for it.

To the consternation of the owner of Inverleigh and the owners of Neumayer Valley, the Williams brothers took possession and brought with them their small herd of two hundred cattle. This had occurred just a few years before FE and William Cain bought Inverleigh, and provides an illuminating instance of a legitimate method of doffing cattle. The two brothers, knowing that Inverleigh and Neumayer Valley cattle had been and still were watering on Lagoon Creek, were careful to assure their neighbours of their good will by permitting the arrangement to continue. There was far more water than could be consumed by their own herd, and they wished always to be neighbourly. Both generous fellows, they declined to accept payment for the water taken by their neighbours' cattle, and this kindness was rewarded by the increase in their small herd.

The dry season coincided with the time the majority of the cows weaned their calves. At the beginning of the dry season, the cows and their calves concentrated on Wernadinga for the water in the holes along Lagoon Creek and, at the end of the dry season, the cows migrated eastward to fresher pasture leaving their weaned calves behind. In payment for the water taken, the Williams brothers rounded up these calves with their own cattle and branded them with their own brand: it was a fair *quid pro quo*.

There could be no argument about it. It was their country. Their own cattle and their own calves were grazing on it. They possessed every legal right over all unbranded youngsters whose parentage could not be proved because the mothers would have nothing further to do with them.

This was one of the problems facing FE when he tackled the development of Inverleigh. It was definitely not good business to allow others to build up a fine herd at the expense of Inverleigh and its southern neighbour. However, the only way to stop it was to forego that chain of water-holes by erecting a boundary fence - but the water-holes were urgently necessary because this was before the bores were sunk. There was only one sure way left for FE to stop this annual loss of calves and that was to buy out the Williams brothers.

Compared with Inverleigh, Wernadinga was a very small property. Its water supply was greater than its capacity to carry stock, and consequently the property was of greater value to either Inverleigh or Neumayer Valley than to its owners. The Williams brothers knew this well. As usual, FE dispensed with the frills of dealing and bluntly asked the brothers what they would take for Wernadinga.

They did not know. They had not thought of selling. They were not particularly anxious to sell. All was right in their little heaven and – on the quiet – the owners of Neumayer Valley were showing signs of a desire to offer.

To Messrs Wharton and Longwell, the owners of Neumayer Valley Station, they casually mentioned that FE had offered to buy them out, an offer they were considering. Wharton and Longwell mentioned a slightly higher figure, and the Williams told them they would consider that. Then, as if by chance, they met FE and casually mentioned to him the offer made by Wharton and Longwell.

At once understanding this game of silent auction, FE rode to Neumayer Valley. "Look here!" he said to Wharton and Longwell. "These fellows are getting us to bid against each other for their bit of a property. We have contributed in equal measure to building up their herd of cattle, and we desire equally that that should not go on and that we continue to use the water-holes in Lagoon Creek. Let us get together and fix a price to offer them. Let the price be a fair one and, having secured the property, let us make equal division of the area which will give us an equal share of the water."

Wharton and Longwell promptly agreed, and it was arranged that FE should negotiate for the property. The owners of Wernadinga seemed hesitant to part with it, and continued to hope that by this hesitation they might succeed in luring one of the two parties now in combination to offer separately and acquire the whole of the area – and the water. They then offered the property at public auction, but the last bid being less than the standing offer of FE and Longwell and Wharton, the latter eventually bought Williams out.

The division of the land was a simple matter. By running a straight east-west fence through its centre not only was the land divided, but the water-holes were divided too. The male cattle were mustered and sold, the money was divided by drawing a cheque and the unmarketable cows and the youngsters went to Inverleigh by agreement.

6.

Early in 1909, FE's brother-in-law and co-partner in Inverleigh decided that his years demanded the bringing of his affairs within a smaller compass. He suggested the sale of Inverleigh. FE said there would be no difficulty about that as the cattle industry was booming and Inverleigh was on the verge of booming and producing the harvest he had so assiduously sown.

William Cain and FE regarded Inverleigh from wildly different angles. The former was well past the allotted span and he took no personal interest in the progress and growth of his property. Being a much younger man, and having taken a keen personal interest in Inverleigh, FE was reluctant to part with it. A solution was found by FE bringing O'Brien into partnership, when the value of the property was put at £60,000 by agreement, at which price O'Brien bought a third share, giving the two original partners £10,000 each. For O'Brien it was to be a very profitable deal, giving him a profit in one year of £8,666 on a £20,000 investment.

45.   William Cain (1831 – 1914)

William Cain insisted that Inverleigh was remote. He pointed out that probably in the near future FE would find it irksome to pay it the necessary visits, and he argued that now was the time to sell.

Intuitively FE knew that it was not the time to sell, knew that the prosperity line had much further to rise on the graph of Inverleigh. O'Brien, who was not familiar with the property, was inclined to side with William Cain. However, FE felt that he would never forgive himself if intuition failed him in this instance - his partners would suffer the loss of a good bargain, if not actual financial loss - so with reluctance he agreed to find a purchaser. It was against his judgement, but no man is infallible.

Again in Sydney, he visited O'Brien to lay before him the proposal to sell Inverleigh, but before he could broach the subject O'Brien said: "Brodie has got hold of a syndicate who want to buy a big cattle station. Will you sell Inverleigh?"

Relating then what had passed between Cain and himself, FE and O'Brien at once talked to Brodie. Brodie had spent many years in the Gulf country and at one time had owned Lorraine Station, on the Leichhardt River. He said, before Inverleigh was mentioned: "You have now got Inverleigh going well. How much would you take for it?"

"Eighty thousand pounds – one third cash down," replied FE as though this figure had been in his mind for months.

"All right," assented Brodie. "I can get it off."

An offer was given to the principals of the Syndicate which allowed them time to inspect the property and return to Sydney. The following day, however, having got hold of a false report concerning the country, one of the principal subscribers drew out. Brodie then suggested that as the deal might fall through, it would be as well to reduce the price by £5,000.

"Nothing doing," FE said firmly. "I'll take that £8,000 share, and you can let the syndicate know that I am prepared to take the place of anyone and everyone who wants to draw out."

It was partly bluff on his part, although his faith in Inverleigh was strong. No man knew it better, or understood its resources more than he did, and he was prepared to remain in - even to the extent of taking the whole of it on his own shoulders. Had he wanted them, there would have been not the slightest difficulty in finding partners.

The Syndicate procrastinated and finally made an offer of £75,000. FE declined it. He again bluffed when he said that Inverleigh was now withdrawn from sale. He departed at once for Brisbane, prepared to take over Inverleigh from his partners should they be dissatisfied with his actions, and being quite resigned to having to do that in the end. He then allowed a period to elapse before re-opening negotiations with the

Syndicate, thinking that by now they would have made up their minds about it. Inverleigh changed hands for £80,000.

It might well be thought outrageous profiteering to sell for £80,000 a property purchased for £18,000, but consideration must be given to the thousands of pounds spent on improvements, money risked sinking bores which might not give water, and that Inverleigh's flourishing condition was due wholly to FE's management. He found it disorganised and badly managed by a man in Sydney who acted for the widow. She received a better return from the investment of £18,000 than she ever had done from Inverleigh.

7.

In 1911, when Inverleigh was sold to the Syndicate, FE took one thousand pound shares in the Company, and he was thus able to continue his interest in the great cattle station.

About the time of the change of ownership, Inverleigh began a decade of even greater prosperity, proving that FE's intuition was again right. The flowing bores, the big weir, and the lagoons on Wernadinga gave a splendid water supply over the whole area, now 2,567 square miles or 2,242,880 acres, which provided ample scope for increasing herds. For the ten years 1911-1920, the profits were shown as £112,937, a yearly average of £11,293.

It was a fine achievement, this creation of a greater Inverleigh, and stands as a monument to a man's courageous determination when the sky over the pastoral industry was dark, to his foresight and his confidence when others despaired and to his energetic activities which took no account of physical discomforts.

In 1919, the Queensland Government began buying cattle stations in anticipation of a world shortage of beef, and Inverleigh was put under offer to the Government at a price which worked out at £172,250. The Government's Inspector reported favourably on the purchase, and there is no doubt that the sale would have been effected if FE had still been the managing partner, or even if he had been the Chairman of Directors of the Company. It revealed, however, the hesitancy of the original Syndicate, and their delay in following the usual procedure in the case of a Limited Liability Company was fatal.

The sudden slump in cattle values not only deprived the Company of the chance of a brilliant winding-up and liquidation but, its policy having been to distribute the large profits during the bumper years, recourse had to be made to the bank to obtain the money for the final settlement of the purchase price to the vendors, since the original capital subscribed had been only £38,000.

Having raised Inverleigh from the dust of the semi-desert to a proud position in the pastoral industry of Australia, FE sold his thousand one pound shares at the cost to the buyer only of the stamp duty.

CHAPTER NINETEEN

Years 1906 - 1926
'... and now Sheep!'

1.

One of several effects of the great drought, with its prolonged suffering of helpless animals and the mental strain it placed on the men who owned them, was the tendency of those pastoralists who had survived to get out of the industry. They were fearful of risking everything in another such experience; properties all over Queensland - and in New South Wales, too - were thrown on the market at very much less than their nominal value.

The moment for a courageous man to act is when others fear.

FE had taken up temporary residence at the Gresham Hotel in Brisbane when one day Daniel Morgan came in and said: "Hullo, FE! Do you want to buy a station for forty thousand?"

"Yes. Where is it?" asked FE.

Morgan grinned. Then: "Langlo Downs, near Charleville. The actual price is forty-one thousand pounds, and there are about fifty thousand sheep on it."

The state of the money market was frigid. Buyers were few and cautious – all except FE, whose belief remained strong that the time to buy is when everyone wants to sell. Patrick O'Brien, that other courageous man, was still in Sydney, retired from active life but still capable of getting a kick out of a deal of this kind. O'Brien's faith in Queensland was like a shining star. FE knew quite well what O'Brien's answer would be when he received a wire asking if he cared to join FE in the purchase of a sheep station.

Together with Mr Millar, who had managed Langlo Downs for many years, FE inspected the property.

"Are all these sheep station-bred?" he asked, when they were sitting in a station buggy looking at the flocks.

"Yes. All of them" Millar replied.

FE's gaze swept over the flock. It took in the surrounding land. To him it was familiar, this land to the north-east of Charleville, these rolling hills forming the northern extremity of the Paroo Range. Not far away were Fairlie Station, once owned by John Howie, and Williams' Station, once owned by Ridley and Bob Williams. FE had worked for the Williams brothers, and then for John Howie back in the days when he had left Albermarle to seek the pot of gold. Then it had been cattle. It had been cattle ever since. Now it was sheep.

"No country can be bad which can breed such good sheep," he said. "I am satisfied to close for the place at forty one thousand pounds. Being on the telephone to Tambo, you can wire my acceptance."

Forty one thousand pounds! When FE left Albermarle, he could not command the half of forty thousand pence.

In addition to the wire of acceptance despatched to the vendors, FE wired to William Cain requesting Cain to act for him, and to confirm on his behalf the acceptance of the property.

William Cain at once replied: "McCulloch says price is forty-one thousand five hundred."

FE wired: "Never mind. Close for cash."

O'Brien and he now were sheepmen.

2.

1906 was a wonderful season. It rained nearly every month and the grass and herbage were phenomenal. The number of sheep on Langlo Downs proved to be 55,000 and the summer drop of lambs was over 15,000, so within a few months of FE's part-ownership the place was carrying over 70,000. Besides the sheep, there was a small herd of cattle and a number of horses. The first sale of surplus sheep was a mob of 10,000 wethers at 11s per head. The wool clip was a heavy one, filling over eleven hundred bales and selling in the vicinity of £15 per bale. On the first year's operation, the station returned a handsome profit.

FE spent the winter months on the property inspecting its every acre and planning necessary improvements. Some time in September, he received particulars that the adjoining run, Listowel Downs, was for sale at £52,000. The stock comprised 52,000 sheep off the shears, a few hundred head of cattle, riding horses, a valuable plant of teams (both bullock and horse), wagons and everything needed for the working of a big station.

The reader needs little imagination to know what FE did next! He lost no time in inspecting Listowel Downs. The homestead is situated on the Blackwater Creek, centred in rolling downs supporting mitchell grass and lightly timbered. The poorest section of its land lay against Langlo Downs and, the homesteads being only fifty miles apart, FE saw that the two properties could be worked as one.

Yet again wiring to O'Brien that he was on his way with an attractive proposition, FE hurried to Sydney. Together he and his old partner called on the General Manager of the Bank of New South Wales.

"You can have what money you want," he said, and then added frankly: "I have never hesitated to advance money to you gentlemen but, FE, this time you don't pay it back as quickly."

"What! Don't you want your money back?"

"By all means – but not too soon. We like to see our money out on interest, and when it comes back we have to find another honest borrower."

FE closed for the property with Mr Hallimore, the General Manager of the Union Bank in Melbourne, who explained that the shearing was proceeding on Listowel Downs, and that the delivery date must be the last day of the shearing.

"What are you going to do with the wool?" asked FE.

"Ship it to London, as usual," replied Hallimore.

"Would you care to put a price on the clip?"

"Yes. Twelve thousand five hundred pounds, subject to the wool going the usual channels for sale in London."

FE's mind worked with lightning speed. He had had nothing to do with sheep before the purchase of Langlo Downs except for his short apprenticeship to the pastoral industry at Albermarle, but he had habitually followed the wool market and was as conversant with it as he was with the meat and cattle markets.

"Very well" he said swiftly. "I'll buy it at that price and on those conditions."

He paid £12,500 for the clip, which sold in London for £18,000.

3.

In 1907, the sale by auction of Mitchell Downs on August 7 was advertised. It was situated fifty miles west of Roma on the Western Railway, and comprised 30,800 acres of freehold and 300 square miles of leasehold. On it were 15,000 sheep and 4,500 cattle.

FE was then in Brisbane and he found that he could just manage to travel by train to Mitchell Downs, 375 miles out from Brisbane, devote one day to the inspection, return to Brisbane in time to catch the train to Melbourne and be present at the sale at 3 o'clock on August 7th.

The inspection satisfied him, and on his way to the southern capital he called on O'Brien at Sydney. O'Brien still was game to invest, as his confidence in FE was based on the firm foundations of nearly a dozen great pastoral properties, and again they called at the Bank of New South Wales and arranged a credit for a further £50,000. That done, FE continued the journey to Melbourne, where he arrived at 1.30 pm. He lunched at Scott's Hotel, where the auction was to be held that afternoon.

There was only one other serious buyer after Mitchell Downs - Mr Lewis Kiddle, who owned Carabest in New South Wales. FE provided the auctioneer with a start at £30,000. Mr Kiddle bid an advance of £500. FE raised the bidding by a similar amount. Both persisted. When the bidding had risen to £40,000, Mr Kiddle jumped it up by £5,000. FE continued with £500 bids until Mitchell Downs fell to him under the hammer at £46,500. It was a cash sale.

The then manager, Mr F A Deshan, had been in control of Mitchell Downs for about fourteen years; FE was glad to accept the continuance of his service, which were rendered him for the following twenty years.

The seasons now were fair to good until 1914, when many parts of Australia suffered drought. The war broke out and the world was upset for four years and longer. Then came the beginning of nearly a full decade of remarkable prosperity for Australia. Government borrowing rose by leaps and bounds. There was never going to be another trade depression.

4.

Queensland has been tragically unfortunate in its politicians, and that section of the Queensland people which has provided the greater part of the wealth of the State has been the greatest sufferer from their greed for votes and their incompetence. The determination of politicians to repudiate the obligations entered into by the Crown with men who had given their lives and their fortunes to create Australia's greatest industry and upon which hung the people's prosperity or damnation was first born in the

Amendment Act of 1902. A further attempt was made to achieve this dictatorship over the pastoralists in 1915, when the Minister for Lands boldly took up the position that since the Government was so much in need of money and the graziers were experiencing prosperity, the fifty per cent limit of rent increase afforded them should be abolished, and their rents should be assessed by a Court untrammelled by any limitations. The Court was, of course, to accept its order from the Minister.

To counter this menace, a most influential deputation representing pastoralists, grazing farmers, financial institutions and others interested in the land was formed to wait upon the Minister for Lands on December 3rd 1915. Unaware of this, FE reached Brisbane at ten o'clock that day. Shortly after his arrival at his hotel, Mr A D Walsh called to place the facts of the deputation before him and urge him to become a member of it and speak. FE consented, although there were only two hours in which to prepare a speech.

Mr Kirwan MLA introduced the deputation. Mr J A Walsh, solicitor to the Pastoralists' Association, dealt with many of the objectionable clauses in the proposed bill and then came to what the pastoralists regarded as crucial alterations which were contained in clauses 8 and 30. These repealed the restrictive provisions and limitations provided by section 43 and section 109 of the principal Act, whereby rents of pastoral holdings and grazing farms acquired prior to 1902 could not be increased by more than 50 per cent on the preceding period. The deputation considered that three provisions of the principal Act should be retained. From the very start of the land laws in Queensland, it had been recognised that some limitation should be imposed on the raising of rents of pastoral leases. Under the 1869 Act a Promise of Lease was for twenty-one years in three periods of seven years. The first, second, and third periods of the lease were fixed and definite at 5s, 10s, and 15s per square mile. Under that Act there was a fixity of rent and definitions that enabled the pastoral lessees to know exactly how they stood.

Under the 1884 Act the limitation was imposed that the rent was not to exceed 90s. Then came the 1886 Amendment Act, where they had the limitation imposed in similar terms to those in the present Act – namely, that the annual rent for each period after the first year should not exceed the annual rent payable for such preceding period by more than half. Under the Land Act of

221

1897 an alteration was made, and while the limitation was maintained, the 1884 provisions were re-enacted, with the limitation of not more than 90s.per square mile.

Then they had the Act of 1902, which did affect limitation, but provided that the rent should be reappraised in the event of a portion of the lease being resumed for public works. The 1905 Act reimposed the provisions of the 1886 Act, limiting the increase to 50 per cent. Then there was the Land Act of 1910, by which the same provision was again re-enacted in the codification of the land laws.

So from 1869 the principle of limitation of increase of rents had been recognised. They contended, too, that under the 1910 Act certain rights were given to Crown tenants. A contract was entered into by which other Acts were turned out and a fresh start was made, and a contract binding and definite was entered into between the Crown and its tenants. On the faith of that contract, many leases had been taken up, many advances had been made, and the Crown tenants had faithfully carried out their parts of the bargain. They had made improvements on the land, they had improved their herds and the value of the wool, thus bringing the pastoral industry to such a position that it was the leading industry in the State. These being the conditions in the history of the land laws of Queensland, they submitted that it was not the right thing for the Government now to repeal these sections. They went further, and said that it really amounted to a breach of faith with the Crown tenants, and he – Mr Walsh – did not think he would be expressing the true feelings of the deputation if he did not go so far as to say it was clear repudiation.

When Mr Walsh sat down, FE rose to address the Minister for Lands. He spoke deliberately, saying: "The previous speaker has dealt so exhaustively with the different classes of the Bill that I think it will be sufficient if I confine myself to a few remarks on clauses 8 and 30 which affect the limitation of rentals.

"I view with considerable alarm and anxiety the proposal to rescind the clauses of the principal Act. I view with apprehension a clause abolishing the very foundation on which the whole fabric of the pastoral industry has been built – namely, reliance on the good faith of the Government. I venture to say that never could the Queensland pastoral industry have

222

expanded to its present dimensions without liberal land laws and absolute faith that whatever happened the Crown leases or, as was formerly the case, promise of leases, would stand inviolate. This faith also must have been shared by financial institutions, otherwise they never would have advanced the money, without which the country could not have been developed, and when I look back on my earlier years, I can but admire the courage of those institutions which, in the face of many losses and discouragements, continued to back up the pioneers with financial aid.

"The pastoralists have not always had good times, and certainly during my first thirty years in this State the Crown had the best of the bargain. Yet there always was that abiding faith in the Crown, backed up by hope that, if a man stuck long enough, he was bound to come through. If these clauses are rescinded, I would not like to say what the effect will be on public confidence, because we know that commerce and civilisation are based on public faith.

"Then there is the injustice to innocent transferees and people who purchased on the faith of Government leases. Some of these might have given a little more than they otherwise would have done in consideration of a favourable rental and in the faith that the Crown would respect the bargains."

"Do you think there is any sporting chance taken in business?" asked the Minister.

"Yes. Always. That is what we rely on," replied FE. "If we go down, we do not cry. We try again."

"What I infer" persisted the Minister, "is that there is rather not so much faith as the hope that it may not happen."

"I am referring to the faith we have had in our contracts and covenants with the Crown," FE said stiffly. "I say that I look back with pleasure to the confidence and good feeling that existed between the Crown and pastoral lessees many years ago. I would not like to see that confidence destroyed, because it may have a very bad effect, not only in the State, but outside it. To show that the pastoralists have not always had good times, I will go back to the early seventies, when the first run I was connected with (Monkira) was abandoned after sixty thousand pounds had been lost in twenty-five years. In that time upward of ten thousand pounds had been paid to the Crown in rentals, for which was given liberty to the occupier to try and work out his own salvation, and a promise of lease, on faith of which those men persevered until the last shred of hope disappeared.

"The next run with which I was connected had been taken up in the 'sixties (Miranda Downs), soon afterwards abandoned and the lease forfeited. In the early 'eighties, the unexpired term of lease was bought from the Crown at auction and another start made. In twenty years the owners lost sixty thousand pounds of capital and then, disheartened by the apparently hopeless condition of affairs they sold at auction all their interest in the lease, thousands of pounds worth of improvements, and ten thousand cattle for a sum equalling about half of that which had been paid to the Crown in rentals.

"From 1890 to 1902, I was managing partner of two runs in the Warrego district (Riverleigh and Authoringa). The net loss to my firm at the end of that period was twenty-four thousand pounds. It cannot be said that this was through want of enterprise on our part, for we made dams and tanks, erected fencing, and sank three artesian bores which alone cost six thousand three hundred pounds. In 1901, I and a partner purchased a run (Magoura) that had used up the lives and the resources of two men and ruined a third, and I could go on and mention other runs with which I have been personally connected, either as manager or part owner, that have had similar histories. No one of these ventures was very encouraging, but in all cases we went on solely in the faith that whatever happened we could rely on the conditions and provisions of the lease so long as we performed our part.

"In 1901, with a partner, I purchased some scattered occupation licences and blocks held under the Pastoral Leases Extension Act of 1869, together with ten thousand cattle (Inverleigh). The intervening areas were dry, and so the herd could not be increased without costly improvements in the form of artesian bores, dams having proved a failure. After correspondence with the Lands Office and interviews with the Minister, in 1905 we accepted a thirty years' lease under the 1902-5 Lands Act. This latter Act limited increase of rentals to 50 per cent in the several reassessment periods, and, on the faith of that, we accepted all the intervening areas to be included in the lease. This increased our mileage from approximately 1,400 to 2,314 square miles, and of this area, 654 square miles was classed as salt pans and mangrove swamps, so that our rental was very much increased.

"In addition, we undertook to spend six thousand pounds on artesian boring, and in fact we spent seven thousand pounds plus a further eight thousand pounds on fencing and other improvements.

"All this money we expended on the faith in the lease we held. It enabled us to double the number of the herd, and so increase our earnings and the State's production, in which the State benefits as much as the individual. I have been in Queensland for forty-three years – thirty years in the back country – and, in that time, I have for my partners and myself put down twenty-four artesian and sub-artesian bores, at an approximate cost of twenty-two thousand pounds. I have paid to the Crown anything from £50,000 to £75,000 in rentals, and in countless ways I have improved the Crown's domains. All on what? It was on faith. The Crown gave us the use of the land at a rental we thought could not be exceeded beyond the statutory limits. The financial institutions found the money, and they helped us to do the work.

"My excuse for so much ego," FE said in conclusion, "is that the experience of the older pastoralists of the State will be found to be mainly privations and financial reverses during the best part of their lives, but always sustained by that faith in the inviolability of Crown contracts. If this faith is to be upset, it will knock the props from under the whole structure of national credit, and I fear that the injury it would do the pastoral industry would take a long time to repair."

The result of the deputation to the Minister for Lands was that the limitation of increases of rental beyond 50 per cent was not interfered with in the New Land Bill – at least not then.

5.
However, the Official Mind became obsessed with this idea of being free to raise pastoral rents when it wished, and by the increases it wished. Some Treasurers were more influenced than others, but none of them went to the dangerous lengths reached by Mr Theodore.

In 1920 Queensland was guarded from wild and irresponsible legislation by an Upper Chamber - the Legislative

Council - whose members were appointed by the Governor acting on the advice of Cabinet. Under Premier Ryan, though the Lower House passed the Bill to which the deputation to Minister for Lands had successfully objected, the Bill was then thrown out by the Upper House.

On Mr Theodore becoming Premier, however, he succeeded in having a sufficient number of his own partisans appointed to the Legislative Council to create a majority subservient to his will, and again the measure known as the 'Repudiation Act' was brought forward and this time passed by both Houses.

The whole of the press of Australia, excepting extreme Labour, denounced the Bill and described such legislation as seriously damaging to the credit and the honour of the country. A scathing article appeared in the London Times under the heading 'The Pirate State'.

The passage of the Act not only took the lid off, it not only destroyed the sanctity of agreements, but by it the Queensland Government set an example for other Governments in Australia to follow when the first chill breath of adversity blew. The Act went further in giving the Official Mind freedom to do what it liked to its now defenceless victims. It was made retrospective, and thus placed an immediate and a heavy burden on those who had suffered drought, the pests and catastrophes, but who had conquered the wilderness and had played important roles in assisting the State's growth. The Ogre metaphorically licked its chops and got to work.

"Pay or be dammed!" it snarled.

In one instance, the rent was increased by over 300 per cent; to appeal for justice was useless.

The rent increase, the retrospective charges, the costs of appeal concerning those properties controlled by FE accounted to more than £10,000, plus the additional annual charge of £1,203. The official outrage was committed in a good-years period. When the inevitable bad-years period came, rents were not reduced to meet it.

6.

What years they were, the 1920s! Wool prices steadily increased. A line of Listowel Downs' wool brought £54 per bale. Even the rabbit trappers were making money, for rabbit skins averaged 7s per pound, and certain classes rose to 110 pence per pound. There was very little dealing in station properties. Owners would not sell, but selections changed hands time after time, and at an ever-increasing price. Some of them, without stock and just the leasehold tenure, changed hands at over £1 per acre, while others were sold at £2 and £3 per sheep on them.

From the very day of their purchase Langlo Downs, Listowel Downs, and Mitchell Downs proved to be profitable, and reached a peak in 1924, the balance sheet concerning the three properties showing a profit for the year at £90,039.

Men were talking not of the possibility, but of the probability, of wool going to five shillings per pound. Everyone was earning good money – and the majority were recklessly spending it. There was never going to be an end to this prosperity. Wages and salaries were going to increase and increase, always and always. It was a wonderful world, and Australia was an extra wonderful part of it.

The higher prices rose, the greater and more frequent became the loans on the London market. Political parties out-promised and out-borrowed each other, but there were men in banks - unassuming, unheard of men - with their fingers on the financial barometer, who knew what the end of this prosperity would surely be.

They, and FE with them, knew the causes of previous slumps, and they knew that within this amazing prosperity were hidden these same identical causes predicting disaster. FE had not forgotten the bank smashes of 1893, when he had to ride after his drovers with a bag of sovereigns because banknotes were valueless.

Still, there was no good to be obtained by running to meet the Devil. No one could make a reasonable guess as to when the next depression would arrive, and although he played for safety, FE did not believe the crash would come for a year or two yet.

Early in 1925, he took passage for England with Mrs Cobbold and Miss Wish, sister of the manager of Hughenden, giving instructions to the manager of Listowel and Langlo Downs to sell up to fifteen hundred head of cattle before leaving. On his return the year following, he found the weather conditions in Queensland indicative of drought, and he sent instructions to the same manager to sell stock and keep selling. Forty thousand sheep and several thousand cattle were sold off these two properties.

The lease of Mitchell Downs finally expired in this year and, since it was now infested with prickly pear despite all efforts to keep it down, FE did not want an extension of leases for any part of it. Even if he had wanted to, he could not have secured an extension, for there was a brisk demand from selectors to take up the whole run. The market was still firm so the manager, Mr Deshan, was able to dispose of the herd of cattle for £16,000.

There was about 36,000 acres of freehold lands left on Mitchell Downs and 12,000 acres secured under different tenure. Mr Deshan owned a neat little property not far away, and was happy to retire – by then he had been the manager of Mitchell Downs for thirty-four years. FE was determined to sell, and eventually the property was sold on a walk in walk out basis to a Sydney firm for the sum of £91,000 cash.

It will be remembered that the purchase price in 1907 had been £46,000, but in the interim FE had steadily improved the place and increased its stock-carrying capacity; in addition, world prices were infinitely higher in 1926 than they had been in 1907.

46. *Copy of the certificate of marriage between FE's niece Mildred Cobbold and Harold Lowe on 21ˢᵗ July 1925. FE was visiting England at the time and was a witness at the ceremony*

CHAPTER TWENTY

Horses

1.

The time came when FE no longer found it necessary to take an active managerial part in the development of the stations he bought from time to time. By 1910 the pastoral industry had passed beyond the pioneering phase which demanded constant personal attention to all its details. With the advent of wire, windmills, and the internal combustion engine, the working of a run was simplified. The old illiterate shepherds gave way to an intelligent race of stockmen, and the owner-pastoralists gave way to managers whose education included much study of the results which had been procured by the pioneers through bitter experience.

The coming of the internal combustion engine revolutionised the pastoral industry and the outback changed almost overnight. Cobb & Co's horse-drawn coaches and their poetry-reciting drivers vanished, to be replaced by fast motorcars driven by keen-eyed youths wearing English cloth caps back to front. The swearing horse and bullock drivers, with their teams and tabletop wagons, faded from the landscape, their places being taken by the swifter motor trucks. The owner-manager driving his buckboard, accompanied by his blackboy bringing on spare animals, became a figure of the romantic past. His modern prototype covers as much ground in a week in a motorcar as he was able to cover in three months. In the old days men drove behind horses, or rode on horses, to make an inspection of the bores and wells. Nowadays a youth is sent to do the same work on a flashing motorcycle.

The change gave the owner-manager more leisure without loss of efficiency. In fact, the change increased his efficiency because it gave him additional time to be used profitably in other directions.

From those early days of his bush apprenticeship on Albermarle, FE loved horses. We have seen how he took over those mounts broken in by Maori Jack and the Murrumbidgee Sticking Plaster, to ride them until finally they had lost their fear of Men and yet retained intelligent docility. When McGuigan made him a present of Hector, that clean-bred animal of courage, intelligence and stamina, he also gave FE that interest outside one's vocation which goes so far in making life worth living. The Picnic Races of those early years in the Gulf country reveal how clean and wholesome horse-racing can be, how men can follow it in the same clean spirit which animates those playing a cricket match.

Horseracing, unfortunately, has become a Jekyll-Hyde sport, to be followed not only by those whose love of horses provides them with a thrill of pleasure when watching them, but also by those whose interest is not in the animals but in the money to be won or lost on the contest.

That FE is a gambler goes without saying, but he did not contest with the single object of accessing money and has frowned on punting in a big way on or off the racecourses.

2.

FE's greatest horse was one purchased very early in his racing career - or, rather his hobby, because racing was never more than a hobby with him. In 1912 Irving Wheatcroft imported a horse called Cesarion from America with twelve of his yearlings. The pick of them was destined to make his mark as Conquistador. During the two years and nine months prior to his departure for Australia, Cesarion was represented by fifty-two two-year old winners, whilst he himself was a great race-getter, having raced for six seasons and winning thirty-six races.

FE purchased one of the two colts brought to Australia and it is well worthwhile producing part of an article on the colt and its owner written in a Brisbane sporting paper:

'Prescott's History of Peru tells us that the Spaniards of old who sought fresh fields in South America were known as the conquistadors of Peru. Conquistador (the native pronunciation is Conkistador) is Spanish for conqueror. Appropriate, is it not, that we should have the most consistent horse racing in Queensland today so admirably titled? Conquistador has been the all-conquering horse of the metropolis since the inception of the new racing year. Nomenclature of horses is quite a fascinating subject, and in Mr F E Cobbold, owner of Conquistador, it has an interested student. Three names were chosen before he was finally 'christened'. The other two – Circassion and Centurian – were not acceptable to the Registrar for the reason that they already appeared in the official register

... The alliterative 'C' in the names Conquistador, Circassion, Centurian can be appreciated when it is pointed out that Mr Cobbold follows the plan of beginning the names of his horses with the same letter that characterises the sire. Hence it is that we find his colt Bradbury blending in letter with the sire Benzonian; likewise Minchinhampton, a son of Martian. Bradbury's name was selected from one of a volume of sporting magazines of the nineteenth century which were heirlooms left by Mr Cobbold's father, and which were printed as early as 1820.

'Ever since the establishment of horseracing as a sport, racing and betting have gone hand in hand – in fact, gambling is its very essence. But, glad to say, there are many high-minded and right-spirited gentlemen associated with it who do not make the noble animal 'an instrument of gaming'; nor do they become infatuated with the passion of 'picking winners'. Mr Cobbold is one of them, and it is such men of stainless honor and true sporting instincts that imperishably stamp their names upon the records of turf, of which they form such a welcome part. Just before the Stanley Plate was to be run at Ascot on Saturday last, I chanced to hear Mr Abe Barrington jocularly ask the owner of Conquistador whether he cared to be accommodated to the extent of £3,000 to £4,000. ... Mr Cobbold appreciated the 'leviathan' suave invitation, but adjourned to the totalisator and made a modest investment on his horse. As he sagely remarked to me later, 'I patronise the £5 ticket window when my own horse is running, and the 10s window when I back the other fellow's horse'. ...

'What I set out to tell was something of Conquistador's breeding and performance, unique as his achievements on the Queensland turf have been. When Mr Irving Wheatcroft, a well-known American sportsman, decided four years ago to ship his entire stud to Australia, Conquistador then was very young, having been foaled on May 23rd 1911. He was bought by Mr Cobbold at the sale of the American stock in January 1913, in Sydney, for 190 guineas. He started racing, rated as a three-year-old, before his third birthday, and all through a conspicuously successful career has been placed at the disadvantage of 'being foaled to English time'.

Conquistador is a beautifully proportioned, rich brown horse, He is by Cesarion (2) from Yelonda (19), by St Florian from Involved .... It is pleasing to know that Brisbane offers sufficient inducement to Mr Cobbold, who does not propose to send Conquistador out of the State in search of a wider field for conquest.'

To complete the combination of a fine sportsman and a fine horse there was the trainer, W Prosser - a man short of stature, short of speech and able and more than willing to keep his own counsel - and, lastly, the jockey Tucker, who was a good rider and who rode the horse in all his many races in Brisbane.

On May 2nd 1914 Conquistador ran in the Walter Handicap at Ascot, Brisbane, and gave a great battle to Rolad, being beaten by only a length. He was described as 'a grand little chap' when he won the Trial Handicap on Cup Day at the Queensland Turf Club's Meeting on June 5. With twenty-three competitors against him, he won by three quarters of a length

after a terrific struggle against Mulgawillah. At the QTC Meeting on August 8, he won the Ascot Handicap by a length and a quarter from King Cleo; and then in Tattersalls Flying Handicap on August 16 he won an exciting race and finished brilliantly by beating Ruinall by a short head.

47. *Oil painting of Conquistador*

'Conquistador strikes Form' the papers said when he won the First Division at Albion Park. 'Conquistador Wins Again' the papers cried when he won the First Division again at Albion Park on September 4. Winning the QTC Flying Handicap on October 2, the papers headlined him 'The Brilliant Conquistador', and 'Conquistador a Top-Notcher' they said when he won the First Division on October 30 at Albion Park.

On October 6, he won the Spring Stakes, Weight for Age, at the QTC Meeting, meeting several of the very best horses. In the King's Plate on November 13 Conquistador came in second, but on December 11 he won the QTC Stanley Plate, Weight for

Age, winning by a length from Loveacre - the papers roared – 'Conquistador a Crackajack!' Then again, at Albion Park he won the first Division Race in fine style in July of the following year.

Conquistador was then retired from the Brisbane turf and taken to Sydney where he always carried big weights and where he met the best company. He won the Flying Handicap at Sandwick, and the Rosehill Prince of Wales Stakes. In other races he gained four seconds and two thirds, and in his nine races in Sydney was only once out of a place.

His was a brilliant career, and finally he was retired to the stud at Hughenden, where he mated with ordinary station mares and sired a large number of successful country performers.

3.

FE paid three hundred guineas for Bradbury in Sydney. A New Zealand importation, this colt promised to be something out of the ordinary. He made his debut in Brisbane at the spring meeting of the Queensland Turf Club, and at his first start, ran third in the Hopeful Stakes. A week later, he ran second in the principal two-year old Stakes, while a fortnight after that, he won the Champagne Stakes. Subsequently he broke a blood vessel and was ruined.

Then came Minchinhampton, another New Zealand importation by Martian, New Zealand's premier sire. FE paid three hundred guineas for him, but he proved to be a rogue and no good for racing, although on account of his breeding he became a useful station sire.

Ormiston was bought for one hundred and fifty guineas. He was described as 'A Promising Youngster' and won his first and only race in good style at Albion Park Races in the Fourth Division Handicap on July 17. He was a horse of great promise, sired by Royal Artillery from Crafton Lassie, but unfortunately died of a twisted bowel. Paynim was another colt of promise, but his performance was disappointing. Yet another was a Cardinal Beaufort colt, and this horse and others were trained by Albert Carr whose misfortune it was to have a succession of FE's failures. Subsequently, in other hands, they did no better.

Tom Splendour, sired by Tom Wedgwood from Miss Splendour, was purchased for two hundred and fifty guineas. He was a lovely brown colt, with a small star, and not a fault

233

could be found with him. He was a real Splendour horse, upstanding, with a fine body, fore and hindquarters, and a head indicative of intellect and gameness. Nevertheless, this horse turned out a disappointment, and FE sold him to a Tasmanian sportsman for whom he won a number of races.

After taking up permanent residence in Melbourne in 1919, FE made another venture by buying a Comedy King yearling for eight hundred and fifty guineas. It was a fine-looking colt, but after winning a Trial Handicap at Flemington and a Corinthian Handicap at Mornington, he showed so little promise that FE put him in the auction room and so severed the connection.

FE's run of bad luck in picking winners was broken with his purchase of Taras, sired by Sea Prince from Kyaree. The price paid for this yearling colt was four hundred and fifty guineas, but he was worth it, for his mother's ancestry went back to the famous old Sappho.

Taras won the Geelong Gold Cup, Moonee Valley Caldermeade Handicap, and the Argyle High-weight; the QTC Welter, Stewards' Mile, and May Day Handicap; the Kyneton Maiden Plate, Mornington Purse; ran a dead heat for Aspendale Park Welter; ran second in VATC Charity Meeting Butler Welter, the VEC Benevolent Fund Welter Purse, Moonee Valley Edward Naylor Gold Cup, and other races. In the most important of these races, the Geelong Gold Cup, he carried 7 stone 6lbs. His winnings amounted to about £2,500, and eventually he was pensioned off to Hughenden Station.

The next to appear was Alesus, by Sea Prince, for which one hundred guineas was paid, but he gave such little promise that he very soon stepped off the stage. After him came a black colt by Devizes from the good old mare Kyaree. His career was a short one – one day he was sent out for a spell after having been broken in, but ran into a fence and broke his neck.

4.

After Taras, the next horse that performed creditably was Centauri by Great Star from Torbrooke, bought as a colt for two hundred guineas at Flemington. Broken in as a yearling, Centauri showed considerable promise, but after running two races fairly well as a two-year old he developed a suspicious knee. The vet advised a rest, and he was sent to Listowel Downs where he sired several foals. The knee trouble disappeared and FE sent him to A G Anderson at Brisbane; from April 1932 to August 1935 he won six races and was placed ten times, the money prizes amounting to just under one thousand pounds.

Danilo had an eventful career, winning between £1,400 and £1,500 in stakes and placings. FE leased this brown colt with the option of purchase for 500 guineas, exercising the option after the horse won the Doona Trial at Caulfield, on September 2nd 1933. In February and March of this year, Danilo had run a second at Williamstown, gained a third place in a race run at Caulfield and second place in the Gibson Carmichael Stakes at Flemington.

By Chivalrous from Operetta, Danilo turned out a good horse, and he might have gone far had not misfortune ended a promising career. On March 9th 1933, he won the Carnival Handicap at Flemington. On the 11th of the same month he ran third in the Batman Stakes at Flemington. In January 1934 he gained third place in the C F Orr Stakes at the Spring Meeting at Williamstown and then he came out a fortnight later to win the St George Stakes at Caulfield, where he met some of the best company in the land.

48. *Danilo winning the Carnival Handicap in 1933*

This brilliant race was followed by the Australian Cup in which he met trouble after the start. It was felt necessary to turn him out for a spell, and then he contracted a suspicious leg. FE decided to put him to the stud at Hughenden for a short season and watch how the leg progressed. Further misfortune occurred with the ship in which he was sent to Brisbane. The ship ran into a succession of heavy gales off the east coast, during which the animal was so knocked about that it had to be landed at Sydney where it spent three months in the veterinary hospital before being sent on up to Hughenden.

49. *Frank Cobbold and Danilo*

Villius, by Gay Lothario from Violet Hays, was purchased at the March yearling sales at Flemington for 350 guineas. A handsome chestnut colt, he revealed little promise at the beginning of his racing career, being an Also Ran in his first five races. Then on January 29th 1934, he went out in the Juvenile Handicap at Williamstown at about 30 to 1 and won with ease. In the following May, he ran second in the Juvenile Handicap at Williamstown, and then, after several races in which he showed poorly, he came out at Flemington on March 8th to win the Carnival Handicap, also at about 30 to 1. It is a strange coincidence that Danilo won the same race at the same time the same Thursday in the previous year.

50. *Villius winning the Carnival Handicap, 8th November 1934*
at the Melbourne Centenary Cup Meeting

In December 1934, Villius brought off the Laluma Handicap, the principal race at Koonee Valley, at about 20 to 1. On the 25th December, he ran second in the Hopetown Handicap at Caulfield, and ten days later he won the principal race at Ascot - The Commonwealth Handicap. Keeping in the ruck until

236

the entry into the straight, Villius came on with wonderful pace to overhaul everything ahead of him before the winning post was passed.

51. *Villius after winning the Laluma Handicap, 8ᵗʰ December 1934*

5.
FE's conviction was that horseracing is not the prerogative of rich men. It is when a horse owner bets heavily that he is almost sure to come out on the wrong side of the ledger. Any man having moderate means, who punts moderately if at all, and given a sound trainer and a knowledge of horses, may keep ahead of his expenditure.

FE just about paid his way, and in consequence he enjoyed a good deal of pleasure at little or no cost. Even in his racing, he had partners in the persons of the trainers, the jockeys, and the stable boys, for he gave them one-third of the horse's winnings in addition to the usual percentages and tips. Further, he never interfered with the trainers, so that the partnership was a happy one and everyone involved with the horse in the race was vitally concerned with his performance.

The major interest taken in his horses lay not in their actual racing performances, but in their growth and training from colts onward. And when all is said and done, that is the chief interest taken in horses by all lovers of the turf.

CHAPTER TWENTY-ONE

Years 1911 - 1935
Home Ports

1.

F A Brodie occupied an important position in FE's long business career. The two men had first met at the head of the Carron River in the Gulf Country when FE was on his way to create Miranda Downs from the wilderness. Brodie, accompanied by Lands Commissioner Warde, was then searching for good cattle country, and through the years he graduated to Stock & Station Agent at Croydon, and then at Sydney.

It was through Brodie's instrumentality that FE purchased several of his stations and sold his greatest property, Inverleigh. On his return from a trip to Europe in May 1911, FE met Brodie in Sydney.

"Do you want to buy a sheep station?" Brodie asked, the question having almost become a habit.

"Yes," promptly replied FE, "Where is it?"

Brodie produced the particulars of Hughenden Station situated a short distance from the township of that name, and some two hundred and thirty miles south-west of Townsville. It comprised 10,160 freehold and 84,962 leasehold acres and 1,614 acres for grazing - 96,736 acres in all.

The leasehold had just over 16 years to run at 36s per square mile rental and the grazing farm had 9 years to run at 2d per acre rental. It was stocked with 36,315 mixed sheep, 9,469 mixed lambs, 25 working bullocks, 86 mixed cattle and 111 mixed horses. The price was £41,000 cash.

FE was referred to Messrs Dalgety & Co, but the firm was unable to give him first offer as the property was under consideration by another buyer. However, on the chance that the intending buyer might not do business, FE took a second offer, and left at once for Hughenden by train to Brisbane, then by boat to Townsville, and finally again by train. The evening before reaching Townsville, he asked the Captain what time it was expected that they would berth, as it was vital that he catch the 7.20 am train for Hughenden.

"It will be worth ten pounds to me if I make the connection," he said.

"You'll catch the train all right," the Captain assured him.

FE did catch the train and that ten-pound note enabled him eventually to purchase Hughenden.

All day he was on the train, arriving at the township of Hughenden at nine o'clock in the evening and putting up at the Central Hotel, from which he telephoned Mr Cory, the manager of Hughenden Station. The next morning he was driven to the homestead in the station buggy in time for breakfast, and after that Cory drove him out on to the run. What he saw during the drive of only five miles from the homestead convinced him that the proposition was a good one because there was scope for much improvement. The methods of working it were antiquated, and consequently the labour costs were excessive.

"That will do," FE told Cory. "Drive back to the homestead. I wish to wire acceptance to Dalgety at once in case the other buyer has done so."

Since the owner of the property was on his way to England in a liner approaching Colombo, the situation was a little involved. The agents, Messrs Dalgety, asked £41,000 cash, but the other buyer was one jump ahead of FE. This buyer had recently inspected the place and had given Cory the impression that he intended to chase for it. But, after leaving Hughenden, the other buyer must have deliberated, because he wired his offer for £40,000 – one thousand pounds below the price asked.

The ifs in this case are illustrative of FE's success in life.

Having decided to inspect the property and to offer for it if satisfied, FE delayed not one unnecessary moment. If he had not taken the second offer, if he had delayed his departure from Sydney, if he had missed the connection at Townsville and if he had delayed wiring his offer from Hughenden, without doubt the matter would have turned out differently and four people would not have made the money they ultimately did through his direction.

On receiving the first offer of £40,000, Messrs Dalgety cabled it to the owner – Robert Gray - at Colombo. The reply Gray sent read: "Declined. Withdraw. Do not re-offer." FE's offer of £41,000 reached Messrs Dalgety at about the same time they received the owner's cable, but they cabled the second and higher offer, together with the assurance that a cash sale was certain. Gray received this cable just as his ship was leaving Colombo, and he had time to cable his acceptance.

Robert Gray was one of the early pioneers of Queensland, and his volume of reminiscences, published in 1912 and dedicated to 'my wife who was the first white woman at Hughenden', vividly describes the hardships and the tribulations encountered by those first courageous pioneers.

Gray took over Hughenden from his cousin Ernest Henry and lived there until FE bought the property. Physically a small man, Gray had a big heart. When he left the army in India he had attained the rank of captain, but his small capital was always inadequate to develop properly the enormous leasehold area he had acquired. He needed all his pluck, tenacity and resourcefulness, and when FE first saw Hughenden, he quickly grasped the peculiar financial difficulties Robert Gray had faced. He saw that money had been and was being spent unnecessarily because of lack of capital with which to carry out improvements and thus reduce wastage. The late owner had developed the place to a point and then had been forced to stand still, when it would have been better to have sold or relinquished part of his holding and to have concentrated on a smaller area.

To finance the purchase of Hughenden was beyond FE's resources at the time, as all his spare cash was employed with other properties. There was never any doubt of obtaining all the money he wanted from the bank, but as it happened, Mrs Cobbold expressed her desire to sell her shares in the Brisbane Tramway Company. These offered her a profit, and she was happy to re-invest in a concern which, in her husband's hands, she was convinced would also return a profit.

William Cain, who had got out of Inverleigh with fifty thousand pounds although he never saw the property, had died and left his fortune to his three sons. FE suggested to them that they might like to take a share in Hughenden or, alternatively, advance ten thousand pounds at bank interest. Aware of their uncle's flair for making money for his sleeping partners, they elected to take over a share between them. Consequently a partnership of four members came into operation, the division being nine-twelfths to Mrs Cobbold, and one-twelfth each to Robert, W H, and W C Cain. FE agreed to act as Managing Director.

He had then recently undergone an operation and, in partnership with O'Brien, he was the active managing director of

240

three other great properties. There never appeared to be sufficient outlet for his energies. The life he was living was not dictated by necessity; his tastes were simple and inexpensive. He had made a fortune sufficient to provide him and Mrs Cobbold with what are termed luxuries of life. The mere amassing of money had never controlled his thoughts, and his energies were never directed to that end. None of his many partners suffered loss or ever regretted their association with him. The bank was ever willing - almost anxious - to advance him money, and in this way became his partner. O'Brien, after his retirement to Sydney, did not hesitate to enter into partnership with him again. William Cain, through his partnership with FE, made fifty thousand pounds, and his sons were each to receive £15,000 for the one-third interest in Hughenden. It is an undoubted fact that FE made more money for his partners than he made for himself and, in addition, he did all the planning, all the work, all the

> William Cain's eldest son was Robert Cobbold Cain, born about 1880, went to Christchurch College, Oxford, became a barrister and died unmarried in 1935.
> William (Willie) Nicholas Cain was born in 1882 and married his cousin Dorothy (Dot) Sarah Cobbold in 1920. They both died in 1978 leaving two daughters, one son having predeceased them.
> Walter Cobbold Curphey Cain was born in 1884 and fought WWI in the RFA Special Reserve with 23rd Army Brigade, Australia Corps. He married Lily Shaw Parsonage in 1928 but died without issue.

necessary travelling, without taking account of the seasons or the weather discomforts. He begrudged his partners not a pound; he wanted only freedom of action, and in this lay the secret of his success.

Some men delight in creating the characters in a book, and others delight in portraying people and scenes on canvas. FE delighted in taking hold of a cattle or a sheep station, surveying its disadvantages, planning improvements, and creating a very much finer property. The Profit and Loss Account measured the accuracy of his vision, the success of his planning, and in that lay his satisfaction. The fact that he made one thousand, fifty thousand, or one hundred thousand pounds for a partner was of less concern than the fact that the money proved his plans and ideas, his recommendations and his judgements to be well founded.

52. *First day cover issued by the Isle of Man recognising the achievements of William Cain*

As with these many stations in which he had been actively interested, so FE retained freedom of action with Hughenden and threw himself into the labour of making it modern, and making it carry two sheep where earlier it had carried only one.

The only permanent water was in the Flinders River and the Mount Devlin Bore. A second steam pumping plant lifted water from the 1,100 feet deep Devlin Bore, since the level of the water in it was 250 feet below ground level. Fourteen miles from the homestead was Mount Walker Dam, now rapidly silting up, as were the several other dams of low capacity. One other bore had been put down, another partly put down, and the site for the fourth had been selected.

This site had been chosen by a water diviner named Corfield and, when referring to it, Mr Cory the manager said it was a pity that it was a mile away from the intersection of four paddock fences, from which a good water supply would provide water for stock in four paddocks.

"Shift the bore-site peg to the four corners," FE ordered.

"But the diviner …"

"We'll have the bore sunk at the intersection of the four fences," persisted FE.

The bore was sunk and an excellent supply of water struck. About a year later, FE met Corfield in Brisbane, who said:

"I see it reported in the paper that a big supply of water has been struck at my Number Four Site."

"Your Number Four site was moved a full mile to the adjoining corners of four paddocks," FE informed him, with a disarming smile!

In FE's experience of Queensland, divining for water is pure farce. Anywhere over the Artesian Basin water may be got by boring. Three further bores were put down on Hughenden where water was most needed, and in each case a good supply was obtained at around the expected depth.

At the Mount Devlin Bore, a receiving tank had been excavated from the earth from which the stock drank water pumped into it with a Marsh Pump. This pump was operated by a 14 hp boiler requiring forty pounds of steam to work it. During the dry periods, the receiving tank had to be filled every six weeks, and this necessitated the services of an engine driver and a bullock driver and team to cart the required furnace wood. This, plus the constant moving of the shearing shed engine to the river and back again, plus the wages of a man carting water in a tank on a dray, raised overhead charges beyond excuse, because windmills had arrived.

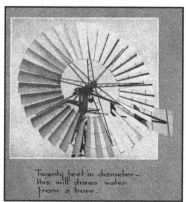

53. *Typical windmill fan*

"You'll never raise water two hundred and fifty feet with a windmill," FE was told by those who thought they knew.

He ordered a windmill which had a twenty-seven feet diameter fan-wheel, and this was erected to operate the Mount Devlin Bore and to raise water into receiving tanks from which it was piped into lines of drinking troughs. All the mill required was a little oil now and then. The old steam pump affair, demanding the wages and keep of two men and a bullock team, could be applied to other and more profitable tasks.

The water supply system on Hughenden was both antiquated and costly. Gray had attempted to get water by sinking a well on the ridge itself, when he would have been successful by sinking it on the river flat between the river and the ridge.

"It's no use sinking wells here," they told FE "Gray sank one and didn't strike water. You've got to bore for water here."

"Gray's well was sunk into clay for sub-artesian water. I'll sink a well nearer the river for river soakage water. If water can be got by digging a hole in the river bed, a hole to be filled in when the river flows again, it should be got off the river bed by a well that will not be filled in every time the river comes down," argued FE.

The shaft went down only thirty feet before water was reached. It was continued a few feet further to ensure a good supply, and then a 16 feet Hercules windmill was erected over the well. The mill pumped an endless supply of water to the receiving tank on the ridge, from which it gravitated to the several necessary supply points at the homestead and through pipes onwards to the shearing shed and the shearers' quarters. To this day the well serves all purposes at the homestead, and the high labour costs were replaced with the expenditure on a little oil.

The Well Boring Company went on sinking bores, seven in all; all were successful. Huge areas within the boundaries of the run were thus brought into stock use. Prior to FE's management, during the dry periods the stock were forced to hang about the Mount Devlin Bore and the wretched water-holes in the river, and every day to walk many miles out to feed and then many miles in again to water.

The last bore was put down in a part of the run known as Big Top which, being so far from water, had rarely been grazed over. A drought threatened, and FE was anxious that the bore should be completed before the summer was well advanced. He was in Brisbane when he received a wire from the manager, then Mr Wish, saying: "Bore down seven hundred and fifty feet. Struck water. Saltier than the sea." FE called at once on the manager of the Inter Colonial Boring Company.

"Salt water! That will demand boring elsewhere," said the manager.

To move the plant to another site would take time, and to put down another bore would take even longer. Time was a vital factor. The locality of Big Top was in splendid feed condition, whereas other portions of the run were denuded of feed growths. Before the bore plant could be moved and another bore sunk, the summer would be over and most of the stock would be dead of starvation. Here on Big Top feed was abundant, but without water it could not be brought into use. On the assumption that salt water floats above fresh water, FE took a chance. He telegraphed his manager: "Begin pumping at new bore at once. Keep pumping day and night until I arrive."

Reaching Townsville, on the way to Hughenden, there was a message waiting for him: "Have pumped three days and nights. Now pumping fresh water."

The new bore had tapped a small cavity of salt water lying above the vast store of fresh water, as FE had thought might be the case.

In the summer of 1915 all the stock at Hughenden was put into Big Top country to water at the last bore put down. They did remarkably well on this untouched country – 35,000 sheep and the cattle and horses, all herded together. Four thousand lambs were born during the period - and those 4,000 were bigger and stronger and heavier fleeced than any sheep Hughenden had ever bred. It proves how wonderful the Hughenden district was before the overstocking wiped out many of the indigenous shrubs and herbage and grasses.

When the seven bores had been equipped with self-acting pumping appliances and earth tanks had been excavated for standby reservoirs, FE turned his attention to the shearing shed, which was so eaten by white ants that every time the machinery was run it threatened to collapse. Plans were drawn up. The frame of the new shed was T-section steel built, fitted in Melbourne under the direction of a carpenter who had worked for William Cain on his railway constructions. The carpenter and his son then moved to Hughenden to erect the shed.

By the expenditure of capital, most of which would be returned when the final resumptions were made, FE achieved two results. He cut down what was an unnecessarily high labour bill, and he brought miles of country into use which was formerly lying idle and semi-idle, at the same time putting a stop to the body-wasting in animals which were forced to walk many miles to water and to feed.

The 1910 resumption from the Hughenden leasehold was effected at the time FE purchased the property, and in the beginning of his management he was faced with the loss of 17,701 acres. The remaining portion of the lease had just a few years to run, and when this was resumed – it was most unlikely that the lease would be renewed – the freehold property left, plus a priority selection block, would reduce operations to a minimum. Interest on the capital invested had to be made and the capital secured before the final resumption took place. The money spent on improvements such as fences and bores was secured in that the selectors would be required to pay the valuation before taking them up, the valuation being made by the Crown Land Ranger. In the event of disagreement between the outgoing and the incoming tenants on the valuation made by the Crown Land Ranger, the matter was settled by the Land Court. In consequence of this time schedule, FE had to make every post a winning one.

Back in 1870, when the runs in Western Queensland were held under the Act of 1869, Robert Gray had availed himself of this clause in his lease for making 10,160 acres freehold. Those leases were granted for fourteen years with the right of purchasing, without competition, 2,560 acres for every block of twenty-five square miles held. The opportunity in Gray's day of acquiring freehold did not last long because of official jealousy, and the Act of 1884 provided that re-issued leases should not contain the right of pre-emption.

With Hughenden, there was the 1910 resumption of 17,701 acres, leaving a freehold of 10,160 acres dependent on 80,000 acres of leasehold. FE had sixteen years to regain the capital invested, plus interest, before Hughenden lost something like 60,000 acres, and became reduced to a large selection. When Gray first held it, it stretched thirty miles above the homestead and thirty miles below it and was about twenty miles wide.

When FE bought the lease in 1911, the rent for the whole leasehold area was £236 19s 0d per annum. On the 23rd November 1917, it was increased from 36s per square mile to 54s per square mile, a total of £358 8s 6d per annum. There was no appeal allowed. No post-war Dictator has held greater power than that held by the Queensland Minister for Lands. On May 21st 1920, the Land Court determined the rent at 85s 10d per square mile, or £569 14s 4d per annum for the whole. The insatiable Government considered that the Land Court had not gone far enough, and in the following October the rent was again increased to 102s 6d per square mile – and then £2,123 retrospective charges back to 1914 were added. Had FE bought the property the year before, he would still have had to pay the retrospective charges.

Men have suffered the hangman's rope for robbery under arms. There is no moral difference between robbery under arms and robbery under the law when the law has been created through gerrymandering. The victim in the first instance had no appeal when a pistol was pointed at his head: he had no appeal when the threat of confiscation was presented in the second instance. If he should refuse to pay the extortion, he would be deprived of his leasehold and the surcharges deducted from the value of his improvements. That the leasehold system operating in Australia is rotten to the core will be obvious to anyone not obsessed with politics. That it causes Australia grave disadvantages in competition for world markets with Argentina, where the pastoralists know just where they stand with regard to the land they command, is also clear.

The leasehold system has created uncertainty and insecurity among the people. We have seen how it was when FE watered the Big Top and the 4,000 newborn lambs did remarkably well on virgin country. In less than one hundred years the heart has been eaten out of Australia. One hundred years on, unless the land occupiers are given security of tenure provided by freehold so that they can put back into the land what they have to take out of it, the stock-carrying capacity of Australia will be exhausted.

In 1922, with seven years of the lease to run out, FE found that the sheep numbers totalled nearly fifty thousand, in addition to a prolific drop of lambs. Before he left for England on June 6th, he gave orders to the manager to sell and keep selling; when he left, 13,000 sheep had been sold at good prices. On account of this selling, the dividends he distributed to the four partners amounted that year to £30,000.

Towards the end of the lease, the necessary disposal of the stock maintained the dividends. FE became anxious with regard to carrying on the freehold with only some twenty thousand acres of leasehold to support it after the final resumption. He therefore wrote to the Cain brothers explaining the situation, and giving his opinion that what would be left of Hughenden would be profitable only for a resident owner who would attend strictly to his business. The considerable profits in the past had been won from the leasehold of approximately 90,000 acres and at an average cost of about three halfpence per acre, and this had had to assist in carrying ten thousand acres of freehold at the cost of about nine pence per acre, including interest on the capital value of the land, rates and taxes. In short, the profits had been won from the leasehold, and the freehold contributed only a very small proportion. Further to this, FE pointed out that he did not think he could go on with the supervision, and he asked them all to say how they wished the firm to be wound up. The sale of the sheep off the leasehold land and the sale of the improvements to the incoming tenant selected was effected, and in 1934 a dissolution of the partnership was agreed on whereby Mrs Cobbold purchased the interests of the others at a valuation made by the Hughenden manager of the firm Winchcome, Carson & Company.

54. Hughenden Station

2.

Towards the end of 1913, FE saw the particulars of a property for sale in the west of Victoria named Yarram Park. It seemed likely that Mrs Cobbold was at this time beginning to rebel against the constant movement from one station homestead to another. What was the breath of life to FE, with his tireless brain and equally tireless body, had long lost any attraction it might have had for a lady like Mrs Cobbold, who naturally desired a real, permanent home, and a garden in which she could cultivate flowering shrubs and blooms. Staying at one homestead for a few months, to be followed by a period of hotel life, and that to be followed by another period of station life, was a manner of living which no woman in the world would find charming for very long.

Since he first set foot on the *Ann Duthie* FE had been constantly on the move. The Island of Sandwich had held him for some time – because there was no possible means of getting away from it. Monkira had held him for a year or more, but Monkira was the size of an English county over which he could ride and camp.

Perhaps it was the growing conviction, hateful though it was, that he would have to settle down sometime, that caused him to consider the purchase of Yarram Park. It was not in keeping with his past life. He was still determined never to retire if that could possibly be avoided. 'Go on or go under' had been his comfortable working philosophy. Yarram Park does not lie in the bush proper, nor does it possess any of the characteristics of an inland sheep or cattle station.

Situated at the foot of the Grampians, 180 miles west of Geelong and 220 miles from Melbourne, Yarram Park extended across 22,000 acres, and it carried some 15,000 sheep, 60 to 70 cattle, and the usual complement of horses, including enough draught horses to work the few hundred acres under wheat and oats for the working horses and the milking cows. For years Yarram Park had been noted for the growing of fine wool merinos, and in this connection it held a leading position from the early days of settlement.

The house was decidedly comfortable – a roomy villa built of stone and brick and roofed with slate – and costing £5,000. In all, it was a beautiful estate, suitable for the breeding of high class sheep and horses and a little mixed farming, but it was not a place to retain FE's interest for long, nor to restrain that questing spirit of his.

Accompanied by his eldest nephew, Robert Cain, he was present at the auction of the property. On his uncle's behalf, Mr Cain opened the bidding at £60,000. FE knew that the bid was not high enough to secure the property, and indeed it did not sell as there were no other serious bidders in a room full of spectators. By private treaty, FE then purchased Yarram Park for £79,000 which, according to the valuation of adjoining properties, was cheap.

A permanent water supply for the homestead was wanted urgently, and he began to rectify this drawback first. In Queensland he had been accustomed to putting down open tanks of from 12,000 to 16,000 cubic yards: here he found it difficult to find men who understood the peculiar work of dam making and, moreover, those who possessed the necessary plant.

In time a tank was excavated and the first of the winter rains provided a splendid sheet of water containing 6,000 cubic yards. Then, under the supervision of an architect from Hamilton, FE planned the addition of two small wings to the house and installed an improved lighting system, spending altogether a further £2,000.

It so happened that the first summer spent by FE and Mrs Cobbold at Yarram Park was the hottest for many years. They both found the humid heat of western Victoria much more trying than that of Queensland. With the purchase of Yarram Park, there followed a routine similar to that with which Mrs Cobbold was well acquainted, but which was not so wide in scope. She and FE spent the winter months at Hughenden and the summers at Yarram Park.

What woman would not tire of the everlasting setting up house, of moving from homestead to homestead, and being unable to make either of them a real home? Notwithstanding this, FE was reluctant to part with Yarram Park. It was a beautiful property. The seasons in western Victoria are regular. The wool clip from Yarram Park was regular. Drought was rare, and there was a certainty of steady income from it commensurate with the capital invested.

55. Yarram Park, Victoria, 1913

However, despite the attractions listed, after he had improved the property Yarram Park did not appeal to FE. It was neither a station nor a dairy farm, but something between the

250

two. Why, he could hardly move about on Yarram Park without having to open a gate! He had never become used to gate opening on those great properties of one thousand square miles and more on which he had spent most of his life.

Yarram Park would have ideally suited an English country gentleman used to viewing the boundaries of his estate from the top windows of his mansion. By a family arrangement, the property passed to the Cain brothers.

3.

In 1916, that grand old fighter Patrick O'Brien began rapidly to fail in health. He was then living at Leura, in the Blue Mountains, and for a year FE spent as much of his time as possible with this staunch partner, the last of the famous 'dividing mates'.

At this time O'Brien and FE were partners in Listowel Downs, Langlo Downs, and Mitchell Downs, but O'Brien's pleasure at welcoming FE had less to do with the business of these properties than in the prospect of recalling the old days at Green Hills, Forest Home and the wonderful Cumberland Mine.

In 1917, on the day he died, O'Brien signed the last Codicil to his will, with his doctor and his gardener witnessing his signature. FE received the news of Patrick O'Brien's death in Sydney that afternoon, and he returned to attend the funeral.

A clause in the deed of the partnership laid it down that the surviving partner had the option of buying the deceased partner's share in the pastoral properties at the values last appearing in the balance sheet. In consequence FE gave notice to the Executors of his intention to exercise the option but, at the request of the grandchildren who were the beneficiaries through their father, he withdrew the notice. Thus the beneficiaries retained their grandfather's share in the old partnership and, by the terms of the will and the articles of association, FE remained in sole control.

And so passed first William Steele, then Edward Hunt, and lastly Patrick O'Brien, three men who had pooled all their resources and taken equal shares out of that 'dividing mateship'. That is the most amazing partnership Australia has to offer against the rugged background of its early years of discovery.

251

4.

In 1919, Mrs Cobbold was still having to set up house for short periods at various homesteads, and FE was still being urged ever onwards by the same restless spirit that had roamed the South Seas and Northern Queensland. Advancing age made no difference to him either physically or mentally. In this year he was sixty-nine.

When he decided to make a trip to Tasmania, Mrs Cobbold elected to stay on at Petty's Hotel in Sydney. When he arrived in Melbourne, however, FE found the city quarantined because of a virulent outbreak of pneumonic influenza. Being placed at a loose end, he decided at long last to look about for a 'real home'.

Both Toorak and South Yarra attracted him, containing as they did many of the most beautiful homes in Southern Australia. An inspection of a score or more available houses left him cold, however, and he became determined to rent a flat from which he could wait for the opportunity to buy the kind of house he wanted.

He went to visit the estate agents, Kate Gardner & Lang, and fortunately he saw the lady member of the firm, who asked:

"Is it a flat you want?"

"No" replied FE "I want a house, and am tired of searching for one."

"Have you seen one you like?"

"Yes"

"Where is it?"

"The address is Number 7 Fulham Avenue, South Yarra, but there is no 'For Sale' notice there."

"We can sell it for you," the lady then said, and FE closed.

Miss Gardner proved to be a near neighbour, and afterwards she and Mrs Cobbold became friends. Their two houses joined at the rear and, when Miss Gardner retired to devote her energies to her garden, and Mrs Cobbold delightedly saw what was to be her garden, they set out in friendly rivalry to produce the most gorgeous blooms.

56. *Magnificent rhododendrons at Tilehurst, 7 Fulham Avenue, Melbourne*

> *In moving to Fulham Avenue, FE was close to Christ Church, South Yarra which had benefited from his brother-in-law's generosity. William Cain had given the font to the church in 1886 and the Baptistery was presented for the Church's Diamond Jubilee in his memory in 1916.*
>
> *But that was by no means the end of the connection. FE's niece Aida Arkins nee Cobbold (1898-1979) embroidered 40 kneelers for the Church, a font footstool with the Isle of Man emblem and a Minister's seat cushion and kneeling stool, which have been in use since 1968.*

5.

At long last Mrs Cobbold was able to enjoy the amenities provided by a real home, from which she could accompany her husband – at a lesser rate of speed and with less frequency – to Europe every three years, and to Hughenden for four or five months every winter. This 'settling down' came hard to FE, however. In Melbourne for seven months of the year, he missed something which the city could not give him, for which even his interest in his racehorses could not compensate. The indefinable, haunting charm of the Australian bush never relinquished its hold on him; the soft, alluring call of the bush lands forever called him back. It is a voice so much more powerful than the sea, so much more powerful than one's native country. As has been said before, onetime bushmen sit in offices and throw down their pens and relax into happy reverie if the caller mentions the bush.

Still interested in pastoral properties, FE sought the opportunity of acquiring a station or stations within easier reach of Melbourne than those in Queensland, and the opportunity occurred in November 1933, when he saw that Woorooma West, near Deniliquin, was for sale. After having inspected the place he attended the auction, but as the bidding did not reach the reserve, the property was withdrawn for private sale. Before he could act, it was purchased by the Vickery brothers of Sydney. Within a few weeks, he heard that the Table Top Estate, near Albury, was for sale following the death of the widow of the late James Mitchell. The Mitchell family had possessed the estate for nearly a century, and had occupied the place all that time. After protracted negotiations, FE bought Table Top - 19,000 acres freehold with 26,000 sheep and several hundred head of cattle.

Then he heard that Woorooma West was again on the market, and this time he bought it with its 23,660 acres of freehold and 10,000 sheep. These two estates, each being one day's motor run from Melbourne, and one day's motor run from each other, provided him with sufficient occupation and interest outside the partnership properties in Queensland, the supervision of which demanded an ever-dwindling amount of his time and energy.

57. *The homestead, Table Top Estate near Albury*

On 20th April 1934, Frank Cobbold typed the following letter to his niece, May Kerr, who lived in Frinton on Sea, Essex:

TELEPHONE
WINDSOR 2023

7 FULHAM AVENUE,
SOUTH YARRA S.E.1,
VICTORIA.
20th April 1934

Dear May

I have to acknowledge your letter of 6th March just after you had returned from a round of visits, the last one with the Francis Cobbolds at Ipswich; I am not surprised you like them both for they are both genuine, and she charming.

Dear old Waldringfield, I spent many happy summers there, and for many years I cherished the hope that some day I would return and buy the old place. I recollect one autumn my father, Lord Alfred Paget, and John Hill taking their guns down the river marshes and coming back with full bags of snipe. It was in the old shed at the back of the house where the duck punts used to be housed in the summer months for use in the winter for wild duck shooting on the marshes, I also remember the big room on the third story of the house with the big telescope for spotting the flighting ducks coming across the Deben River to settle on the marshes, then there were the mud pattens strapped to the feet of the sportsman to enable him to walk over the mud flats without being engulfed; those were bonny days.

... Yes the Hughenden partnership is dissolved. The brothers put £10.250 in to the venture in 1911 and have now taken altogether out of it £43.869 but would have come out of it better if they had taken my advice to dissolve before the expiration of the lease and the resumption by the crown of three fourths of the land, since then instead of a substantial annual profit the accumulated losses in the

years 1930/31/32 have been £4806/13/2 and for
1933 a profit of £38/3/9- not much to divide
amongst four, and not much hope in the future.
While the place was enjoying good seasons and
the average dividend was 24 per cent on the
invested capital it was a joy to me to
distribute the fat dividends, but after the
loss of the land I knew it to be impossible to
make the place a dividend payer for absentee
share holders, it was in 1920 or 21 Robert just
before leaving Melbourne for the Isle of Man
offered to sell me his share of the place which
I refused, for the next three years their
dividend amounted to £12,900.

     Three weeks ago poor faithful old Tim Wish
died, suddenly, his sister had gone up to nurse
him, he appeared to be getting better, when he
lay back and expired, it was mainly on his
account that I was reluctant to let the place
pass away for he had been for years a confirmed
invalid, and strangers would have turned him
out, it was forty years ago that he first came
to me, the manager was away in Sydney getting
married, the woman cook in Hospital with
pleurisy, poor Miss Wish left in that state but
good Samaritans from the town went out to her,
she is still there, went into the kitchen and
took the sick woman's place.

     ... I daresay Walter will tell you I have
taken more responsibilities in the purchase of
two properties both are within a days motor
journey from here and a days journey from each
other, one, Table Top Estate had been in the
one family for about 70 years and is close to
Albury, the railway to Sydney goes through the
Estate, the other place is about 80 miles from
Madowla on the Edwards River that had been
practically in the same family for about the
same time, Motoring over the Estate (they are
both freehold) about a fortnight ago ... everywhere we went there were flights of wild duck.

When I can get out of Queensland it will be my
desire to spend my winters there for there is
plenty of fishing in the river and shooting in
the paddocks. Your Aunt Bea likes Table Top
best there is a fine garden and a beautiful
view on every side Albury is only ten miles
away, and the town of Moulamein ten miles from
the other place Woorooma West, so I hope the
day is not far distant when I can exchange
Queensland for one or other of the two places
for my winter sojourn.

    Just while I am writing a letter has come
from Miss Wish saying she cannot return as she
has taken on the cooking until the old cook
returns from Townsville where she has gone to
recuperate after her illness, I am going to
give very imperative orders that she leaves
them to cook for themselves.

    ... Those poor things Mirabel and her
husband, could they not have got some thing to
do in South Africa that would have given them
food and shelter which I would think would be
easier obtained there than in England, but
perhaps there is no Government help there as in
England, If I were down and out I would go to a
warm climate, few clothes are required and food
is much easier got.

    Janie is still the same old self comes
smilingly to see us every week

    ... Danilo didn't win the Australian Cup
and is now on holiday for a time.

    Villius has only won one race which has
paid his expenses for a year but we have hopes.

    Last and most important of all we are
sorry to hear your eyes are giving you trouble
it seems the best alleviation is to rest them
as much as possible.

               Well I must now close
               Our love to you
               Your affect uncle
                 Frank.

A few months later, he wrote what may have been his last letter to his niece:

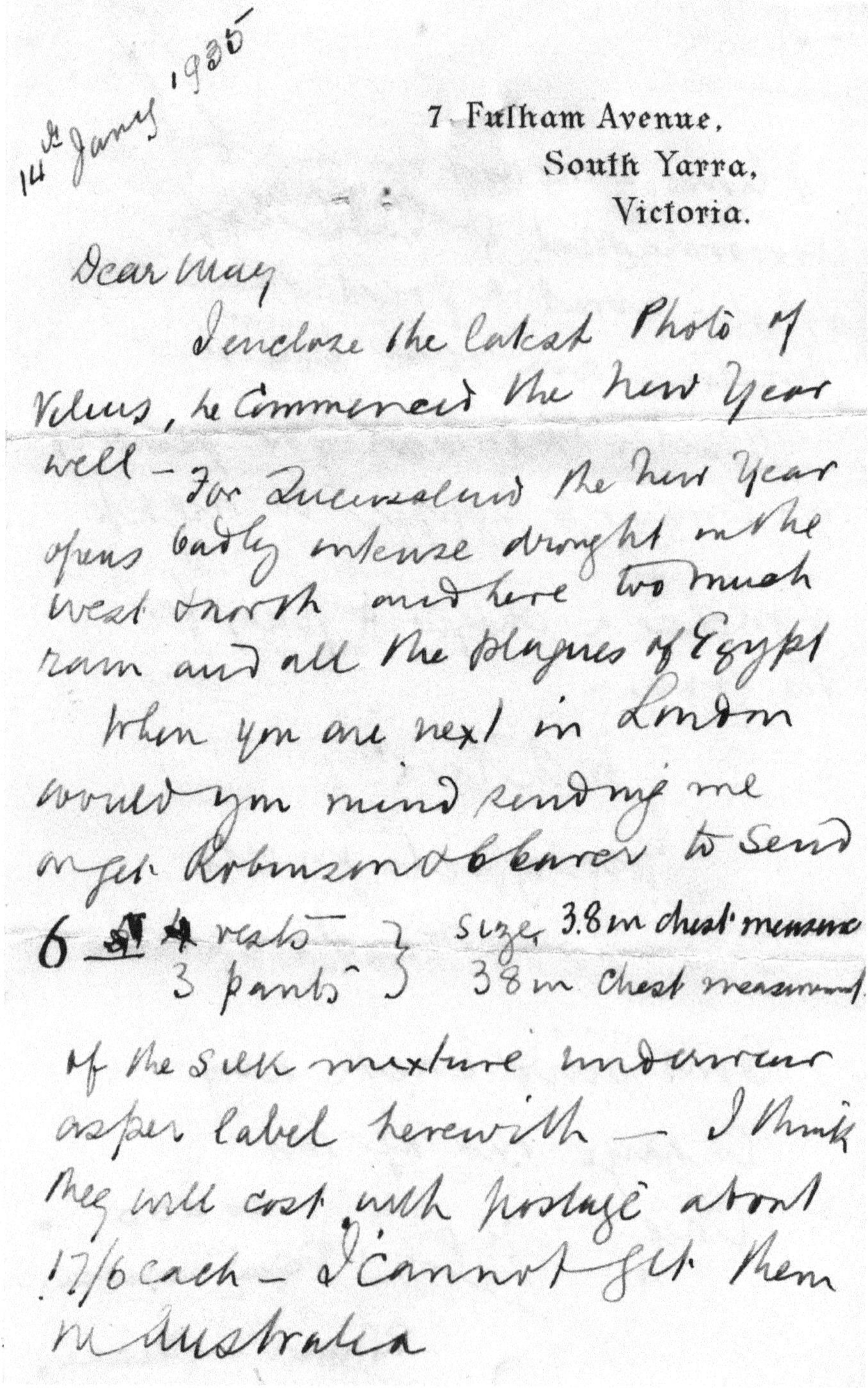

14ᵗʰ Jany 1936

7 Fulham Avenue,
South Yarra,
Victoria.

Dear May

I enclose the latest Photo of Vilius, he commenced the new Year well — For Queensland the new Year opens badly intense drought in the west & north and here too much rain and all the plagues of Egypt

When you are next in London would you mind sending me or get Robinson & Cleaver to send 6 vests ⎱ sizes 3.8 in chest measure 3 pants ⎰ 38 in Chest measurement of the silk mixture underwear as per label herewith — I think they will cost with postage about 17/6 each — I cannot get them in Australia

258

I leave to morrow morning for
Wowoomattest & Table Gap –
I motor about a great deal and
Sometimes am very tired –

Walter & Lily and Mr Spenning
are coming to supper to night
I enclose a cheque to pay for
the goods –

With love
Your affect uncle
Frank

Don't send back any
Change out of the
Cheq.   DO 5.6 0
            JEC   Refund underwear

                  Robinson – Cleaver.

259

CHAPTER TWENTY-TWO

Farewell

A visitor to 7 Fulham Avenue in 1935 would notice that, despite being eighty-four years old later that year, Francis Edward Cobbold carried his years well. Being still tall and straight, one would imagine him to be no more than seventy. Indeed, following him along the corridor and down the narrow stairs to the quiet, cool study at the rear of the house, the estimate would be sixty. He is a man of sixty who asks the visitor to be seated and seats himself at the writing table.

The lie of the ground slopes to the rear and beyond the windows may be seen a beautiful lawn girdled by flowering shrubs and beds of flowers. On the walls of the study, reminiscent of a ship's captain's cabin, hang picture after picture of Taras, Danilo and Villius winning their many races. Upstairs hangs an oil painting of the great Conquistador.

When the man of sixty speaks there is no doubt left in the visitor's mind that he knows exactly what he is talking about. When asked about the past, FE goes back in an instant, not only in the spirit but as though in the flesh. The years slip off him like a tired lady's cloak. How many cattle were there on Inverleigh when he bought it? How many tons of cement had to be taken to Station Creek with which to build the weir? What were the provisions of such and such an act? FE can at once supply the desired data. One forgets absolutely that one is in the presence of a man of four score years and three. The pleasant room fades, and one is sailing with him in that open boat across the Kandavu Passage, rafting his traded goods down the Rewa River, shooting pigeons in the jungle of Sandwich Island, pushing the hide boat in company with two blackboys and a white stockman across the five-miles-wide Diamantina River in flood, and with him in the little bush telegraph offices sending those messages to his partners: 'I am on my way with an attractive proposition.'

He is still controlled by the wanderlust. In the heat of the summer, a car tour of his pastoral properties, during which he covers anything from two to three hundred miles a day, is no more to him than those buckboard drives across North Queensland. Every week he receives reports from his station managers, and types out his own letters and instructions to them. He is as intimately acquainted with everything concerning those properties as ever he has been.

The visitor leaves the room and his presence with regret, for one has not been conscious of the passage of time. In racing circles, FE Cobbold is widely known as a good sportsman. In Australia's major banking institutions, he is known as the client who has never failed to keep his contracts. Enemies he has none. No one of his partners ever regretted being associated with him.

And so we say farewell.

58. Frank and Beatrice Cobbold, Frinton on Sea, Essex, 1934

FRANCIS EDWARD COBBOLD 1853 - 1935
BEATRICE COBBOLD née CHILD 1869-1951

261

EPILOGUE

It is clear from reading his remarkable story that Frank Cobbold had many gifts.

Physically he was a tough, determined, gritty man of boundless stamina who survived typhoid and many other challenges. In business he needed no gimmicks; he relied upon intuition, trust and integrity. His word really was his bond and, in modern parlance, he always delivered.

I would have liked to have met him. As it is, from reading his life story, I am sure he would have been proud of the use that Independent Age has made of his generous legacy. We remain enormously grateful for it.

Hamish Bryce
Chairman
Independent Age

THE GIFT OF INDEPENDENCE

After leaving a life interest in his estate to his wife, Beatrice, Frank Cobbold left his residuary estate to the Royal United Kingdom Beneficent Association (Rukba). He directed that it should be used to fund 'FE Cobbold' permanent memorial annuities of £36 for residents of Suffolk who were eligible under the charity's Royal charter.

His legacy was the largest the charity, now called Independent Age, has ever received, and it would not have been able to help so many people without it.

But who was Rukba and what difference did his gift make?

Frank Cobbold was ten years old when the United Kingdom Beneficent Association was founded. In those days the wives and children of gentlefolk could be made destitute and homeless if the breadwinner died and another male relative claimed the family property. Unmarried daughters depended on their fathers and the only acceptable work for them was as governesses or companions. The last resort, the workhouse, was unthinkable.

So in 1863, six philanthropists set up a society to assist middle and upper class folk over 40 and in difficulties. It paid lifetime annuities. One of the first people it helped was a 47 year-old woman whose clergyman father had died. She was so desperate she pawned her clothes and wedding ring to pay for food and would have starved to death in a rented room if the organisation hadn't come to her rescue.

In 1911 the charity received a Royal charter and it became the *Royal* United Kingdom Beneficent Association (Rukba). Why did Frank Cobbold choose to help this particular charity?

The most likely theory is that his solicitors recommended Rukba as an organisation that could be relied upon to meet the conditions of his bequest. His lawyers approached Rukba before the Will was written to ask if the charity would be prepared to accept such a specific gift. As Sir John Maude wrote in *The Story of the Royal United Kingdom Beneficent Association, 1863 to 1963*: 'It is scarcely necessary to record the reply to this letter'.

The gift was duly made and when Frank Cobbold's wife Beatrice died in 1951, the money passed to Rukba. The charity invested the money wisely, abiding by the stipulation in the Will

264

that required the capital not to be spent and only the interest earned would go to support the beneficiaries in Suffolk.

It soon became clear that the bequest was far larger than would be needed to help people in Suffolk, so Rukba applied to the High Court for permission to extend the conditions of Frank Cobbold's mandate and use the surplus to help people in other parts of the British Isles.

'The effect of this magnificent legacy on the development of the activities of the Association can hardly be over-emphasised,' wrote Sir John Maude. 'Not only has it enabled the Committee to increase the normal annuity of Suffolk annuitants from the £36 specified in the bequest to £108, but it has also made it possible for the scope of the Relief Funds to be widened.'

As well as £22,500 a year to be distributed among Suffolk beneficiaries, there were benefits for Rukba's other annuitants. Those in care homes received £1 a week pocket money and those in receipt of National Assistance received a Christmas gift of £5.

In 1954, an impressive 404 older people joined what Rukba called its *family*. It brought the total number of beneficiaries to 3,574, a new record.

Frank Cobbold also left Rukba his two Australian sheep stations. Ever the astute businessman, he was not content to bequeath the fruits of his labours without also bequeathing some sound financial advice. He made it a condition of the gift that Rukba set aside part of the yearly profits from each station to ensure their survival in years of poor return.

By 1960, the amount received from the Cobbold legacy was well over half a million pounds, excluding the stations. In 1965, the first sheep station, Table Top in Albury, was sold for £226,000. The proceeds enabled the charity to increase the value of annuities, which were being eaten away by inflation.

Eight years later, Rukba sold the second sheep station, Wooroomera West in Deniliquin, for £450,000. Just one of the many uses it found for the money was buying its new headquarters in Avonmore Road, west London.

The sale of the two stations roughly doubled the original value of the legacy and marked a turning point. With such considerable assets, Rukba needed to appoint an expert investment panel. Under the new panel's guidance, the FE Cobbold Trust Fund thrived and by 2007, was able to pay out £190,000 to beneficiaries while retaining a capital value of £9.6m.

265

Much of what the charity has achieved over the years is down to prudent investment of Frank Cobbold's gift. The charity's administration model has been so successful that today it manages a number of sister charities including the United Beneficent Society (UBS) and the Florence Nightingale Aid In Sickness Trust (FNAIST). This enables it to help people who do not meet Independent Age's criteria.

Frank Cobbold might be surprised at all the changes that have taken place since he made his Will.

The Rukba he left his money to changed its operating name to Independent Age in 2005. Its new name allows it to become better known and attract many more supporters, volunteers and potential beneficiaries. The charity now focuses its help on people over 70 from any background, provided they do not have income above its limit, have served their community by paid or voluntary work, and live in the UK or Ireland.

The £700,000 he left in 1951 is equivalent to £1.2m in today's money. The charity has multiplied the original investment eight and a quarter times.

In 1939, Rukba supported 3,260 beneficiaries. Today, 6,200 people are financially independent thanks to Independent Age, and 1,200 caring volunteers visit and befriend them.

When Frank Cobbold wrote his Will, the life expectancy of a male was 76 and of a female, 78 years. Today, it is getting on for 81 and 84 respectively. By the late 1980s the Government realised that people were living longer and it wouldn't be able to afford their care home fees. In 1990 it passed the Community Care Act to provide care for older people in their own homes for as long as possible. Frank particularly wanted his legacy to be spent on assisting people to stay in their own homes. His wishes will be respected as Independent Age develops help-in-the-home services and initiatives to keep older people involved in their communities.

Over the years, many inventions have arrived to make older people's lives easier - from powered bath seats to sophisticated personal alarms. In 2007, Independent Age supplied 4,500 beneficiaries with gadgets and equipment they had selected from its catalogues to keep themselves independent. It issues grants for unexpected costs such as taxi fares to hospital, new central heating boilers and convalescence breaks after surgery.

266

The charity also helps out in emergencies. So in July 2007, for instance, it came to the aid of a 94 year-old woman washed out of her Warwickshire home in the freak floods.

But this story began in Suffolk where Frank Cobbold wanted the proceeds of his lifetime's earnings to be spent. So it's to his home county that we return as we read about just one person helped by Independent Age.

Eighty-nine year old Mary Oakley* couldn't be more deserving of the regular extra income she receives from Independent Age. It helps people who have served others through paid or voluntary work, and she has done both.

An ARP nurse during WWII and married to a former Desert Rat, Mary was widowed at 42, with two children to bring up on her own. Despite these challenges, she went on to teach in an infants school from 1966-1988 and was a carer to her mother-in-law for a decade and a half. Incredibly, she also found time to be an active member of her parish council and church, and to run the district branch of the cub and scout movement.

But she struggled financially and when she saw a leaflet about the charity's work, she approached it for help. The volunteer who met her, reported: 'Mrs Oakley has devoted her life to helping others … Her flair for organization and leadership has led her to do a great deal of work with children and young people. Despite (lists Mary's difficulties), she has always found time to offer care and support to others'.

Independent Age's regular income gives Mary considerable peace of mind in her later years. She said: 'Thank you once again for your kind attention to me.'

In Suffolk alone Independent Age helps 200 people like Mary to live independent, fulfilled lives in their own homes. Thanks to shrewd investment of Frank Cobbold's legacy, it'll be helping people like Mary, throughout the UK and Ireland, for many years to come.

'Mary Oakley' is not her real name

If you would like more information about Independent Age, please write to: 6 Avonmore Road, London W14 8RL, call 020 7605 4200, email charity@independentage.org.uk or visit www.independentage.org.uk.

THE CATTLE AND SHEEP STATIONS
MANAGED/OWNED BY FRANK COBBOLD

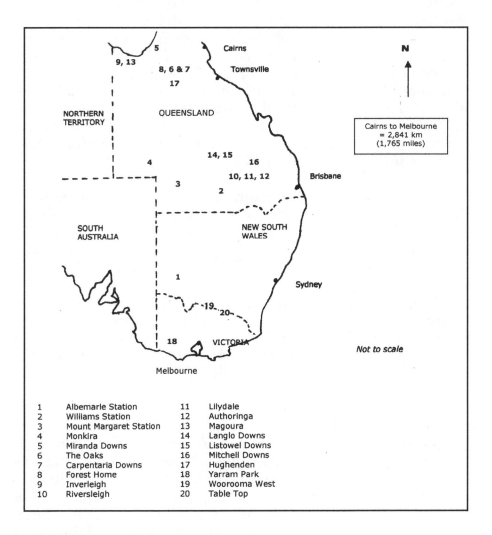

1	Albemarle Station	11	Lilydale
2	Williams Station	12	Authoringa
3	Mount Margaret Station	13	Magoura
4	Monkira	14	Langlo Downs
5	Miranda Downs	15	Listowel Downs
6	The Oaks	16	Mitchell Downs
7	Carpentaria Downs	17	Hughenden
8	Forest Home	18	Yarram Park
9	Inverleigh	19	Woorooma West
10	Riversleigh	20	Table Top

ACKNOWLEDGEMENTS and EDITOR'S NOTES

There are several people without whose contributions this publication would not be as it is today and to whom I am therefore very grateful. In alphabetical order, they are: Sonia Desmond, who copied the (lengthy, and at times illegible) original manuscript into an electronic format; Sheila Marchant, who owns the original oil painting of Conquistador and arranged for it to be digitally copied; Pat Reid, who clarified the information about her grandfather, Arthur James Cobbold; Sylvia Stoltz, who researched a great deal of information about the stations in Australia and confirmed some genealogical points; and Roberta Taylor, the source of direct information about her uncle, Frank Edward Cobbold.

All pictures, maps, diagrams and textboxes have been added for this edition. The photographed painting of Frank Cobbold on the cover is by Janet Agnes Cumbrae Stewart, who was born in Victoria in 1883. She studied at the Melbourne National Gallery School under Bernard Hall and F McCubbin and in 1905 was awarded second place in the National Gallery travelling scholarship competition. Janet Cumbrae Stewart devoted the most significant section of her work to pastel studies of the female nude; she exhibited regularly in America and Europe, as well as Australia, and lived in South Yarra, Melbourne from 1947 until her death in 1960.

The following institutions kindly gave permission for images to be reproduced in the book and their contributions are specifically itemised at the end: Aberdeen Art Gallery & Museums Collections, Cornell University Library (John M Echols Collection on South-east Asia); the Director of the Public Record Office of Northern Ireland and the depositor, Ms S Armstrong of Ballmoney; the Fiji Museum; the State Library of Queensland; the State Library of Victoria, and the National Library of Australia.

Sandra Berry
September 2008

6

LIST OF ILLUSTRATIONS, MAPS AND PHOTOGRAPHS

Figure

The cattle and sheep stations managed/owned by Frank Cobbold

SOURCES OF ILLUSTRATIONS etc:

Grateful thanks are due to the following for their kind permission to reproduce the images named:

Fig 7	Copyright Aberdeen Art Gallery & Museums Collections
Fig 10	Copyright Aberdeen Art Gallery & Museums Collections
Fig 13	Courtesy of The Fiji Museum
Fig 16	Courtesy Cornell University Library, John M Echols Collection on South-east Asia
Fig 21	Courtesy of the Director of the Public Record Office of Northern Ireland and the depositor, Ms S Armstrong of Ballmoney. D/2412/D/1
Fig 22	Courtesy of the Director of the Public Record Office of Northern Ireland and the depositor, Ms S Armstrong of Ballmoney. D/2412/D/1
Fig 24	Courtesy of the State Library of Victoria
Fig 26	Courtesy of the National Library of Australia Prospectus: Lake Speculation and Darling River Scheme/Broken Hill & District Water Supply Co Ltd, by Broken Hill & District Water Supply Co; Publ: [Sydney: The Company, 1891] section 3 Historical Overview, p40 Figure 17
Fig 42	Courtesy of the State Library of Queensland
Fig 45	Courtesy of the State Library of Victoria
Fig 47	Sheila Marchant, who owns the original oil painting
Fig 54	Roberta Taylor, who owns the original photograph

THE COBBOLD FAMILY HISTORY TRUST

The COBBOLD FAMILY HISTORY TRUST has three main purposes. Firstly, to collect and preserve, safely and permanently, family memorabilia: books, pictures, photographs, papers and artefacts. It was started to accept the settlor's own collection but has since grown by acquisition and gift. Donors have often expressed relief and satisfaction that lifelong and treasured possessions have found a safe and permanent home. The Trust is non-aggressive; it does not seek items with which the owner does not wish to part, but it actively seeks items that would otherwise be lost, destroyed or fragmented.

Secondly, the Trust wishes to grow the family tree to the point where it can be beneficially published. Thirdly, and resulting mainly from the first two objectives, the Trust provides a substantial resource for family members and family historians in this and future generations.

In this fast changing world of expendability, obsolescence and disposability the remarkable and historically important family possessions of the past will vanish unless we bring them together and make them safe now. To achieve this the Trust relies solely on donations from friends and family members.

For further information on the work of the Trust see the website at **www.cobboldfht.com**

As building a family history is inevitably a step-by-step process, readers who feel they have a contribution to make are positively encouraged to contact the Cobbold Family History Trust at:

14 Moorfields, Moorhaven, Ivybridge, Devon PL21 0XQ, UK
Phone: 01752 894498   E-mail: anthonycobbold@tiscali.co.uk